THE LINGERING SHADOW OF NAZISM: THE AUSTRIAN INDEPENDENT PARTY MOVEMENT SINCE 1945

MAX E. RIEDLSPERGER

EAST EUROPEAN QUARTERLY, BOULDER
DISTRIBUTED BY COLUMBIA UNIVERSITY PRESS
NEW YORK

1978

EAST EUROPEAN MONOGRAPHS, NO. XLII

Max E. Riedlsperger is Professor of History at
California Polytechnic State University

Copyright 1978 by East European Quarterly
Library of Congress Card Catalog Number 77-82397
ISBN 0-914710-35-4

Printed in the United States of America

EAST EUROPEAN MONOGRAPHS

The *East European Monographs* comprise scholarly books on the history and civilization of Eastern Europe. They are published by the *East European Quarterly* in the belief that these studies contribute substantially to the knowledge of the area and serve to stimulate scholarship and research.

1. *Political Ideas and the Enlightenment in the Romanian Principalities, 1750-1831.* By Vlad Georgescu. 1971.
2. *America, Italy and the Birth of Yugoslavia, 1917-1919.* By Dragan R. Zivojinovic. 1972.
3. *Jewish Nobles and Geniuses in Modern Hungary.* By William O. McCagg, Jr. 1972.
4. *Mixail Soloxov in Yugoslavia: Reception and Literary Impact.* By Robert F. Price. 1973.
5. *The Historical and National Thought of Nicolae Iorga.* By William O. Oldson. 1973.
6. *Guide to Polish Libraries and Archives.* By Richard C. Lewanski. 1974.
7. *Vienna Broadcasts to Slovakia, 1938-1939: A Case Study in Subversion.* By Henry Delfiner. 1974.
8. *The 1917 Revolution in Latvia.* By Andrew Ezergailis. 1974.
9. *The Ukraine in the United Nations Organization: A Study in Soviet Foreign Policy, 1944-1950.* By Konstantin Sawczuk. 1975.
10. *The Bosnian Church: A New Interpretation.* By John V. A. Fine, Jr., 1975.
11. *Intellectual and Social Developments in the Habsburg Empire from Maria Theresa to World War I.* Edited by Stanley B. Winters and Joseph Held. 1975.
12. *Ljudevit Gaj and the Illyrian Movement.* By Elinor Murray Despalatovic. 1975.
13. *Tolerance and Movements of Religious Dissent in Eastern Europe.* Edited by Bela K. Kiraly. 1975.
14. *The Parish Republic: Hlinka's Slovak People's Party, 1939-1945.* By Yeshayahu Jelinek. 1976.
15. *The Russian Annexation of Bessarabia, 1774-1828.* By George F. Jewsbury. 1976.
16. *Modern Hungarian Historiography.* By Steven Bela Vardy. 1976.
17. *Values and Community in Multi-National Yugoslavia.* By Gary K. Bertsch. 1976.
18. *The Greek Socialist Movement and the First World War: the Road to Unity.* By George B. Leon. 1976.

19. *The Radical Left in the Hungarian Revolution of 1848.* By Laszlo Deme. 1976.
20. *Hungary between Wilson and Lenin: The Hungarian Revolution of 1918–1919 and the Big Three.* By Peter Pastor. 1976.
21. *The Crises of France's East-Central European Diplomacy, 1933–1938.* By Anthony J. Komjathy. 1976.
22. *Polish Politics and National Reform, 1775–1788.* By Daniel Stone. 1976.
23. *The Habsburg Empire in World War I.* Robert A. Kann, Bela K. Kiraly, and Paula S. Fichtner, eds. 1977.
24. *The Slovenes and Yugoslavism, 1890–1914.* By Carole Rogel. 1977.
25. *German-Hungarian Relations and the Swabian Problem.* By Thomas Spira. 1977.
26. *The Metamorphosis of a Social Class in Hungary During the Reign of Young Franz Joseph.* By Peter I. Hidas. 1977.
27. *Tax Reform in Eighteenth Century Lombardy.* By Daniel M. Klang. 1977.
28. *Tradition versus Revolution: Russia and the Balkans in 1917.* By Robert H. Johnston. 1977.
29. *Winter into Spring: The Czechoslovak Press and the Reform Movement 1963–1968.* By Frank L. Kaplan. 1977.
30. *The Catholic Church and the Soviet Government, 1939–1949.* By Dennis J. Dunn. 1977.
31. *The Hungarian Labor Service System, 1939–1945.* By Randolph L. Braham. 1977.
32. *Consciousness and History: Nationalist Critics of Greek Society 1897–1914.* By Gerasimos Augustinos. 1977.
33. *Emigration in Polish Social and Political Thought, 1870–1914.* By Benjamin P. Murdzek. 1977.
34. *Serbian Poetry and Milutin Bojic.* By Mihailo Dordevic. 1977.
35. *The Baranya Dispute: Diplomacy in the Vortex of Ideologies, 1918–1921.* By Leslie C. Tihany. 1978.
36. *The United States in Prague, 1945–1948.* By Walter Ullmann. 1978.
37. *Rush to the Alps: The Evolution of Vacationing in Switzerland.* By Paul P. Bernard. 1978.
38. *Transportation in Eastern Europe: Empirical Findings.* By Bogdan Mieczkowski. 1978.
39. *The Polish Underground State: A Guide to the Underground, 1939–1945.* By Stefan Korbonski. 1978.
40. *The Hungarian Revolution of 1956 in Retrospect.* Edited by Bela K. Kiraly and Paul Jonas. 1978.
41. *Boleslaw Limanowski (1835–1935): A Study in Socialism and Nationalism.* By Kazimiera Janina Cottam. 1978.
42. *The Lingering Shadow of Nazism: The Austrian Independent Party Movement Since 1945.* By Max E. Riedlsperger. 1978.

Contents

	Preface	ix
1	Introduction: The Historical Background	1
2	The Reemergence of Democratic Political Life	11
3	Crystallization of the Opposition	27
4	The "Third Force" Becomes a Political Reality	39
5	Isolation, Impotence and Renewed Hope	75
6	Broadening the Basis?	107
7	The Fragmentation of the "Third Force"	129
8	Conclusion and Epilogue	161
	Appendixes	169
	Notes	183
	Bibliography	201
	Index	208

List of Tables

I	Comparison of the Number of VdU Votes Cast with the Number of Former *Minderbelastete* National Socialists Reenfranchised by the Amnesty Law of April 22, 1949	69
II	Comparison of the Numbers of National Socialists Admitted to the 1949 *Nationalrat* Elections with the Number of Votes Cast for the Various Parties	70–71
III	Results of the 1953 *Nationalrat* Election and the Difference for Each Party Relative to the 1949 *Nationalrat* Election and the 1951 Presidential Election	122
IV	Results of the 1953 *Landtag* Elections in Styria, Carinthia and Burgenland and the Difference for Each Party Relative to the *Landtag* Elections of 1949	123
V	Comparison of the Results in the *Gemeinderat* and *Nationalrat* Elections of 1949 and 1953 in the City of Salzburg	136
VI	Comparison of the Villach *Gemeinderat* Election Results of 1953 with Those of 1949	137
VII	Comparison of the Results in the *Landtag* and *Nationalrat* Elections of 1949 and 1953 in Tyrol	138

VIII Comparison of the 1954 *Landtag* Elections in 1) Salzburg, 2) Vorarlberg, 3) Vienna and 4) Lower Austria with Previous *Nationalrat* and *Landtag* Elections   146

IX Comparison of the 1949 and 1955 *Landtag* and the 1949 and 1953 *Nationalrat* Elections in Upper Austria   156

X Comparison of the *Nationalrat* Election Results of 1956 with Those of 1949 and 1953   162

List of Illustrations

Figure 1   Comparison of the Percent of the Vote for the Various Parties with the Percent of *Minderbelastete* Nazis According to Province   72

Figure 2   Comparison of the Percent of New Voters Voting the Various Parties with the Percent of New Voters Who Were *Minderbelastete* Nazis According to Province   73

Preface

Scarcely four years after the fall of Hitler's Third Reich, the swastika again cast its shadow over Austrian politics. But in 1949 it no longer symbolized the ascendant Austrian dreams of a united Germandom. Rather, it was a stigma the established parties attempted to affix to a nascent political movement independent of the three political parties officially sanctioned by the Allied Occupation in 1945. The purpose of the research upon which this study is based was to analyze the independent party movement in Austria since 1945 to determine the degree to which it in fact represented a revival of National Socialist sentiment as was widely charged.

In the immediate postwar years, the legacy of National Socialism dominated the political life of the re-created Austrian state and strongly shaped its reestablished republican government. De-Nazification extended to all areas of public life: from the incrimination of all members of the NSDAP and its affiliates, to press censorship and limitations on the free formation of political parties. The strictures the Austrian Allied Control Commission placed on Austrian political activity and the techniques developed by the three sanctioned political parties created a rigid government coalition, elected democratically, but ruling virtually by fiat on the basis of an artificially constructed three-party system controlled by absolute party discipline. Indiscriminate application of the de-Nazification laws to all former Nazis, regardless of whether they were involved in war crimes, excluded approximately half-a-million individuals from their generally middle-class existence. When the families of these incriminated are included, de-Nazification directly affected over twenty percent of the entire Austrian population. Excluded from the franchise and discriminated against in all areas of private and public life, these second-class citizens were a brooding, silent force, unable to exert direct political influence, but possessing a numerical significance that could not be long ignored. When the de-Nazification methods demanded by the Allied Control Commission and dutifully conceived and enforced by the Austrian government proved abortive, all parties responsible gradually came to the realization that persecution had to be replaced by integration if Austria were to heal the wounds in its body politic and become a united state. As a consequence, the de-Nazification laws of the immediate postwar years were gradually relaxed, and that silent, previously excluded force of ex-National Socialists was transformed into a significant political bloc within the Austrian electorate. By 1949, a sizable number of ex-Nazis had gained the vote and had joined with unincriminated, but nevertheless bitterly dissatisfied, middle-class voters to form a portentous third-party movement that aimed at exerting a "third force" as an alternative to the rigid two-party coalition that postwar conditions had fostered.

In 1949, the "third force" took political form in the *Verband der Unabhängigen* (VdU),[1] a third-party movement that was widely reviled as a revival of National Socialism. When only the VdU constituency is taken into account, this accusation was partially valid. Nevertheless, the leadership and many supporters of the "third force" had no previous association with National Socialism. Therefore, to label this movement neo-Nazi simply because a little more than half its members were ex-Nazis is to oversimplify the product of a political movement of which Nazism was only a transitory part. Although it would likewise be inaccurate to underestimate the National Socialist legacy to postwar Austrian political life, the roots of the postwar third-party movement go far deeper in Austrian political history than Nazism, whose extremism was the latest, but by no means either the inevitable or the final, culmination of the national-liberal movement that has traditionally constituted the "third force."

What follows is an account of the genesis and disintegration of the League of Independents as the only potentially significant representation of the "third force" in Austrian politics since 1945. Owing to the contemporary nature of this topic, the Archives of the Austrian Government as well as those of the occupying powers are still closed. My primary sources, therefore, were contemporary newspapers (both independent and party), published and unpublished government statistics, memoirs, and personal interviews.

I wish to express my gratitude to the Austrian Ministry of Education, the Austrian-American Fulbright Commission, and the University of Colorado for grants that enabled me to spend a year in Austria to conduct research on this movement. A generous grant from California Polytechnic State University aided me in the final stages of completion of this manuscript. I am also grateful to Drs. Viktor Reimann and Herbert Kraus, and *Nationalrat* Gustav Zeillinger for the interviews they graciously granted me. I am also indebted to the faculty and graduate students of the *Historisches Institut der Universität Salzburg* and to the staffs of the Salzburg *Studienbibliotek* and *Universitätbibliotek* for helping me obtain necessary sources.

In conclusion, I wish to thank Professor Stephen Fischer-Galati, who supervised this study as a dissertation, and finally my wife Deanna, who tolerated the inconveniences and provided me the encouragement to see the task through.

San Luis Obispo, California, 1977   Max E. Riedlsperger

I

Introduction: The Historical Background

As in other areas on the European continent, the nineteenth century dawned in the ramshackle empire of the Habsburgs to the stirrings of a new age, to forces that gradually eroded the aging mortar that in another era had effectively built the solid edifice of a great European power. During the nineteenth century, the gradual awakening of the various nations constituting this polyglot dynastic state rendered its previous governmental structure increasingly obsolete. Under the stimulus of the French Revolution and the Wars of Liberation against Napoleonic domination, the Germans of the empire experienced a birth of national consciousness parallel to that of their "brothers" in the "Germanies" to the north. But the arbiters of post-Napoleonic Europe were not sympathetic to the demands for change within their own lands, which they regarded as parallel to those responsible for the past upheaval in France. Under the leadership of its foreign minister, Prince Clemens von Metternich, Austria became a chief architect of a European peace based on the containment of the forces of liberal, social, and above all national revolution. To this end, the great powers designed a system of conservative collective security, which in the "Germanies" took the shape of a German Confederation. Wielding its power as chairman, Austria used the confederation to thwart the development of the nationalism it so feared.

Until almost mid-century, nationalism as a significant political movement was held in check by the conservatism of the German princes. In the "pre-March" period prior to the revolutions of 1848, however, there began to develop in the Habsburg Empire a number of heterogeneous middle-class factions with no clear unifying ideals, but nevertheless interest in the unity and supremacy of Germans in Central Europe. Even at their most militant, however, these sympathies and aspirations were merely literary and journalistic expressions of opposition to the rigidly controlled Austrian state.

But in 1848, when opposition to German national unification was temporarily immobilized by the revolutions which chased princes from their thrones or momentarily made them subject to the will of their subjects, Germans were briefly permitted to toy with the creation of a unified, constitutional nation-state. The Frankfurt Parliament, which met in this power vacuum for one exciting, optimistic year, raised a problem that has plagued all subsequent generations of German nationalists: the role of Austria in a united Germany. Out of the debates in Frankfurt emerged a dichotomy between the *grossdeutsch* and *kleindeutsch* solutions, which divided German nationalist thinking for the next quarter century.

For Austrian Germans, these terms referred to the manner in which they were to be included within the desired German Reich. Exclusion was unthinkable! For the *Grossdeutschen,* the unification of the German *Volk* was to be predicated on the perpetuation of the geopolitical unity of the Habsburg Monarchy as the basis for a German-dominated *Mitteleuropa*. Opinions varied as to whether the Habsburgs, Hohenzollerns, a federation of dynasties, or even republics should govern this state, but the principle of an economically, politically, and militarily unified central Europe based on the primacy of German culture was generally accepted.

In contrast, the *Kleindeutschen,* with similar variations, hoped for the collapse of the multinational Austrian Empire and the *Anschluss* of the German rump to Germany. This group, which followed the intellectual orientation of the so-called "Frankfurt Left" of 1848, was decidedly republican and expressed deep distrust of the Habsburg dynasty and its Viennese bureaucracy, which it regarded as racially mongrelized and increasingly under Jewish influence. This *völkisch* sympathy, which was centered in the highly particularistic mountain provinces of Tyrol, Salzburg, and Upper Austria, found its own ingrained regionalism more compatible with a general German nationalism than with the universalist *Kaisertreue* demanded by the Habsburg dynasty. In the 1860s, this sentiment found additional support in the German borderlands of Carinthia, Styria, Bohemia, and parts of Lower Austria, where Germans were coming under the increasing economic and political pressure of Slavs. In response to thr nascent nationalism among many of its peoples, the government attempted to neutralize these threats by playing one nationality off against another, relying on their mutual antagonisms to strengthen the position of the emperor as the supreme arbiter. But as the Germans in the areas of mixed population were increasingly challenged in their traditional positions of supremacy, they joined their fellow Germans in the western Alpine provinces, looking toward Munich as a counterpole to Vienna. In addition to their support of German exclusivism, these *Kleindeutschen* also rejected Catholicism as a state religion. As the intellectual descendants of the Enlightenment and firm adherents of the liberalism of the day, they regarded religion as a matter of individual choice and therefore not subject to regulation by the state. As a result of this posture, German nationalist exclusivism became allied with the anti-clericalism of the middle-class intelligentsia, creating a second base of the national-liberal movement.

Following the repression of the revolutions of 1848–1849 however, nationalism, whether *grossdeutsch* or *kleindeutsch,* was forced from the center stage of political activism back into the wings of speculation. When nationalism was restored to the arena of real politics, it was as the harnessed creature of Bismarck who used it to forge a "smaller" Germany than even the *Kleindeutschen* had envisioned.

After the exclusion of Austria from Germany in 1866 and its reorganization as a superficially liberal and constitutional Dual Monarchy in 1867, the national-liberal movement underwent a total realignment. For the *Grossdeutschen,* the reality of a unified, if not all-encompassing, Germany ended the hopes for a German *Mitteleuropa* under a single federated government. Most of these were, however, able to convince themselves, particularly after the conclusion of the Dual Alliance with Germany in 1879, that the two empires could together still fulfill a "German Mission" in Central Europe.

The years 1866–1867 signified an end to the political reality of *grossdeutsch* sentiment, but the unification and the transformation of Cisleithan Austria into at least a nominally constitutional state served to crystallize the *kleindeutsch* movement. As a result of the introduction of constitutional government in 1867, the national-liberal camp acquired political significance. Under this constitution, control over internal affairs was almost totally vested in a bicameral parliament, the lower chamber of which was elected by a tightly restricted franchise heavily weighted in favor of the urban middle class. Since Germans predominantly controlled Austrian commerce and industry, parliamentary power thus rested with a bourgeoisie influenced by the contemporary ideals of liberalism, which was incidentally German in nationality. Therefore the Constitutional or Liberal party, formed by the bourgeois delegates to represent their political and economic interests, was a German party.

During this same period, *kleindeutsch* exclusivism, initially centered in the Alpine provinces, began to take hold in those areas of mixed nationality in Bohemia where the economic upheaval occasioned by industrialization brought Germans and Slavs together in desperate economic competition which exacerbated increasingly antagonistic nationalistic tensions. As the German working classes in Bohemia were forming a national and socialist movement, a flamboyant, ethnic Pan-Germanism was gathering impetus in the traditionally nationalist university fraternities. Drawing from social-Darwinist principles of biological superiority of races and rejecting all "unpure" elements as unassimilable, these early Pan-Germans looked upon the rise of Germany as a world power and its corresponding political, economic, scientific and artistic flowering as confirmation of the principle of "survival of the fittest." For these radical students of the 1860s and 1870s, the Habsburg Empire was an obsolete, moribund, mongrelized remnant of the past. Only *Anschluss* to Germany could save the Germans of Austria.

Radical German nationalism found its political *Führer* in 1873, when Georg Ritter von Schönerer was elected as a Liberal deputy to Parliament. Initially, Schönerer showed sincere attachment to the leftwing liberal cause as interpreted by the somewhat nationally oriented Progressive Club of the Constitutional party. But after his reelection in 1876, he gradually adopted the ethnic nationalism and Prussophilia of the Viennese student fraternities. On the basis of his pyrotechnic oratory against the church, the state, the dynasty, and the industrial capitalists, Schönerer became the acknowledged spokesman for radical German nationalism by 1879. In that year of parliamentary elections, he tried to convert the Constitutional party to a nationalist program. Failing that, Schönerer was reelected on a radical nationalist program, which served as the ideological basis for his formal split with the Liberals.[1]

In the same election that confirmed the Schönerer movement as an independent political force, the return of the Czechs after a twelve-year boycott brought an end to German control in parliament. Taking advantage of the split in the Constitutional party, Count Eduard Taafe put together an "iron ring" coalition of Conservatives, Czechs, Poles, and Clerics against the more numerous, but badly divided, Liberals. In the next three years, several attempts were made to reunify the Constitutional party, but neither the old Liberals nor the German nationalists were willing to compromise on the ideological role of nationalism in the party program. On June 28, 1882, Schönerer formally split with the Constitutional party and founded the Union of German Nationalists.[2] The ideological foundation for this association was the *Linzer Programm*, which combined a strong German nationalist posture with a democratic appeal for universal suffrage, progressive social legislation, and broader civil rights.[3] Although anti-Semitism was certainly a part of ethnic German nationalism at this time, it was sufficiently balanced by the social-progressive aspects of the program, permitting such prominent Jewish radicals as Viktor Adler, Heinrich Friedjung, and Alfred Fischhof to participate.

In the next three years, Czech nationalists in Parliament forced the Taafe government to make further concessions to national equality and federalism, which only radicalized the German nationalist movement even more. As a consequence of this renewed upsurge of German nationalism, more nationalists were returned to Parliament in 1885. Again the old Liberals of the Constitutional party tried to unite all parliamentary delegates of the Liberal and nationalist factions into a single party. Although the Liberals and the nationalists found many points of agreement, the Liberals ultimately could not accept the nationalists' fundamental belief that the interests of Germandom coincided with those of the multinational Austrian state. The negotiations were terminated; the old Liberals reconsolidated themselves in the German-Austrian Club in the Parliament, and the nationalists formed their own German Club.

But even in the German Club, nationalism alone could not solidify the movement. Anti-Semitism immediately became an issue within the faction. In his campaign for the 1885 election, Schönerer had added a demand to those outlined in the *Linzer Programm* of 1882: "For the implementation of the reforms stipulated, the elimination of Jewish influence on all areas of public life ... is necessary."[4]

Although the bulk of the German Club, led by a moderate anti-Semite, Otto Steinwender, regarded the Jewish population as assimilable, Schönerer found this intolerable. On October 8, 1885, he founded his own Association of German Nationalists, based on a revised *Linzer Programm*. For the next two years, bitter infighting among the nationalists totally shattered the German Club. In 1887, Steinwender solidified the moderate wing of the German nationalist movement with the founding of the German-Nationalist Association, the predecessor of the future German National party.[5]

The essential structure of the national-liberal camp was established by this split. Although numerous groups were formed within the movement during the remaining years of the monarchy, the division between the radical, extremist followers of Schönerer and the more moderate supporters of Steinwender remained. For the radical Pan-

Germans, the only salvation for the Germans of Austria lay in the destruction of the Dual Monarchy and the *Anschluss* of the rump to the German empire, creating a racially unified greater German nation. They looked across the German border with unabashed and almost mystical admiration for Wilhelmian Germany, whose Prussian conservatism and militarism stood in marked contrast to the revolutionary, democratic, anti-dynastic, anti-conservative tradition from which this radical wing of the nationalist movement had sprung. This German-Austrian love for Germany remained, however, unrequited, for the conservative *Reichsdeutschen* were shocked by the radicalism of the Austrian movement. Even the Pan-Germans of the German empire were embarrassed by its fanatical, anticlerical *Los von Rom* ideology, which discredited Pan-Germanism in the tenuously attached Catholic states of southern Germany.

In contrast to the radical Pan-Germanism of the Schönerer movement, the Steinwender faction followed a policy that conformed to the realities of a responsible German nationalist political party within the context of the multinational empire. Its realistic policy successfully reconciled the ambiguities of German nationalism and Austrian independence and became a prototype for the balancing "third force" of the First Republic. Although emphatic German nationalists, they refused to accept the essentially treasonous posture of the Pan-Germans and combined a strong loyalty and patriotism to the Austrian state with an equally strong avowal of German nationalism. Fearing the incompatibility of anticlericalism and German nationalism in Catholic Austria, these moderate nationalists adopted the traditional liberal attitude of "neither clerical nor anticlerical."

Although repeated attempts were made to heal the breach in the nationalist camp and create a truly mass party in the last years of the monarchy, the movement remained splintered and without any real influence on Austrian politics. Ironically, in 1918 the German-Austrian nationalists' long-desired opportunity for *Anschluss* was almost realized at the very moment of their country's most disastrous defeat. The problem of reconciling the annexation of German-Austria to Germany with the remaining nationalities of the empire disappeared with the dissolution of the monarchy. Christian Socialists, Socialists, and German nationalists alike were amenable to the absorption of the rump into the new Weimar Republic. On this question there was no longer any significant difference dividing the various political parties. For the victorious Allies however, such an enlargement of Germany was intolerable. The Great Powers specifically forbade any such unification of the German *Volk,* and Austria was again excluded from Germany.

This Allied rejection of national self-determination was bitterly received by most German-Austrians who felt that the tiny German remnant of a former great empire could not become a viable state, but rather must become a part of a "greater Germany" in order to survive politically and economically. Thus in the First Republic, *Anschluss* again became the central programmatic point upon which a political movement could be assembled. Although divided, the nationalists collectively sent twenty-six delegates to the Constituent National Assembly elected in February of 1919. In the nearly equal balance of power in the National Assembly between the seventy-two Social Democrats and the sixty-nine Christian Socialists, the nationalists saw an opportunity to play a significant, responsible role in Austrian politics for the first time since the emergence of the national-liberal camp. In 1920, some degree of unity was brought into the movement with the consolidation of all important nationalist elements, with the exception of the peasants and those who later became National Socialists, into the *Grossdeutsche Volkspartei* based on the principles of *Anschluss* and *Volksgemeinschaft* (Community of the *Volk*).[6] The label party was however, overly optimistic, for the *Grossdeutsche Volkspartei* was nothing more than a central organization which coordinated, represented and expressed the political will of a large number of diverse constituent groups. Its only cohesion came on the issue of *Anschluss,* but this binding force was severely compromised by the decision of the party to participate directly in the governing of Austria. This opportunity came only a few weeks after the founding of the party when the elections of October 17, 1920, thrust the Social Democrats from their majority position in the parliament and gave a comfortable plurality to the middle-class Christian Socialist party. Although the Christian Socialists became the largest party in the parliament, they were still four votes short of the absolute majority necessary to pass legislation. The "balance on the scale" between the "red" of the Social Democrats and the "black" of the clerical Christian Socialists was the nationalist bloc of delegates — twenty representatives of the *Grossdeutsche Volkspartei* and eight of the *Deutsche Bauernpartei.*[7] The Socialists, smarting from the repudiation they had received at the polls, bolted the government, leaving the Christian Socialists to create a minority government. In this favorable situation, the nationalists with their decisive bloc of votes followed a "policy of the free hand," by which they were able to control the government's actions on individual parliamentary decisions without committing themselves to the complete program of the governing Christian Socialist party. But without a working agreement to regularize this relationship between the Christian Socialists and the nominally anticlerical nationalists, the situation proved to be unstable, and in 1922 the two middle-class parties concluded a coalition pact. Shortly before the elections of 1923, the newly organized *Landbund* likewise agreed to cooperate. Together, these German-nationalist parties consistently won the support of between ten and twenty percent of the vote and combined with the Christian Socialists in all successful governments until 1932.

In accepting the responsibility of sharing power in coalition with the Christian Socialists, the nationalists essentially decided to compromise the principles of the national-liberal movement for the good of the Austrian state. In cooperating with the Christian Socialists in the face of the irreconcilability of the Socialists, the nationalists undoubtedly delayed the disintegration of the First Republic by a decade. For the fragile structure of the *Grossdeutsche Volkspartei* however, this compromise was suicidal. By accepting responsibility for the austerity programs of the Ignaz Seipel government necessitated by the economic realities of the 1920s, the *Grossdeutschen* bore a growing public enmity with the Christian Socialists. Perhaps even more devastating however, was their acceptance of the Geneva Protocols of 1924, under which this *Anschluss*-committed party sacrificed the central point of its program in return for the economic aid necessary for the survival of the state. The result was that although the *Grossdeutsche Volkspartei* continued to prominently support the principle of *Anschluss,* its sellout convinced many *Grossdeutschen* that the only hope for the realization of unification with Germany was in more radical quarters. Furthermore, for many anticlericals, cooperation with the Christian Socialists was unacceptable. As a result, the self-compromise of the *Grossdeutsche Volkspartei* combined with the general antidemocratic, *völkisch,* corporative and fascist ideas gaining ground throughout Europe to weaken the democratic interpretation of the national-liberal movement and to make its constituency susceptible to the radical right.

Late in 1930 and early in 1931 however, it seemed that the nationalists were at the peak of their power. In the November 9 election, the nationalists won their greatest electoral victory and with nineteen representatives in the *Nationalrat* were able to command a prominent position in the new government with their most prestigious figure,

Johannes Schober, occupying the important posts of vice-chancellor and foreign minister. In a politically popular and economically sound move, Schober secretly negotiated an agreement for a customs union with the Weimar Republic. German nationalists were jubilant, perceiving this as the first step towards ultimate union with Germany. This possibility was also recognized by France and Italy, but with a decidedly different emotional reaction. They protested that this customs union was a violation of the peace treaty and of the Geneva Protocols, a position which was subsequently upheld by the World Court at the Hague. Barred even from economic integration, many nationalists despaired of any legal, peaceful realization of their desires, and defected to the National Socialists. In the chaotic year that followed, the representatives of the nationalists in the government tried to pursue a German-oriented foreign policy, but foundered on the strengthened opposition of the Christian Socialists. The political climate was further radicalized in May of 1931 by the collapse of Austria's largest bank, the *Creditanstalt*. In the financial chaos that followed, businesses failed and unemployment soared while each party sought political capital at the expense of the other. In January 1932, the *Grossdeutschen* finally decided that the conditions of the Christian Socialists for further cooperation were unacceptable and the coalition was terminated.

In March 1933, the "self-dissolution" of the parliament created the basis for the conversion of Austria into a "clerical-fascist" state by the Christian Socialists. The end of party-political activity in Austria combined with a stream of Austrian-German nationalists to National Socialism (stimulated by Hitler's rise to power in Germany) caused the *Grossdeutsche Volkspartei* to reevaluate its position under the new conditions. On May 15, the party announced its unity of purpose and action with the National Socialists. With this pronouncement, the party surrendered its political independence to the National Socialist party, for which they planned to serve as a cover in Austria.

In the period between 1930 and 1934, almost the entire nationalist camp was swallowed up by the burgeoning National Socialist movement. In 1934, when Chancellor Dolfuss imposed his "fatherland front" under Christian-Socialist dictatorship to restore stability to Austria, the national-liberal third-party movement disappeared, along with Socialism and Communism, in the "clerical-fascist" one-party state. In 1938, the "black" dictatorship of the Christian Socialists was exchanged for a "brown" dictatorship made in Germany, to the delight of the nationalists, who saw the realization of a truly united Germany.

In the next seven years however, the German nationalists of Austria saw their dreams turn into a nightmare. Thus in 1945, when the Allied victory for the second time imposed state independence upon Austria, her German nationalists were again confronted with the century-old dilemma of reconciling Austrian state independence with the obvious "German-ness" of her people. In the post-World War II era however, the continuing thread of a national-liberal political movement was given an added dimension: the legacy of National Socialism and the Third Reich.

II

The Reemergence of Democratic Political Life

In March 1938, Austria disappeared from the political map of Europe to become the *Ostmark* of Adolf Hitler's Thousand Year Reich. If the scenes of delighted public delirium were true witness to the prevailing mood, the Austrians were a people joyously bent on state self-destruction. Seven years later, they began to gather the pieces of shattered state independence to again make Austria more than a "geographic expression."

Even as the Russian and German artillery echoed through the streets of Vienna in April of 1945, activities were underway to form a provisional government for the liberated republic. But due to the refusal of the Schuschnigg government to leave before the *Anschluss* of 1938, Austria, unlike the other countries absorbed by Nazi Germany, lacked a government in exile to return to provide a sense of legitimacy and continuity.

In the years before the *Anschluss* however, there had been a large exodus of left-wing political leaders from Austria; the Communists fled from the political repression of the Dolfuss-Schuschnigg regime to the Soviet Union while the Revolutionary Socialists sought refuge in England. The moderate Socialists remained behind to maintain an underground movement, but many were imprisoned after 1933 as violators of the one-party regulations of the "fatherland front." They were later joined by more of their comrades and even many of their erstwhile captors when Austria changed dictators in 1938.

These former political leaders returned to active political life in 1945 as individuals with neither a formal organization nor a previously agreed upon plan for the political future of Austria. A common goal had, however, developed among those who had shared the rigors of past political repression. Christian Socialist and Socialist alike had learned that their bitter and uncompromising enmity of the First Republic had brought catastrophe for themselves and for their homeland. Rigid political ideology was discarded for a realistic commitment to cooperation for reconstruction of the Republic of Austria.

In the political vacuum resulting from the total destruction of the former Austrian government, a modicum of organization did exist in the Austrian Resistance Movement. But political hostility extended even to the underground, so there was little effective contact between the Socialist and Christian Socialist resistance organizations.

As the future political leaders of Austria returned home from the concentration camps, from exile or simply from their basement refuges in their ruined cities in the spring of 1945, they were confronted with a blank slate upon which they could write the political destiny of their homeland. They came carrying only their personal reputations and the ideological baggage of their thoroughly discredited political parties. They came optimistically however, these former "clerical-fascists" and would-be proletarian dictators, for they had learned from their disastrous mistakes of the past that a stable democracy is built not on the dominance of any one ideology, but rather on the cooperation of all the political representatives of its citizenry.

Much of the hope for a free and independent existence for Austria emanated from a declaration by the Allied powers signed at Moscow on October 31, 1943:

> The Governments of the United Kingdom, the Soviet Union and the United States are agreed that Austria, the first free country to fall victim to Hitlerite aggression, shall be liberated from German domination.
> They regard the annexation imposed upon Austria by Germany on March 15th, 1938 as null and void. . . . They declare that they wish to see reestablished a free and independent Austria, and thereby to open the way for the Austrian people themselves as well as those neighboring states which will be faced with similar problems, to find that political and economic security which is the only basis for lasting peace.[1]

Building upon this promise, the Austrian political leaders who emerged in April 1945 quickly began to sketch the shape of the new republic.

After the evacuation of the city by the *Wehrmacht* and before the imposition of the Russian military occupation, there existed a political and personal freedom which had not been known for years. But Vienna, although gladly free of the Nazi yoke, scarcely received the Russian "liberators" with jubilation. The rebirth of Austria, in marked contrast to its disappearance seven years before, was greeted more with a profound sense of relief than with any great celebration. The hard reality of survival preoccupied most Viennese in these first days of occupation.

Soon after the Red Army had occupied the northern and western parts of the city on April 7 and 8, brutalization reached its peak and left a bitter legacy to be reaped by the Austrian Communist party in subsequent years. As remembered by future Minister of Interior Oskar Helmer:

> In the night of April 8 and the morning of April 9, the horrible night visits of the occupation soldiers to the houses and apartments began. They took place for the most part about midnight. Since there was no light, the electricity had been out of order for days, these visits, which for the most part were aimed at the rape of women, had the effect of a sport played in Hell. The superfluous indulgence in wine and *Schnapps* only added to the picture.[2]

In this city reduced to the most primitive level of existence, the political pulse of the long-dormant Austrian political life began to quicken. Former political party functionaries became conscious of the necessity of forging some kind of political organization with which to confront the occupying Soviet military forces. Thus, in addition to the hazardous task of providing the most basic means of sustenance, shelter and protection for their families, the future political leaders of Austria began to make their way to their former meeting places in order to establish the contacts necessary for the recreation of civilian government.

These first discussions were in no way prearranged and frequently crossed party lines, as in the case of the meeting on April 14 between Socialist Oskar Helmer and former Christian Socialist and future chancellor Leopold Figl. Trying to make the contacts necessary to reestablish the provincial government of Lower Austria to provide some kind of basic order for the Soviet-occupied territory, both men had made their way through blockaded and rubble-strewn streets to reach the former seat of government. In the cold, battered, windowless *Landhaus* these two men of opposite political views encountered each other, discussed the problems confronting the future Austrian Republic and decided upon a course of common action to reestablish the administration for Lower Austria.[3] Similar meetings were taking place throughout Vienna, and by the end of the first week of Russian occupation a network of associations had been formed which permitted the organization of provisional political agencies and the reestablishment of political parties.

In this period of almost total anarchy, the only organized political force was the resistance group "05".[4] From its Viennese headquarters in the Palais Auersperg, this group coordinated efforts of various military and civilian resistance units with the intention of hastening the liberation of Austria by the Allied armies.[5] Although the Communists were weakly represented in the leadership of 05, they nevertheless were able to seize control of the organization in the first hours of the occupation. With the aid and influence of the Red Army, the Communists hoped to establish a provisional municipal government in Vienna which they intended to use as the basis for a widespread seizure of political power throughout all of Soviet-occupied Austria. Their tool for this maneuver was to have been former Social Democratic councilman Anton Weber, whose support of *Anschluss* in 1938 had alienated most of his former party colleagues.

On April 12, in a meeting called by the 05 leadership Weber discussed with Socialist Adolf Schärf the threatened conversion of the renowned "red" of traditionally socialist Vienna into a hue "made in Moscow." They decided that the only possible prevention of a Communist seizure of power lay in a strong countermaneuver by the numerically superior Socialists.[6] To reawaken the dormant strength of Viennese Socialism, Weber and Schärf arranged a meeting of all their party colleagues for the next day in the so-called "red salon" of the City Hall. Immediacy was added to the already tense situation when the Communists established offices in the same building and began to issue declarations stamped: "Office of the Mayor of the City of Vienna."[7]

The divisions of the 1930s dissolved and the former leftist Revolutionary Socialists closed ranks with their more moderate comrades. Confronted with a united Socialist front, the Communists agreed to accept a provisional City Senate with fifty percent of the seats in the hands of the Socialists along with a Socialist mayor, Theodor Körner.[8] The selection of Körner was a brilliant move on the part of the Socialists for his military posture as a former imperial general commended him to the more conservative elements, while his service to the Socialist *Schutzbund* during the First Republic endeared him to the Socialists. Most important perhaps, was the fact that his military bearing and his ability to speak Russian won him more respect from the Soviet military authorities than could have been commanded by any strictly civilian party politician. Thus, by April 14, the immediate threat of a Communist seizure of Vienna had been removed and the first of many coalitions began the monumental task of providing order for the ravished city.

On the same day that the Socialists beat back the Communist challenge for political control of Vienna, they also decided to bury the rigid ideological enmity of the past and founded a new Socialist party, based on the nascent spirit of cooperation revealed in the struggle against the Communists. The name of this new party, The Socialist Party of Austria, SPOe (Social Democrats and Revolutionary Socialists), as well as the parity between the two factions on the provisional Executive Board, reflected the change in the image of the Socialist party from its interwar predecessors. These Austrian Socialists who fled into exile had learned, either negatively from their observations of Soviet socialism, or positively from their experiences in the West, that the social justice they sought for Austria might best be achieved by democratic reform based on broad political cooperation among people of varying political persuasions. Thus when they returned to Austria in 1945, the Revolutionary Socialists were ready to pursue a more moderate evolutionary socialism than they had been willing to accept under the First Republic and the Social Democrats were willing to work with them in achieving this goal. Those who retained their more radical convictions gradually drifted into either the Communist party or one of several left-wing splinter factions which formed a common front with the Communists. Symbolic of the new brand of Austrian socialism that emerged following World War II was the selection of Adolf Schärf as SPOe chairman. His pragmatic, non-ideological approach to party politics was primarily responsible for the creation of a party which was able to work with its conservative coalition partner through the difficult times confronting Austria after 1945.

Perceiving the growing strength of the Socialists in April 1945, the former Christian Socialist members of the O5 leadership determined that a rapid reconstitution of a middle-class party was absolutely necessary if a leftist domination of the Viennese provisional government was to be avoided. As a consequence, they sent out a call for a general meeting of former Christian Socialists to establish a new conservative political party.[9] Among these representatives from non-socialist labor, business and agriculture there was common agreement that a truly new party must be created to avoid inheriting the bitter legacy of the old Christian Socialist party. At the suggestion of Lois Weinberger, leader of the middle-class Viennese underground, the name Austrian People's party (OeVP) was accepted. An organizational fabric was adopted with separate associations within the party to represent big business, the peasantry, as well as labor and the white collar workers. The decision of former vice-chancellor Vinzenz Schumy not to reestablish his *Landbund* as a separate political faction left the nationalist and either Protestant or anticlerical peasantry and urban *Kleinbürger* with little choice but to support the OeVP.[10] But the de-emphasis of the confessional character of the new party made this a tolerable alternative after 1945 as the OeVP leadership committed itself ". . . to support a really new party from all groups of working peoples of Austria based on the broad principles of Christian mentality and a clear avowal of Austria. . . ."[11]

The new image of the People's party was a happy development for Austria; a party of the old Dolfuss-Schuschnigg orientation could never have achieved a coalition with the Socialists. In 1945, both parties were vividly aware of the catastrophe which their mutual animosity had brought upon Austria in the interwar period, and were therefore determined not to destroy the Second Republic as they had the First. The coalition which they pieced together in 1945 persisted until 1966 and was dependent on this spirit of pragmatic cooperation.

The third party of the 1945 coalition had already made its appearance when the Viennese Communists tried to take over the municipal administration. These early leaders of the Austrian Communist party were insignificant functionaries who were quickly replaced by a party leadership formed from among the Austrian Communists in exile in Moscow. Led by Johann Koplenig and Ernst Fischer, the Communist party of Austria (KPOe) demanded and received parity with the other two parties in the provisional government, partially due to the pressure of the Red Army. There was recognition among all Austrian politicians that the Communist party had grown in strength during the "illegal period" since 1934 and was therefore entitled to equal representation. Furthermore, the super-Austrian patriotism of Ernst Fischer in support of ". . . united strength . . . by which we overcome the difficulties and make out of our homeland what it deserves: a country of freedom, of peace and of creative humanity,"[12] helped to convince even such conservatives as Weinberger ". . . that many of our Communists and above all Ernst Fischer, were convinced to work in their Communist way for salvation."[13] This dream was painfully shattered for Weinberger and many others in the coming years, but in 1945 was responsible for the creation of the three-party coalition. This inclusion of the Austrian Communist party proved to be a decisive factor that prevented the Iron Curtain from being lowered over the Russian-occupied sector of Austria, for the Soviets hoped to win control over Vienna through the KPOe and thereby over Austria through democratic means.

The tool which the Soviets felt would help them in this political coup was Karl Renner. That the name Karl Renner was again announced as the provisional head of an Austrian Republic emerging from the ruins of a second lost world war is one of those coincidences that leads to oversimplified, cyclical views of history. But in 1945, if the name was the same, the circumstances were totally different. After World War I, the victorious allies permitted the Austrian people to guide their own domestic political destiny and Karl Renner, a prominent, mediating figure in the powerful Social Democratic party, was a natural choice as provisional state chancellor. But as Dr. Renner took up the task of rebuilding a conquered homeland a second time, he did so not as the representative of the Austrian people, but rather under the influence of the occupying Soviet military forces. That he did not become the puppet intended is a credit to his own political acumen and to an Austrian people unwilling to submit to the pressure of the Soviet military presence.

The fact that Karl Renner even came on the world political scene for a second time was pure chance. In April 1945, when the Red Army overran the Lower Austrian town of Gloggnitz where the seventy-four year old pensioner was living in retirement, Renner was concerned for the welfare of his fellow townspeople. With political ambition far from his mind, Dr. Renner made contact with the local Russian commandant in order to plead for more humane treatment by the occupying forces. Among the local staff command were several officers who recognized the name Renner and knew of his leading role in the history of European socialism. Fortunately for Austria, these officers with a sense of history communicated the news of the arrival of their eminent guest that undoubtedly reached the Kremlin. While Renner was comfortably, but forceably detained for the night, the wheels of Soviet decision-making turned with unaccustomed speed. The next morning, Renner was respectfully received by a large staff of officers and questioned extensively about his ideology, his past, and his hopes for the future of Austria. Apparently pleased with his replies, the Soviet authorities asked him if he would be willing to become the head of a new provisional Austrian government.[14] This must have seemed a strange turn of events for a man who had belonged to the moderate wing of the Social Democratic movement and who had been excoriated by Lenin as the ". . . most despicable lackey of German imperialism . . . and a traitor to Socialism."[15] The fact that Renner had been a personal friend of Trotsky during the latter's exile in Vienna could hardly have endeared him to Stalin, yet for Soviet purposes in 1945, his appearance must have seemed a golden opportunity. As described by an English journalist four years later in the *London Observer:*

> He seemed to be just the man whom the Russians needed: old, very old, very popular, long inactive in practical politics, a connection with the past, a respectable facade for a "Peoples' Front" Government, which would quickly be conquered by a few young energetic Communists.[16]

In this evaluation however, the Russians deceived themselves.

Two weeks after Renner had accepted the position as head of the provisional government, he was state chancellor in name only. Until the Soviets permitted him to go to Vienna, Renner had absolutely no contact with any other political leaders. He did however, write to his Socialist party colleague Adolf Schärf and to former Christian Socialist finance minister Josef Kollmann informing them of his appointment by the Soviets and outlining his plan for recalling the last legitimate Parliament of 1933 as the basis for the new coalition provisional government.[17] When Renner reached Vienna, representatives of the new SPOe, OeVP and KPOe quickly convinced him that this plan was impractical. Since the political parties had already constituted themselves, Renner agreed ". . . to establish a provisional state government through the parties and to reerect the Austrian Republic again as an independent state and to create anew all its agencies and offices."[18] On this all parties were agreed. How this government was to be constituted however, became the first crisis of the still unborn Republic. That the Communists were to be included was clear. But the demand by the KPOe for the critical positions of deputy chancellor, minister of interior and minister of education exceeded all bounds of reason.[19] Fearing that Communist control over the police functions of the Ministry of Interior and the propaganda power of the Ministry of Education would severely compromise the democratic efforts of the provisional government and would give the western Allies an excuse to refuse recognition, Renner and the OeVP and SPOe representatives refused to submit. After three days of fruitless negotiations, Renner reached a solution based on the prevailing spirit of cooperation. Instead of one deputy chancellor, Renner proposed three state secretaries without portfolio, one from each of the three parties, to advise the state chancellor on party-political matters. In the State Chancellory each of the nine ministries was to be headed by a state secretary with two under-secretaries from the other two parties to scrutinize the activities of their superior.[20] In this manner Renner was able to accede to the demands of the Communists for the leadership of Interior and Education without delivering total control into their hands. With this formula the *Proporz* principle of proportional representation in the coalition was established and enabled the Provisional Government to get on its feet without a crippling withdrawal of the Communists.

On April 27, this unwieldy, but universally acceptable government was received and recognized by Soviet Commandant Tolbuchin. With this sanction, the state chancellor and the representatives of the three parties made their way to the ramp of the Parliament from which a much younger and less experienced Renner had seen the First Republic called to life. In a conscious reenactment of that scene, Dr. Renner renounced the validity of the *Anschluss* and all subsequent National Socialist legislation and on the basis of the Moscow Declaration of 1943, he proclaimed the independence of Austria to a jubilant crowd of ten thousand Viennese.[21] Two days later Renner and his Provisional Government were formally installed in a solemn ceremony in the Viennese City Hall from which they made their way to the half-destroyed Parliament to officially mark the birth of the Second Republic.

Despite this optimistic declaration of independence the reality of the situation was quite different. In practice, the new government applied only to Vienna, Lower Austria and those parts of Burgenland and Styria already occupied by the Red Army. The remainder of Austria remained in German hands and the Western Allies were readying themselves for what they anticipated would be a difficult assault on the much-touted Alpine fortress. The fortress however, proved to be nothing more than a highly effective piece of German propaganda.[22] By May 8, when the Germans capitulated, most of Austria had been liberated and in the wake of the rapid German collapse in the first week of May, political activity similar to that which had taken place in Vienna was underway in the western provinces. In May and June, provisional governments were constructed, varying according to the local political conditions. However, due to the four-power liberation of Austria, no united organization was possible. The Western Allies looked with grave suspicion on the Provisional Government in Vienna and regarded Renner, as did the Soviets, as a tool for the establishment of a People's Democracy of Austria. The Soviets likewise distrusted the provisional governments in the western provinces, because Communist participation there was virtually nonexistent. This lack of unity was further intensified by the traditional distrust by the largely conservative, agrarian monolithic German west of socialist, industrial, cosmopolitan Vienna. As State Chancellor Renner anxiously explained: "the remaining provinces were not only to be considered on the basis of their long-standing legal status and arbitrariness, they were also at that time under three different occupation powers, each of which was oriented by a different concept of state."[23] Rumors were spread that a separate Alpine Austria would be created in the territory occupied by the western powers with Salzburg as its capital.[24] If this division had taken place, it is probable that Austria would have suffered the same fate as Germany. These separatist tendencies were difficult to oppose, due to the lack of communication between the various zones. "Even the state chancellor was forced to smuggle his envoys to the provincial capitals like spies in order to gain an impression of the course of events throughout the country."[25]

This fragmentation of Austria eased during the summer of 1945 when agreements were reached by the four occupying powers on the nature of the Control Commission and the borders of their various zones of occupation. In August the first forces of the Western Allied Command occupied Vienna and at two o'clock on the afternoon of September 11, the Allied Council met for the first time to declare its assumption of "supreme authority" in Austria to be exercised through each of the four powers in their respective zones.[26] At this first meeting there was a portent of the future friction between the western bloc and the Soviets when a vigorous debate developed between the Russian High Commissioner Konev and British High Commissioner McCreery over the wording of a "Proclamation to the Austrian People" which included a statement extending the authority of the Provisional Government throughout Austria. McCreery refused any implication of acceptance of the Renner government, which he felt was a puppet of the Soviets. Konev, equally obdurate, argued that the Renner government existed and should be recognized until such time as free elections could be held. The U.S. High Commissioner General Mark Clark threatened to issue the proclamation excluding the offending paragraph. When the meeting almost broke up over this disagreement, Konev suggested that a recess be called to give the political advisors an opportunity to work out a compromise wording.[27] After the recess, agreement was reached on a "Proclamation to the Austrian People," declaring:

> "The Allied Council bases itself on the Moscow Declaration in which the Governments of the United Nations declared their intention to see restored a free, independent and democratic Austria.
> . . . .

The Allied Council considers the next task to be the creation of a firm political, economic and cultural foundation for the reestablishment of a truly democratic, free and independent Austria and for the safeguarding of a lasting peace.

The most urgent task is the unification and economic rehabilitation of the country, the elimination of the after effects of war and Hitlerite misrule and of German influence in the whole life of Austria.

... The Allied Authorities will grant democratic parties the freedom of expressing their political views through the medium of press, radio and in meetings as an essential step towards the holding of free elections. These elections will be held as soon as the necessary conditions exist."[28]

To accomplish these goals, the Allied Council sanctioned the activity of the Austrian People's party, the Austrian Socialist party and the Austrian Communist party. Designated as "anti-Nazi and democratic," these three parties were committed by the Allied Council to ". . . maintain democratic principles and the absolute fight against Nazi ideology in all its aspects and forms in political, social, cultural and economic life."[29] All other parties were forbidden unless specifically sanctioned by the Allied Council.

Despite the tacit acceptance given to the Provisional Government by the proclamation, the western allies still wanted a clarification of the relationship between the provincial governments and Vienna before granting formal recognition.[30] The western provinces were likewise apprehensive about their relationship to what they regarded as a Soviet puppet government and had already begun to formulate conditions for their recognition of Renner's State Provisional Government. On August 20, the representatives of all the provinces occupied by the western allies met in Salzburg and decided upon a common policy by which the provinces would ". . . enter into contact with the Vienna government, but also demand its expansion by the inclusion of delegates from the western territory."[31] In this fashion they not only hoped to gain representation for all Austria in the Provisional Government, but also to dilute the Communist influence on Renner.

One of the principal leaders in the west was Dr. Karl Gruber, who as head of the Innsbruck 05 resistance group had played an important role in the founding of the conservative Tyrolean party immediately following the Allied liberation. In order to effect the decision made at Salzburg, Dr. Gruber travelled to Vienna where he found Renner aggreable to the demands of the western provinces.[32]

While in Vienna, Gruber also contacted Leopold Figil who had recently assumed leadership of the People's party. Figil, who had been vigorously trying to extend his party to the entire country, eagerly seized the opportunity to confer with the first important western political leader to appear in Vienna. As a result of this meeting they agreed to merge the Tyrolean party into the People's party. On September 18, a second meeting was held in Salzburg to formulate the specific demands to be presented at a general assembly of all the provinces to be held later in the month at Vienna. Another result of this second Salzburg conference was the completion of the merger of all Austrian conservative parties with the OeVP.[33]

The question remained, however, whether the Soviets would even permit the general Conference of the Provinces to convene in Vienna. When the Renner request for permission to hold the meeting was discussed in the Allied Council, Soviet High Commissioner Konev refused to accept any statement which implied that a *new* government was to be created to extend to all of Austria. Although the Russians had long pressed for the extension of the authority of the Renner government throughout the country, what they wanted was the imposition of the leftist-dominated Provisional Government on the west, not the inclusion of representatives from these conservative provinces. Finally Konev accepted a statement about the reorganization and enlarging of the Provisional Government,[34] but to discourage this the Soviets severely harassed the Conference delegates. Despite this pressure, the Conference was held September 24–26 and in the words of OeVP participant Lois Weinberger became "... a kind of provisional Austrian parliament," roughly representing all parties and areas of the country.[35]

Having failed to block the Conference, the Soviets then tried to obstruct the broadening of the Provisional Government through the Austrian Communist party. At the Conference, Communist speakers played on the very real fears of the SPOe and OeVP that any far-reaching revision of the government would not be tolerated by the Soviets. Many delegates preferred to accept the existing government with its admittedly disproportionate Communist representation rather than risk the imposition of a Communist puppet regime throughout the Soviet sector. The western delegates refused to endorse the existing government and the Conference seemed on the point of collapse after the first day. Finally it was suggested that three new offices be created: Undersecretary for the Interior to carry out the election, Special Commissioner for Public Security, and Undersecretary for Foreign Affairs, all to be staffed by "westerners."[36] The "westerners" agreed to this compromise, convinced that the "Communist ban had been broken."[37]

Even the Communists accepted this arrangement without a struggle, apparently confident of their control over the police and optimistic about the election which was tentatively scheduled for November 25.

Acting on the direction of the First Conference of the Provinces, Dr. Renner communicated this proposal to the Allied Council. In subsequent conferences electoral regulations were worked out and on October 20, 1945 the Allied Council formally recognized the Provisional Government subject to the stipulation that elections be held no later than December.[38] The authority of the Renner government was then extended to all Austria, under Allied control. On October 28, the Renner government issued the electoral proclamation calling:

> "Citizens! Men and Women of Austria!
> ... elect your national representation ... and prove by your complete support of the elections that the citizens of Austria stand solidly behind their State, the free and independent and democratic Republic of Austria."[39]

Quite naturally, the aura of National Socialism hung over the elections of 1945 and was reflected in the electoral law as well as in the campaigns of the competing political parties. The franchise law, worked out jointly by the Provisional Government and the Conference of Provinces, was based on that of the First Republic, but excluded all members of the National Socialist party or its military affiliates.[40] This unconditional restriction of all ex-Nazis was opposed by the OeVP which argued that exceptions should be made in the case of those "... who had joined the NSDAP ... without ever having accepted the National Socialist ideology."[41] The Communists however took a hard line against former Nazis[42] and were ultimately joined by the Socialists for both ideological and personal reasons.[43]

The reason for this uncompromising attitude by the Communists on the National Socialist question soon became apparent in their election propaganda that was much more a campaign against fascism than against the other two parties. As the final days before the election approached, the KPOe swung this emotional weapon into action against the People's party, which was accused of being "soft on fascism" and justified this allegation by reference to the OeVP's plea for leniency on the electoral law.

The SPOe, in line with its new party image, ran primarily on its social welfare record in Vienna during the interwar period and soft-pedaled its ideological commitment to international Marxism.

The OeVP, campaigning with a new name and new faces, played down its clerical heritage by discouraging political activity by the clergy. With no other parties competing for the middle-class vote, the OeVP was able to present itself as the unity party for the non-Marxist population, gathering into its ranks many anticlerical conservatives who had previously voted for one of the splinter parties of the national-liberal camp.

The elections of November 25 were conducted in remarkable freedom and tranquility, probably due to the fact that the Communists were confident of significant support[44] and were eager not to spoil their democratic image. But the results brought the KPOe a stunning defeat and essentially reestablished the traditional ratio of the First Republic between right and left. Of a total of 3,217,354 valid ballots cast, the vote was distributed accordingly:[45]

Party	Votes	Seats in *Nationalrat*
OeVP	1,620,227	85
SPOe	1,434,898	76
KPOe	174,257	4

On the basis of this clear victory with a majority of five seats, the OeVP could have constructed a one-party government. But all Austrians had learned from the catastrophic lessons of the past that a one-party government and a radically alienated opposition had only divided the country. To avert any future polarization all three parties had already agreed before the election to continue the cooperation of the past six months.[46] While brandishing the club of the OeVP majority over the two left parties should they choose obstructionism, party head Leopold Figil offered to construct a new coalition government based on a *Proporz* determined by the election results.[47]

The coalition which resulted was a radical departure from the previous pattern of Austrian politics. Although the political parties which reemerged in 1945 differed from their predecessors, they nevertheless inherited the rigid party images of the past. All three parties were based on radically different political *Weltanschauungen,* with widely varied religious and social attitudes and a totally different approach to the process of political change. This strong distinction between parties was further reflected in a strong loyalty to party discipline. The party member voted not for the man, but for a list of candidates determined by the central party organization. There was little sense of personal relationship between the *Nationalrat* delegate and his constituency. The result was that the representative felt himself much more bound to his club in Parliament than to the people he represented. Thus citizen pressure on individual legislators was virtually unknown. Party policy on legislative matters was decided in secret debate behind the doors of the parliamentary club and, although dissenting opinion might be presented during the debate on the floor, the faction voted as a bloc. Violators of this procedure were severely punished by their colleagues and were occasionally read out of the party. The party machine played an enormous role in Austrian politics.

Because of this rigid, compartmentalized structure, Austrian politics during the First Republic had been marked by uncompromising, antidemocratic tactics that led to total polarization and ultimately dictatorship. Standing on the ruins of a shattered country and on the threshold of a Soviet-dominated Eastern Europe, the Austrian political leaders of 1945 realized that they could not afford doctrinal intransigence. The rigidity of the party-political system necessitated a very special type of arrangement to expedite the compromise required by the tense postwar situation. Because individual compromise was virtually impossible due to the monolithic control of the party apparatus, the system of *Proporz* was applied at all levels from the cabinet to the lowest administrative posts in the bureaucracy, and was spelled out in specific pacts secretly worked out by the coalition parties.[48] The politicization of Austrian life was virtually total.

Three days after the election, State Chancellor Renner dissolved the Provisional Government,[49] and by mid-December Figil had put together a government acceptable to the Allied Council.[50] This first *Proporz* differed somewhat from its successors; in addition to the seven OeVP (including Chancellor Figil) and five SPOe (including Vice-Chancellor Schärf) ministers, there was one Communist.[51] This Communist participation in government ended in 1947 when the lone KPOe representative resigned his post in the course of a stormy debate regarding currency evaluation, carrying his party into permanent opposition.[52]

The Socialist party cast its lot with the middle-class camp and the black-red two-party regime, which locked out all oppositional influence and controlled Austrian politics until 1966, was installed.

Despite the proportional representation of all parties in the Figil-Schärf government, there were many Austrians who were not politically represented by the three-party government. Just as significant for the future balance of Austrian politics as those who cast their ballots for the three coalition parties in November 1945 were those who were not permitted to vote. In the 1945 election some 670,000 fewer Austrians were franchised than in the last democratic election in 1930, despite the population increase of the past fifteen years. This drop was due to the disenfranchisement of former Nazis and the significant population dislocation caused by the war. By the next *Nationalrat* election four years later, this disenfranchised mass of second-class citizens had developed into a considerable silent opposition. In addition to those barred from the polls there was a substantial body of traditionally opposition-oriented voters who were forced to select one of the parties thrust upon them by the three-party structure comprising the Austrian political system. As normalcy returned, the independent press provided a forum for the disenfranchised force to express its discontent, and became a "Fourth Estate" in the truest sense of the expression. Ultimately, this journalistic opposition evolved into a "third force"[53] that wanted political representation for the reservoir of independent voters who balance and swing the political scale in Austria between right and left. Today, this "third force" finds expression in a relatively small opposition party and a large, fluctuating body of independent voters. In the first decade following the war however, it threatened to become a significant, stable political force. The growth and disintegration of this movement form the focus of this study.

III

Crystallization of the Opposition

For some Austrians in the tense years following World War II, the politican world seemed almost the realization of a historical dialectic in which traditional enemies were locked together in a unity of self-interest, providing half-solutions for the partners and no alternatives for the disenchanted. The cry for a "third force" therefore carried a strong emotional appeal for those who longed for a new synthesis to replace the "unity of opposites" which dominated both domestic and international politics.

In an era in which nationalism had been totally discredited, the nationally conscious Germans of Austria dreamed of a resurgent Europe taking its place between the superpowers of East and West. In this vision, cultural nationalism was to be maintained and encouraged, while political integration was to become the vehicle by which the equality, if not the superiority of Europe could be established vis-à-vis the "culturally inferior" Americans and the "barbaric" and "brutal" Russians.

The call for a "third force" developed out of an ardent desire for a viable alternative to the *"Demokratur"*[1] which, although democratically elected, was so bound by the dictates of party discipline, *Proporz* and Allied control that it seemed unresponsive to the desires and best interests of the Austrian people.

Traditionally the vehicle for the expression of such dissent had been the "third force" of the heterogeneous collection of middle-class parties that had made up the German national-liberal camp. But there had been little unity within this constellation and political sympathies ranged from near socialism on the left, the liberal *Grossdeutschen* and conservative-clerical *Heimwehr* elements on either side of the center, to the extreme right of the radical nationalist anti-Semites. The only common denominator was the desire for inclusion within the German Reich. When the collapse of the old monarchy in 1918 made annexation a logical alternative, the victorious Allied powers forbade *Anschluss* and thus converted the legitimate goal of German-Austrian nationalists into a crime against the peace. The difference between the shattered dream of 1918 and its realization twenty years later was that Austria became a part of the Third Reich of Adolf Hitler rather than the Weimar Republic. This however was lost on many German nationalists of Austria in 1938 who enthusiastically supported the *Anschluss* even if they did not actually join the NSDAP. During the next seven years however, many German nationalists gradually discovered that the Third Reich was not the *Grossdeutschland* of which they had dreamed for almost a century. In reality, the *Anschluss* was more a conquest than it was a unification of the German nation. As the *Ostmark* in the "new order," Austria was reduced to a "geographic expression" and was politically and economically exploited by the *Altmark*. This subordination was intolerable to many Austrians who, despite their protestations of membership in the German *Volk,* nevertheless considered themselves historically and culturally superior to the *Piefka.*[2] As the "swollen" tones of northern German dialects became increasingly common in important political and military offices throughout Austria, the initial enthusiasm for the *Anschluss* began to wane.

Under the rigid controls of the Nazi state, many *Grossdeutschen* and *Deutschnationalen* were alienated by the unscrupulous disregard for the principles of the *Rechtsstaat* long cherished by this largely liberal camp. The strong anti-church posture of many Nazi officials further antagonzied many German nationalists who held strongly Catholic views. The dream of a *Mitteleuropa* under the benevolent paternalism of the economically and industrially superior Germans turned into a nightmare under the brutal enslavement and extermination policies of National Socialism. In retaliation against this tragic distortion of their ideals, many Austro-German nationalists withdrew their support from Hitler's interpretation of *Grossdeutschland*. This alienation led some into the Resistance Movement and others into concentration camps for their outraged expression of betrayal.

Following the war, this fragmented and disillusioned group might have been, and to some degree was successfully assimilated by the major parties of the right and left. This assimilation might have eliminated the German nationalist camp but for the clumsy handling of de-Nazification by the government coalition.

The political leaders of the new republic who had suffered imprisonment or exile under the Third Reich, as well as the occupying powers, had a natural desire for revenge against the incomprehensible inhumanity of the Nazi regime. There was little argument that extensive measures were necessary to deal with the residues of a system that had committed countless crimes against humanity and had so deeply indoctrinated the millions of people under its sway. The crimes had to be punished and the indoctrinated re-educated to the ways of democracy. Vigorous disagreement arose however, on the means and the extremes to which this process should be carried.

One of the first priorities of the Renner Provisional Government was to provide the legal basis for de-Nazification. On May 9, 1945 it passed the *Verbot* Law dissolving all National Socialist organizations and setting procedures and penalties for the prosecution of war crimes.[3] In application, the *Verbot* Law directly affected over 500,000 members of the NSDAP and when the impact on their families is considered, de-Nazification can be seen as a factor of massive significance in postwar Austrian society. When fully implemented the *Verbot* Law barred 65,834 officials from returning to their posts and was responsible for the release of another 83,207. Of this total of 149,041, only 23,588 had been members of the party during the so-called illegal period before 1938;[4] the remainder joined after the incorporation of Austria into the Third Reich. This indiscriminate punishment of all party members without trial and conviction on specific grounds placed a collective guilt on more than half-a-million people, on the basis of a law applied retroactively. It incriminated not only war criminals who mostly were able to escape prosecution, but also the inconsequential party member whose only crime was to give his loyalty to a party which became criminal in the wake of a lost war. A joke current at this time well characterizes the plight of many former Nazis:

> A respectable old gentleman was trying, with much effort and little success, to sweep up litter on Vienna's Stephansplatz. Another man stopped to observe the former's struggles, following him around, offering advice on how the street should be swept properly. Finally, the old gentleman sighed, "Look, I'm not really a street cleaner at all by profession. I was a university professor, but I was a Nazi and am not allowed to teach anymore. If you can do this job so well, why don't you sweep?" To which the critic replied, "I was a street cleaner by profession, but you see, I was a Nazi too and . . . ."[5]

In general, the *Verbot* Law too severely punished the insignificant party member who shared no direct responsibility for the crimes of

National Socialism. The result was the exclusion of more than 500,000 Austrians from their normal middle-class existence and the creation of a deeply embittered second-class citizenry with little loyalty to the government that had inflicted this plight. Within a year the Austrian government discovered the impracticality of the *Verbot* Law and grew dilatory in enforcing it. In response to protests by the Allied Council about the progress of de-Nazification,[6] the *Nationalrat* modified the 1945 law,[7] which after revision by the Allied Council,[8] was promulgated on February 6, 1947.[9] Under the terms of the new law, ex-Nazis were divided into two groups, the *Minderbelasteten* (less incriminated) and the *Belasteten* (incriminated), and subject to penalties varying according to the degree of complicity. Despite an easing of penalties for the vast majority of those affected, the continued application of the principle of collective guilt still embittered those touched by the law. Fearing that this alienation might provoke a dangerous underground revival of Nazism in response, and desirous of prodding the Austrian government into prosecution of the really important former Nazis, the Allied Council urged a general amnesty for the *Minderbelasteten*.[10] The *Nationalrat* quickly drafted amnesty laws for all ex-National Socialists born after December 31, 1918[11] as well as for all *Minderbelasteten*.[12] In suggesting and then sanctioning these revisions in the de-Nazification Law, the Allied Council implicitly agreed to the enfranchisement of these former Nazis for the parliamentary elections the coming year, but maintained control over the situation by reasserting the right to reject any new political party that might emerge as a result.[13] In any case, the *Minderbelasteten* were returned to normal political activity and the degree to which they supported or rejected the government became a critical factor in the subsequent political development of Austria.

In addition to the Austro-German nationalists, there was a second traditional element of the "third force" composed of old classic liberals. They came from the urban middle class and the non-Catholic peasantry of the former *Landbund* of western Austria where the legacy of the Christian Socialist party was weak. Both elements had supported German nationalism, but were less inclined than the strictly nationalist groups towards membership in the NSDAP. Thus, they emerged from the war relatively untouched by the stigma of National Socialism. Nevertheless, due to their strong anticlerical and anti-Marxist tradition they found little comfort in the black-red coalition and together with the former nationalists desired a viable alternative.

A third element of the Austrian opposition movement was that indefinable group which can best be classified as dissatisfied. It included the above-mentioned traditional elements, but was augmented by an army of displaced persons who formed the human debris of the war. Most were the *Volksdeutschen* of the succession states of the interwar period who had welcomed incorporation into the Third Reich. With the end of the war they fled or were driven into exile. Gathering in Austria, these refugees of diverse backgrounds, religions, and political persuasions were united in the misery of poverty and homelessness. To these could be added the veterans straggling home from the detention camps to an occupied homeland where their military service was regarded almost as a crime and where the better employment and housing opportunities were already taken.

From this rather diverse raw material, the smoldering distrust of a government seemingly blind to the needs of its people gradually forged these disparate elements into a coalition of frustration. Crying out for recognition, this gathering opposition found expression through the extra-parliamentary representation of the "Fourth Estate." The voice of this opposition emanated naturally from the west where the national-liberal movement and subsequently National Socialism had been the strongest. Here too was the strongest concentration of displaced *Volksdeutschen* seeking refuge from the Soviet occupation. In these years immediately following the war, Salzburg was able to displace Vienna as the journalistic center of the country due to the stringent restrictions on the freedom of the press by the four power occupation in the capital. Under the relatively liberal press control in the American zone of occupation the *Salzburger Nachrichten* was able to exploit the prevailing journalistic vacuum and become the country's leading independent daily. Under the sympathetic editorship of Gustav Canaval, Assistant Editor Dr. Viktor Reimann set forth an independent editorial policy committed to the protection of the rights of the individual within the party-dominated state and to the shepherding of these parties on the path towards a true democracy.[14]

Following the lead of its independent newspaper, Salzburg developed into a center of opposition against Vienna and became, according to political analyst Alexander Vodopivec, a kind of unofficial second capital city of Austria.[15] This was not merely resistance against the capital as such, although a certain element of the old hatred of "Red Vienna" remained. Rather, it was a resistance to what was regarded as a rampant economic and administrative centralization of the state by the coalition. In the minds of many, particularly in the more conservative west, the black-red *Proporz* seemed intent on using its political monopoly position to "outsocialize" even the Peoples democracies of Eastern Europe.

Although the conservative OeVP held the majority in the government, like other conservative parties across Europe it realized that the magnitude of reconstruction required capital and organization which only the state could mobilize. Furthermore, the OeVP was additionally motivated by the fear that obstruction in this sector could drive the SPOe out of the coalition and into the arms of the Communists, creating the specter of a People's democracy along the East European pattern. As a result, the People's party accepted the principle of ". . . state influence on the economy only insofar as it is appropriate from the standpoint of the economy as a whole."[16]

For the SPOe, cooperation with the OeVP meant compromising its Marxist ideology and some of its more radical social programs, alienating some of the more radical Socialists and the Communists in 1946. Far from weakening the SPOe however, this confirmed the policy of cooperation and led to the passage of the first nationalization law in 1946.

If the OeVP was able to justify its concessions to socialism on the basis that nationalization was the best means of rebuilding Austria's wartorn economy, many of the western traditional liberals could not. The black-red *Proporz* locked out any alternative for opposition and forced them into the political pot known as the "party of those without a party."

As early as 1945, a lead article in the *Salzburger Nachrichten* noted the lack of a fourth party to represent those unable to find a comfortable home in any of the three existing parties. The article observed that although this "party of those without a party" undoubtedly consisted in part of former National Socialists who had been justifiably disenfranchised, by far the more important part was composed of fully enfranchised citizens who refused to vote for either of the tweedle-dum or tweedle-dee alternatives.[17] This and subsequent editorials in a similar vein did not initially propose the formation of this "fourth party," but rather the reform of the existing parties and loosening of the rigid bonds of the *Proporz* to provide a greater variety of political alternatives within the existing three-party structure.

Another editorial campaign conducted by the *Salzburger Nachrichten* was directed against the unrealistic de-Nazification policies of the government which the editors regarded as dangerously divisive to the Austrian population at a time when unity had to be restored. Despite their opposition to the *Verbot* Law none of these journalists could be viewed as sympathetic to Nazism. On the contrary, Reimann and Canaval, both of whom had been imprisoned during the Third Reich for their outspoken criticism, conducted a vigorous campaign to undercut and destroy all remnants of National Socialist sympathy.[18] Yet their appeals for an end to the persecution of former Nazis and a demand for their reintegration into society won them a large personal following among the disenfranchised or unrepresented members of the "party of those without a party."

While Reimann's and Canaval's sensitive and realistic editorials were widely read (and building an international reputation for the *Salzburger Nachrichten*), a different kind of journalism was creating a second Salzburg-based support for the developing "third force." In the spring of 1946, Dr. Herbert Kraus established the Austrian Research Institute for Economics and Politics to ". . . supply the facts which in the lack of official statistics of scientific investigation are difficult to obtain and to provide the precondition for the reconstruction activities."[19] Although the Institute claimed to be objective and nonpartisan — it did publish articles from members of both major parties in its organ *Berichte und Informationen* — the analyses clearly supported the conclusion, for those who would draw it, that a new political party was necessary. In a series of articles entitled "The Fluctuating and Constant Vote Capital of the Three Major Parties" Dr. Kraus analyzed the ideological and sociological attitudes of the electorate and estimated that roughly thirty percent of the Austrian electorate was not committed to a party. From this he concluded that, depending upon its stance between the two major parties, a fourth party could win support from both the SPOe and the OeVP.[20] Further articles studied the attitudes of the politically dissatisfied and criticized the government policies of nationalization, centralization, de-Nazification and major-party dictatorship.

In 1947 two events took place that later placed Kraus at the head of the third-party movement. An article he wrote in the spring of 1947 severely attacked the National Socialist Law as unjust and potentially capable of radicalizing its victims to the point where they would be susceptible to neo-Nazism.[21] The response to this article was overwhelming, requiring four separate printings of the journal with a normally small circulation.[22]

The second source of publicity that catapulted Kraus into political prominence was his participation in a radio forum on the American controlled station *Rot-Weiss-Rot*. In this discussion Kraus summarized his attack on the *"Demokratur"* and itemized the means by which the *Proporz* had destroyed democracy and had replaced it with a party-controlled bureaucratic apparatus.[23] The public response to this criticism was enthusiastic, indicating the great degree to which Kraus had represented the mood of the public against the government. Embarrassed by this attack, the government put pressure on the American administration of the radio station to ban Kraus from any further forum discussions and finally cited him for "slander, insult and incitement to hate against the state executive."[24] Although these charges were never substantiated, they nevertheless indicated the government's fears of the growing mood of discontent.

About this same time, the political realization of the "third force" became a distinct possibility with the amnesty and enfranchisement of over 500,000 *Minderbelasteten,* from whom a fourth party could expect to draw a sizable percentage of its constituency. By this time, the Canaval-Reimann group of the *Salzburger Nachrichten* was convinced that internal reform of the major parties was unlikely and accepted the necessity of founding a new party to provide meaningful opposition to the tight control exercised on Austrian politics by the black-red *Proporz.*[25] They found a natural ally in Herbert Kraus whose scientific public opinion research had already revealed significant popular sentiment in this direction. In the summer of 1947 the Austrian Research Institute conducted a series of Gallup-style polls to determine the shape of the newly enlarged electorate. The results were revealing:

> In response to the question: "If an election were to be held today and no new party were permitted, for which would you vote?", the response was:
> OeVP 29.8%
> SPOe 27.3%
> KPOe 3.9%
> Withhold vote 36.3%
> No opinion 2.5%

In its analysis of these results, the institute saw the newly enfranchised voters, predominantly the *minderbelastete* Nazis, as the critical factor. Due to their overwhelming middle-class backgrounds, thirty percent would vote OeVP while only nine percent would support the SPOe.[26] With the vast majority of these former National Socialists preferring to withhold their vote rather than support one of the existing parties, the implications for a new party if permitted by the Allies were obvious. The second poll drew these implications even more clearly:

In response to the question: "Do your political wishes and opinions agree with the program and activity of one of the three parties?", the response was

Yes 41.6%
No 53.3%
No opinion 5.1%

and in response to the question: "Would you like to see a new party founded?" the response was

Yes 49.0%
No 46.6%
No opinion 4.4%

An analysis of these responses by profession clearly indicated that strong support for a new party could be found primarily among the middle classes of the cities and towns.[27] The results of these and subsequent polls on various economic, social and political issues unmistakably illuminated a broad field between and beside the major political parties which could be fruitfully tilled by a moderately reformist, nonideological party of the center.[28]

These implications were not lost on the independent Salzburg journalists who openly began a campaign for the establishment of a "third force." Although many of the youthful political individuals who made up the "Salzburg Circle" in 1947 must have had personal ambitions, conditions did not yet permit, or even warrant an overt step into the political arena. For the time being, their efforts were limited to journalistic activities and to lively political discussions that frequently kept the lights burning until dawn in the elegant reception hall of the Fronburg palace where Herbert Kraus based his Research Institute.[29] But out of this fluid circle of about forty journalists, businessmen and academicians emerged the leaders and the basic ideas which ultimately provided realization for the demands of the "Fourth Estate."

By 1948, with the statutory termination of the *Nationalrat* due the coming year, the question of founding a fourth party moved out of the realm of political discussion and journalistic speculation onto the practical political scene. Although not yet personally willing to take the mission, Herbert Kraus intensified his journalistic agitation for a "third force," with an attempt to stimulate the various elements of dissent into the necessary organizational activity to realize this hitherto muzzled political force. Based on his public opinion polls, Dr. Kraus bodly proposed that his institute's findings and its resultant publications actually constituted a kind of political program which could ". . . *serve every newly emerging party.*"[30] Although Kraus, at this point, still hoped to be able either to encourage the existing parties into the necessary reform, or to stimulate the establishment of a reform party from another quarter, he indicated that in the event neither should take place, he was ready to take the necessary action himself.[31]

In fact, an attempt to provide political representation for the coalition of the frustrated that had developed in the former nationalist camp was made. In the summer of 1948, the "Association of those loyal to the Constitution" was formed and in a very short period of time ". . . attracted many of the politically rehabilitated former National Socialists as well as those who since 1945 . . . [had] become disinterested or have rejected the three privileged parties."[32] The Socialists initially welcomed this largely middle-class movement, hoping for a split in the constituency of the People's party. Accordingly Socialist Minister of Interior Helmer sanctioned the activity of the association. But the group was too heavily dominated by former Nazis and its propaganda in *Der Alpenländische Heimatsruf* was too inflammatory to long enjoy the protection of the SPOe. When the OeVP threatened to breach the coalition and construct a single party government over this issue, the SPOe agreed to demand the dissolution of the association on the basis of the "well-founded suspicion" that members of the executive committee of the group had been in contact with a neo-Nazi movement in Graz.[33] Furthermore, the government intensified press control to harass the association's newspaper. When the executive committee of the Allied Council prohibited any further publication of the *Alpenländischer Heimatsruf* on the grounds that it was a neo-Nazi paper,[34] this attempt at party-building was extinguished.

Although this and several other attempts to found a fourth party shattered before government or Allied Council opposition, the sentiment continued to build. Indirectly the Socialists offered all the moral support they could short of angering the OeVP into dissolving the coalition. In repeated statements by Socialist party functionaries, the SPOe piously argued that a real democracy must be built on political freedom, which if necessary might mean the creation of new parties. In contrast, the OeVP, which saw its majority position threatened by a second middle-class party, adopted the hard position that a new party would only further divide the Austrian people and give leverage to the Communists.

In this debate, the independents of the *Salzburger Nachrichten* took a strong stand in favor of the admission of a fourth party and bitterly attacked the dissolution of the "Association of those loyal to the Constitution" as political expediency, a totally unjust and shameless violation of democratic principles.[35]

In November 1948, Dr. Kraus drastically escalated his previously cautious movement towards the establishment of a new party. In an article entitled "The Prospects for the Approaching Election," he rejected the idea, already tested by the "Association of those loyal to the Constitution," that the fourth party could be built on a base primarily of former National Socialists. National Socialism, he argued, was dead and the only unity among the former adherents was caused by persecution.[36] The sentiment for a new party was in no way motivated by a renewed National Socialist spirit, but rather by a desire to wrest control of the government from the parties and deliver it to the people. To place the movement in historical perspective, Kraus envisaged the new party as

> . . . in no way just "national" — the old labels simply do not apply anymore. Today an entirely new feeling has arisen, for example the rejection of the so-called "party economics," the longing for a strong goal-directed political personality, the fear of Bolshevik-forced domination etc. . . .
>
> There is no common denominator for the nationalists such as the representation of the *Landbund* or the *Grossdeutschen* to bring the opposition together. . . . Furthermore, juridical difficulties would be encountered by which they could be painted as neo-Nazis or Pan-Germans.[37]

The leaders of this new party, Kraus maintained, must be totally *new* men ". . . who already have a name among the population, that in Anglo-Saxon is referred to as 'publicity,' and whose names . . . must to a degree signify a program."[38] Then if there was any doubt remaining about his intentions, Kraus quickly dispelled it with his own "Unwritten Program of the Fourth Party." In contrast to the typical Austrian party program which was written along ideological lines to attract like-minded people, Kraus tailored his program to conform to the demands of his potential constituency as they had been revealed through his numerous public opinion polls. The result was a twelve-point program aimed at snaring as many supporters of the major parties as possible without alienating anyone. In summary, the program offered to

> a. the traditional *bürgerlich* liberal class: reduction of the bureaucracy, stimulation of private capitalism, reduction of customs

barriers, reduction in socialized insurance programs and a denationalization of some industries. (points 1, 2, 3, 4, 7.)
b. skilled labor: profit-sharing, encouragement of technical training in the skilled trades (points 5, 6)
c. political independents and ex-Nazis: electoral reforms to end party domination of political and economic life, restriction of de-Nazification measures to war criminals, reestablishment of a just judiciary to provide compensation for the injustices of the past fifteen years. (points 8, 9, 10, 11)
d. the *Volksdeutschen* and other displaced persons: the rapid granting of citizenship and a generous housing program. (point 12)

The program was established. Popular support was apparent. All that remained was for the informal leadership to draw the well-defined threads of opposition together into the coordinated network of a formal political party.

IV

The "Third Force" Becomes a Political Reality

Throughout the fall of 1948, the debate on the question of a new political party dominated the Austrian political scene. Each of the major parties took a firm stand and a virtual press war raged among the various party organs and in the independent press. Accompanying this great journalistic debate was a groundswell of organizational activity in many areas of Austria to exploit the widespread political apathy and discontent with the established parties. Late in November, a number of these diverse and uncoordinated groups met in a "Congress of those without a Party" in Vienna in order to provide a forum for discussions at a federal level. No positive action toward the founding of a new party was taken, but the Congress did elect individuals prominent in the movement to a number of committees to study further action. Conspicuous among these names was that of the Salzburg section leader, Herbert Kraus.[1]

Although the "Congress of those without a Party" was primarily intended by its organizers as a means by which the need for a new party could be publicized at the state level, many of its participants became actively involved in organizational activity. It was at this point that Dr. Kraus finally moved from his journalistic podium into the political arena.

Although Kraus had long been in the forefront of the demand for a "third force" he had never totally rejected the possibility that this force might be exercised through the existing parties. In addition to his demands on behalf of ex-Nazis, veterans, *Volksdeutschen* and other dissatisfied elements, Kraus was also motivated by the fear that if no new party were founded before the 1949 parliamentary elections, large numbers of middle-class voters would simply withhold their ballots and thereby deliver a majority to the Socialists and Communists. This he feared would lead to a leftist coalition and the total socialization of Austrian political, economic and social life. The means for averting this catastrophe Kraus saw in a "third force" exercised either through a special organization within the People's party or by a second middle-class party which would be brought into the ruling coalition. In either case, the middle class would maintain its majority position and could thus prevent any further movement towards socialism.

When Kraus was in Vienna for the "Congress of those without a Party" he was pressured by OeVP State Secretary Graf to abandon his efforts to form a new party. When Chancellor Figil made known his objection to a broadening of the People's party to accommodate the "third force" within its ranks, Kraus returned to Salzburg convinced that the necessary representation for the dissatisfied of Austria could only come through a new political party.[2]

In the next months Kraus and his Salzburg associates coalesced the informal ties they had formed over the past years and on February 4, 1949, held a press conference in Salzburg's Cafe Bazar to announce the founding of the League of Independents (*Verband der Unabhängigen:* [VdU]).[3] The purpose of the league, Kraus explained, was ". . . to provide the opportunity lacking to all Austrians who feel themselves outside the three parties existing today. . . . The league is therefore that which is called the 'fourth party' by the people."[4] The VdU was founded on a coalition of ten groups that felt inadequately represented by the major parties:

1) independent and trade union representatives,
2) respected and unincriminated representatives of the interests of the registered National Socialists,
3) former *Landbund* leaders not absorbed by the OeVP,
4) representatives of the independent press,
5) representatives of the veterans,
6) segments of the Resistance Movement,
7) The Congress of those without a Party,
8) The Democratic Union,
9) The League of Small Savers, and
10) Socialists for a Free Economy.[5]

Several years later, reflecting on the mood of 1949 which moved the "Salzburg Circle" from journalistic opposition into political activity, Kraus wrote:

> As the election of the year 1949 neared, broad circles considered a reform of the existing parties impossible. The system introduced in 1945 did not seem to fit Austria at all. So it came about that the initiative to found the VdU came directly from the people.

> It was not as much the tendency to create a party constellation as prevailed in the First Republic, as to remove those tendencies from the forms of the Second Republic, which were totally impossible and unbearable.
> I mean with this, the complete party-politicalization of public life. The erection of the *Proporz* had led to the fact that every citizen came into a *degrading* dependence on the governing parties.
> ... Mistrust of legal competence, tremendous economic expenditures, heavy tax burdens, destruction of the desire to achieve and of the private entrepreneurial spirit, overwhelming bureaucracy, waste of ERP aid in creating a new productive capacity, wage-price agreements, continual devaluation of the money, fear of those governing to tell the people the truth and incidents of corruption were taking away the rights of the people.
> It was clear to us that all these occurrences could no longer be changed by public exhortation and the creation of a "public opinion," but rather only by the real power of a political group represented in Parliament. We were far removed from falling back on the tendencies of historical development and founding a me-too party, but rather we gathered out of political desire a clear program, not in any way bound with past parties, but rather only aimed at the present.[6]

There was no formal program. Indeed, the founders did not intend to create an ideological party. Rather they wanted to form a viable alternative to the all-encompassing *Proporz* which seemed to govern by corrupt and scheming concession. They wanted a policy of idealism, a democracy free from the inequities of the National Socialist laws, in short a new start for Austria and Austrians. It was not to be a political party as such, but rather a movement incorporating all those elements dissatisfied with the existing party coalition and seeking an alternative.[7] There was no other. As long as the prevailing dissatisfaction remained, the constituency of the VdU was assured.

The reaction of the People's party to the founding of this rival for the middle-class vote was one of extreme anxiety. Hoping to win the support of the newly enfranchised ex-Nazis, for the past year the OeVP had kept up a steady barrage against the movement for a fourth party and had been able to convince the Socialists and the Allied Council alike that all the previous movements had in some way offered a threat to the stability of Austria. The support which Kraus and Reimann had given to the cause of former Nazis, and the VdU demand for the limitation of de-Nazification to prosecution of criminal cases gave the OeVP a point of assault. But unlike previous attempts to consolidate a "third force," the VdU could not easily be stamped with the label neo-Nazi. Although they had argued vigorously for an end to the concept of collective guilt for ex-Nazis, Kraus and Reimann had been just as outspoken in their condemnation of all aspects of Nazism. In addition, Reimann had been imprisoned for more than four years for his involvement in the resistance movement and Kraus had been tried for disloyalty to the Third Reich, and was acquitted only on a technicality.

Initially, the press policy of the OeVP was to ridicule or ignore the League of Independents in hopes that it would disappear. Ideologically the VdU was immune to any attack from the OeVP because it had none and also because it represented roughly the same economic and social orientation. Lacking substantive grounds for opposition, the OeVP relied on an increasingly hysterical tirade against the VdU as a Nazi party, at the same time trying to woo the ex-Nazi vote itself.

In contrast to the emotional response of the OeVP, the SPOe welcomed the new party with overweening tolerance. Confident that the VdU could only help the Socialists, Minister of Interior Helmer, with good democratic conscience, maintained that "on the question of the fourth party, the maintenance of the privilege of the three parties is no longer possible."[8]

A precise evaluation of the public reaction to the founding of the VdU is impossible, but a poll in which the independent *Wiener Illustrierte* requested its readers to fill in a sample ballot and mail it back to the magazine indicated considerable support for the new party. Of those who returned the ballots, 33.16 percent selected the OeVP, 31.12 percent the SPOe and a surprising 20.30 percent wrote VdU into the blank for a fourth party. No other party received as high as five percent, while only an infinitesimal 0.015 percent took this opportunity to register a protest by writing in NSDAP. From this sampling, the editors of the magazine concluded that there was indeed a strong desire for a new party and even allowing for a significant skew in the voluntary poll, estimated that at least 15 to 20 percent of the population wanted to give the VdU an opportunity.[9]

The most critical test for the new party was, however, the reaction of occupation authorities, for a negative sanction by the Allied Council could have completely thwarted any political activity. But the reaction of the Allies towards the VdU was mixed. Some Americans perceived the third-party movement growing in Salzburg, the center of the American occupation zone, as a potential center for a reemergence of Nazism, while others supported the movement as a democratization of Austrian politics.[10] Since there was no consensus, the Americans simply adopted a policy of watchful waiting and close scrutiny of the movement. This close observation later paid dividends to the VdU for it convinced the American authorities that the party did not represent a neo-Nazi organization.[11]

On only two occasions did the American authorities intervene, not against the VdU, but against Herbert Kraus' *Berichte und Informationen* which was banned, once for thirty days,[12] and once for sixty days,[13] on the grounds that it was failing to carry out the "... resolute fight against Nazi, Pan-German militaristic ideology and doctrines...," required by the Allied-imposed press law of 1945.[14] Twenty-five years after the fact, none of the articles cited by the Council appear neo-Nazistic in tone, seemingly justifying Viktor Reimann's contention that the ban was due to pressure from some Americans whose almost paranoid fears of a reemergence of Nazism were skillfully exploited by the OeVP propaganda.[15] Except for these two incidents, the VdU, through its leading functionaries, enjoyed a favorable personal relationship with the American authorities and encountered little opposition.

The British zone of occupation in Styria was also a center of vigorous nationalist sentiment dating from the nineteenth century. Here membership in the NSDAP had been high and the emotional remnants of this tradition were deeply rooted in the population. For this reason, the British attitude regarding the VdU was considerably more wary than that of the Americans. Despite this suspicious attitude, the British occupation authorities considered the VdU in the remainder of Austria as "... much less extreme in their views and were always believed to enjoy some tacit support from right-wing American occupation authorities."[16]

The French in their occupation zone in Tyrol and Vorarlberg pursued a policy similar to that of the Americans.

Even the Soviet attitude was remarkably permissive, due undoubtedly to the hope that competition between the VdU and the OeVP would divide the middle-class vote and deliver control to a left coalition in which the Communists would have significant leverage. It is true that the VdU organization was at its weakest in the Russian zone, but this was partially due to the fact that this was the traditional citadel of the coalition parties where there was little traditional support for the national-liberal movement. To be sure, the VdU had difficulty with its publicity in the Soviet zone where *Berichte und Informationen* was frequently confiscated and the VdU party newspaper had to be mailed in a brown paper wrapper to ensure delivery.[17] Agitation by Austrian Communists in VdU meetings and raids on

VdU offices were also frequent and were tolerated and occasionally financed and equipped by the Red Army. Nevertheless, the movement was not banned.

In this favorable climate of significant public support and toleration by the Socialists and the Allied council, the VdU moved quickly to establish its organizational and propaganda bases for the approaching parliamentary election campaign. On February 24, Viktor Reimann, as editor-in-chief, published the first issue of *Die Neue Front,* the weekly organ of the VdU, designed to publicize the goals, program and activity of the new league. The newspaper was enthusiastically received by the public, reaching a circulation of about 70,000 just before the election and became not only self-supporting, but also an important source of revenue for the VdU campaign.[18] In the following months, *Die Neue Front* carried the message of the league to the politically dissatisfied and established an unwritten program for the coming parliamentary campaign.

On February 25, the League of Independents registered with the Allied Council as a political association. After successfully passing the four week period during which its activity could have been proscribed, the VdU held its constituent general assembly in Salzburg on March 26. Dr. Kraus was elected chairman of the organization while *Salzburger Nachrichten* Assistant Editor Viktor Reimann and former *Landbund* leader and vice-chancellor of the First Republic, Karl Hartleb, were elected as deputy chairmen. In the party statutes accepted at this founding assembly, the league declared its commitment to "... the achievement of pressing reforms ... the establishment of equality before the law ... and the struggle against unconstitutional laws and unconstitutional violations of the rights of citizens."[19]

In the next months, the organization of the VdU established provincial, regional and local leagues. Although this activity was extremely difficult in the eastern provinces due to Soviet harassment, by the time of the election in October every province was organized for the VdU campaign.[20]

Due to the "independent" nature of the VdU constituency, the league did not attempt to build the highly disciplined type of party structure characteristic of the major parties, but concentrated on electing candidates who represented the political orientation of the movement. Frequently these candidates were not even members of the VdU, which maintained its legal existence as an association rather than register as a political party. Due to this deemphasis of party membership, the number of registered members was quite small in comparison to the number of votes that the party slate drew in elections.

Another characteristic of the VdU organization was the diminished role played by the leadership. Although the league had been first assembled from the top down by a leading cadre of publicists, as the years passed, the aversion of the "independents" to the "democratic centralism" of the major parties caused a shift in power away from the center to the local leagues, with a resultant change in policy and direction.

From its inception, the VdU was plagued by the heterogeneity of its constituency and throughout its short history was weakened by the resignation of prominent members unable to tolerate other segments of the coalition. The first and probably most celebrated of these defectors was *Salzburger Nachrichten* editor Gustav Canaval who had been at the center of the initial mobilization of the "third force." While *Die Neue Front* screamed that Canaval had been intimidated by massive threats from OeVP Secretary of Interior Ferdinand Graf,[21] Canaval himself made vague references to "reports" about the person and posture of league chairman Herbert Kraus.[22] But Canaval was a long-time acquaintance of Kraus and "new revelations" of this sort seem highly suspect. Furthermore, Kraus and Reimann, both long absent from party politics, maintained in independent interviews some two decades later that Canaval was indeed put under pressure from the People's party through the Catholic Press Organization which controlled the printing house of the *Salzburger Nachrichten*.[23] This, added to the personal and professional rivalry between Reimann and Canaval, provided ample reason for the latter's resignation and subsequent bitter opposition and intrigue against the VdU.

But many resignations were undoubtedly prompted by the sincere fear that the VdU might become a neo-Nazi organization. Such apprehension was justified, for the reputations built by both Kraus and Reimann in their editorial attacks on the government's de-Nazification policies had attracted large numbers of former National Socialists. When that following was translated into a party-political constellation, the result was an approximately sixty percent predominance of former Nazis.[24] For most, National Socialism was a dead political issue, but given the depth of the indoctrination of that period it is not surprising that some were guilty of clumsy rhetoric, or nostalgic wishful thinking. Some VdU members undoubtedly saw the movement as a respectable vehicle for the reintroduction of at least some elements of National Socialism. As a result, there occasionally occurred incidents that could be construed as Nazistic in tone, thus driving some individuals out of the coalition and lending credibility to the vitriolic accusations of neo-Nazism by the OeVP.

Despite this bitter opposition and internal instability, the VdU was urged on by the considerable public enthusiasm evidenced at its mass meetings. In July a committee started to write a program acceptable to all the elements of the widely heterogeneous movement. This rather belated move to provide a political program is a clear indication of the nonideological, politically expedient nature of the movement. The VdU was first and foremost a collection of dissatisfied people who held few common convictions save for a unifying disgust with the status quo. The VdU was created when a coterie of charismatic leaders parlayed a negative, anti-establishmentarian reputation into a political movement. Thus the VdU reversed the traditional Austrian process in which a political following was formed around a body of commonly held, fairly well-defined political principles. Instead the League of Independents delayed establishing a firm program until the strength and potential of the movement had provided a pragmatic justification for compromise among its divergent elements. Even with the exciting prospect of a significant impact on Austrian political life, the liberal, social welfare proponents led by Reimann and Karl Hartleb's German nationalist advocates found little common ground. After bitter ideological dispute, agreement was finally reached on a vague, nonideological "action program."[25] This program, accepted at a general assembly of all the provincial organizations on July 22, 1949, was a modernized version of the traditional, national-liberal appeal to the urban middle classes, the nationally oriented and nonsocialist workers, and the anticlerical peasantry. To appeal to the dissatisfied who had provided the initial impetus to mobilize the "third force," the program attacked the government coalition and called for the renascence of a free, democratic, parliamentary democracy.[26] This was not a political program in the traditional Austrian sense, but rather a campaign platform for the coming parliamentary election. But, given the heterogeneous composition of the League of Independents, this mixture of anti-establishmentarianism, national-liberal emotional appeal and popular but vague positive proposals was the only program on which any kind of unity could be reached.

At least as important to a new political party as leadership, organization and program, is its financial support. In this respect the VdU operated under a major, and in the long run, insuperable handicap. In contrast to the coalition parties, the League of Independents had only a minimal registered membership and received very little from dues. Even these were voluntary, but were suggested at not less than one schilling per month.[27] Sale of the party newspaper initially produced enough revenue to support its publication costs and contribute a small amount to the league treasury, but after the election of 1949 this situation reversed and *Die Neue Front* became a financial drain. By far the most important source of revenue for the organization was private donations solicited by Kraus, who, according to Reimann, had a genius "comparable to that of St. Francis of Assisi" in squeezing money out of every source imaginable.[28] These contributions came primarily from businessmen and industrialists who were members of the People's party, but shared with Dr. Kraus the fear that widespread political apathy in Austria would lead to a leftist coalition and ultimately to the nationalization of their industries. Convinced that the creation of a new party would politically revitalize the middle class, a group of Upper Austrian industrialists contributed a total of 120,000 schillings to Dr. Kraus in 1949, which he used to finance the organization and early activities of VdU.[29] In subsequent years, Dr. Kraus continued to exploit the fear of nationalization to obtain contributions from prominent industrialists throughout the western part of Austria. Because these were actually personal gifts to Kraus rather than contributions to the movement, he personally solicited each individual contribution. This was an exhausting, time-consuming endeavor which required the chairman of the league to travel almost continuously. Due to his preoccupation with financial matters, Kraus neglected the internal organization of the league, a fact that was at least partially responsible for his subsequent loss of control. Kraus was able to convince these contributors to forward their donations on a regular basis, but by this time he had already been forced out of his position as league chairman.[30]

Perhaps most important in the founding year of the VdU was the simple question of whether a new party would even be permitted to run for election. In the spring and summer of 1949 this was no moot point. Since 1945, forty-five proposed parties had failed to win the requisite unanimous sanction of the Allied Council,[31] and on at least one occasion, the Austrian Minister of Interior had banned a party.[32] Both of these hurdles had to be cleared if the VdU was to span the breach between political agitation as an association and formal candidacy as a campaigning party.

Since the previous autumn, the OeVP, confronted with the specter of an end to its monopoly position as the only non-Marxist party and the probable loss of the absolute majority in the parliament, had fought bitterly against the authorization of a second middle-class party. Having failed in this, the OeVP tried to frighten popular support away from the VdU. The tactic used was the double-pronged argument that any such constellation would on the one hand appeal to neo-Nazi sentiment, while on the other it would play into the hands of the internationalist Communist conspiracy to convert democratic Austria into a "People's Democracy."[33] As the VdU grew into a threat of considerable proportions during the spring and summer of 1949, the OeVP propaganda grew in intensity in order to convince the Allied Council to bar the new organization from the election.

In the face of this heavy opposition, the VdU would probably have not survived had it not been for the support of the Socialists who innocently argued for the freedom of democratic political expression, privately hoping that the majority position of the OeVP would be destroyed, giving the SPOe greater leverage for its programs in an anticipated two- or three-party coalition. Accordingly, Socialist Minister of Interior Oskar Helmer adopted the position that there existed no legal basis under Austria law which could curtail the free formation of political parties. He contested the right of the Allied Council to intervene by arguing that when it had accepted the Control Agreement of June 28, 1946, it had abdicated influence over all matters not specifically enumerated. Since the power to sanction new political parties was not specifically cited, Helmer concluded that the 1945 regulation regarding "Political Activities of Democratic Parties in Austria" was nullified and that political parties were free to form, subject only to the controls specified by the Austrian Constitution and penal code.[34] The Allied Council, however, rejected Helmer's interpretation and ruled that all decisions remained valid unless specifically abrogated by unanimous agreement of the four powers.[35]

In the meantime, anticipating the Council's action, the VdU found a legal means of circumventing the necessity of even applying for permission to operate as a political party. In two articles published in *Berichte und Informationen,* Dr. Helfried Pfeifer, a professor of constitutional law at the University of Vienna during the Nazi era, explained that Article 26 of the Austrian Constitution, accepted by the Allied Council in its 1946 Control Agreement, made it possible to create an electoral party *(Wahlpartei)* by presenting a petition bearing the signatures of one hundred registered voters within each precinct in which the party intended to run.[36] This clause of the constitution had been designed to dilute the power of the political parties and open the opportunity of political candidacy to unaffiliated individuals at the local level. Seizing this device to escape Allied control as a political party, the VdU chose to retain its legal status as an association and simply campaigned as an electoral party under the label *Wahlpartei der Unabhängigen:* WdU.

Socialist Minister of Interior Helmer, the admitted "godfather" of the new party,[37] concurred with Pfeifer's interpretation of Austrian law and denied that the Allied Council had any jurisdiction in the matter inasmuch as it had itself sanctioned the electoral law upon which the interpretation was made.[38] The Allied Council could have arbitrarily barred the new party from the election. But since the four powers had no unified position on the VdU, the Allied Council chose to accept the candidacy and took no action on the matter in order to avoid testing the delicate constitutional issue.

Towards the end of May, Socialist interest in the VdU moved beyond the limits of simple protection. In a meeting held in Salzburg's 500 year old Hotel Goldener Hirsch, Vice-Chancellor and Socialist party Chairman Dr. Adolf Schärf expressed to Drs. Kraus and Reimann the conviction that the VdU would win a sufficient number of seats in the coming parliamentary elections to reduce the OeVP to a rough parity with the SPOe. Despite Reimann's suggestion that the VdU might hurt the SPOe almost as much as the People's party, Schärf proposed that in the case of a standoff, the VdU would receive the post of Minister of Education in return for its support of Socialist programs.[39] Many Socialists opposed this policy of cooperation with what they regarded as a new Nazi party, while the Socialist press remained restrained and objective in its criticism. In contrast, the People's party responded to the VdU-SPOe collusion with a particularly defamatory campaign against its competitor for the middle-class vote.

Although the VdU had essentially been campaigning since its inception, its real effort did not begin until summer, after its organization had been drawn and its program established. The difficult task of campaigning against the well-established machines of the major parties was complicated by the severe lack of funds. In a year when the major parties plastered every available pillar, wall and kiosk with a variety of propaganda posters, the League of Independents was conspicuous by the simplicity of its one primitive placard bearing the letters VdU and the slogan from the closing appeal of its program: "Justice, Honesty, Achievement."[40]

The principal means by which the more substantive propaganda was disseminated was the party press. In this respect the VdU was severely handicapped in its struggle for recognition and identity. In contrast to the state-wide network of daily newspapers of the major parties, the VdU press campaign was limited to the weekly appearance of *Die Neue Front* and the independent, but sympathetic Graz weekly *Der Alpenruf.* Although *Die Neue Front* under the experienced editorship of Viktor Reimann was a remarkably refined party organ, it was simply unable to publish the volume of propaganda necessary to compete with the press of the three established parties.[41] Almost twenty years after the hectic, exciting experience of founding the VdU, and more than a decade after his last association with it, Dr. Reimann pointed to precisely this problem as the reason for the ultimate inability of the movement to become a meaningful third party:

> The VdU was strictly a journalistic idea and journalists should never try and create a party. If I had it to do over again, I wouldn't; but if I did try again, I would make sure that I had enough money for a respectable press, a daily and a weekly party organ which I could run in the red for two years before having to become self-supporting.... Given the lack of money and the lack of a daily press, the VdU had to go *kaputt.*[42]

After the election success of 1949 seemed to confirm the viability of the third party movement, Reimann tried to rectify this weakness by founding an independent daily, *Die Österreichische Allgemeine Zeitung,* committed to the program of the VdU, but with neither financial nor editorial direction from the league. Although the newspaper found a relatively good public response, it simply did not have the capital reserve to survive the time period necessary to build circulation to the point of self-sufficiency. After four months Reimann had to terminate publication, leaving himself and Kraus with a personal debt to the Steyrmühl Paper Factory which had underwritten the project.[43]

Despite the lack of an adequate party press, both Kraus and Reimann emphasized, in retrospect, the success of mass meetings as a means by which the VdU partially mitigated the deficiencies in its campaign publicity. The impact of these meetings was severely discounted by the opposition press at the time and was not recognized by Dr. Gläser in her 1951 study of the campaign.[44] But if contemporary VdU claims supported by photographs in *Die Neue Front* and the recollections of Kraus and Reimann as well as rank and file VdU supporters are even nominally accurate, it would seem that at least in the 1949 campaign the energetic, youthful leaders of the movement were able to significantly exploit the non-ideological dissatisfaction, their greatest single campaign weapon, through direct, personal contact.

A major problem with this direct, personal campaigning was, however, the lack of central VdU control over the individual speakers who traveled the length and breadth of the country. On numerous occasions inflammatory rhetoric by some VdU speakers which Dr. Gläser found reminiscent of "dialectic mass suggestion a la Dr. Goebbels"[45] embarrassed Drs. Kraus and Reimann who felt that demand for change should be the rallying point for the movement, not an appeal to quasi-Nazi, nationalist sympathies. Nevertheless, there was a significant segment of the VdU constituency which demanded this strongly German nationalist posture and the demand was enthusiastically met by some VdU speakers led by former Nazi journalist Dr. Fritz Stüber, ex-Nazi Law Professor Dr. Helfried Pfeifer and ex-*Luftwaffe* hero Colonel Gordon Gollob. Although they assiduously avoided any statements that could be directly proven to be neo-Nazi, their vitriolic attacks on the government's de-Nazification measures and their ringing avowals of membership in the German *Volk* were enough to stimulate their audiences to rousing cheers. These meetings were only too reminiscent of the mass hysteria attending Hitler's speeches and seemed to confirm the neo-Nazi label which the OeVP, the Austrian Communist party, and to a lesser degree some Socialists, attached to the VdU.[46] In 1949 however, this kind of sentiment held only a minority position in the league and on the whole the mass meetings were moderate in tone. Kraus's and Reimann's claims for the significance of these meetings can be measured by their high attendance[47] as well as the success of the league in winning broad electoral support away from six other "fourth party" competitors and the major parties. This success was undoubtedly due to the VdU's ability to exploit the prevailing political dissatisfaction as well as the personal charisma that Kraus and Reimann brought to the movement. Many Austrians were disgusted with the existing parties precisely because of their isolation from the people and the mass meeting was the vehicle by which the VdU could best dramatize its intentions to change the situation.

The VdU campaign was a combination of a broad, if rather ill-defined "attack" program on the one hand and a continuing denial of charges of neo-Nazism by the People's party on the other. The "attack" campaign was a curious mixture of a strong negative assault on the policies of the government parties and a positive appeal based on the league's modernized version of the traditional national-liberal program emphasizing 1) bourgeois economic principles, 2) a modernized German nationalism and 3) an updated anticlericalism.

The economic appeal was aimed principally at three definable socioeconomic groups: the urban middle class, the non-Marxist working class of western Austria and the nationalist, anticlerical peasantry. To the traditionally liberal middle class, the VdU stressed the importance of a free market economy subject to government interference only when necessary for the good of the people. It vigorously condemned the OeVP-SPOe coalition's policy of nationalization of major industries which was responsible, it contended, for excessive bureaucratization, inefficiency, inflation, low wages and the general inability of the Austrian economy to even approach the "economic wonder" that was gathering strength in a much more war-devastated Germany. By releasing the market economy from the strait jacket of inflationary wage-price agreements negotiated virtually every year by the coalition for their own constituents, the VdU argued that free competition would promote efficiency and at the same time create a favorable climate for economic expansion. This emphasis on "economic policy" rather than "economic planning" was of obvious appeal to small businessmen and the non-union working and agrarian classes in opposition to the entrenched economic concentrations of the socialized industries on the left and the monopolistic tendencies of big business on the right. The VdU program was a definite breach with the economic principles of National Socialism with its *modus vivendi* between totalitarian government and big business in a strange mixture of private and state capitalism. Although the VdU pitched its appeal to the same middle- and lower-middle constituency that had formed the backbone of National Socialism, it was expressed in the traditional middle-class values of "justice, honesty, achievement" rather than the nonrational, *völkisch* catchwords of Nazism.

In addition to this strong middle-class orientation, the VdU also devoted considerable energy to wooing segments of the working class. This effort was directed primarily at the industrial areas of the west, where industry had developed relatively late and had expanded dramatically under National Socialism. The VdU held little hope for winning the support of the class-conscious proletariat of eastern Austria, but in the west where a typical proletariat in the Marxist sense had never existed and where Socialist organization had been significantly retarded by the controls of the "fatherland front" and National Socialism, the league saw bright prospects. Because industrialization in western Austria was so recent, most of the workers had close ties with their lower middle-class or peasant socio-economic roots and were affected by *grossdeutsch* sentiment as well. Here also were employed large numbers of former middle-class professionals barred from their former positions by the restrictions of the de-Nazification laws. An additional segment of this western working class was made up of *Volksdeutschen* who had flooded into western Austria to avoid the Soviet occupation. Since these displaced persons came primarily from the German-speaking areas of the succession states, they had supported the incorporation of their states into the Third Reich and were therefore *persona non grata* with the Soviets and their puppet East European regimes. Typically middle class in their personal lives and bitterly anti-Marxist in their political beliefs, these *Volksdeutschen,* like the Austrian *Grossdeutschen,* were highly susceptible to the appeal of the VdU.

In order to attach this working-class element to the third party movement, the league constructed a labor policy that was "neither middle class nor proletarian." Appealing to the anti-Marxist common denominator in this group the VdU argued that it was the policy of the Socialists to keep the worker a proletarian for fear that individual achievement would lead to the fragmentation of the class and the end of power of the party. "But our workers do not want to remain proletarian," the league argued. "What the league wants is to escape the present miserable situation and then allow the worker unhindered possibility for improvement."[48] To achieve this, the economy must be released from government planning and control. The resultant free market would restore efficiency and achievement to the productive process. Free competition would end party privilege in employment and bring increased production, increased employment and higher wages along with a reduction of prices and an end to bureaucratic inefficiency. The consequence of this application of traditional liberal economic policy, the league contended, would be a general prosperity in which the worker would share according to his ability and achievement. Collective contracts were condemned except to establish a subsistence-level wage floor, and profit-sharing was proposed as the means by which the worker could escape the class-conscious proletarian mentality. To the middle-class oriented workers of the west these proposals had a strong appeal. In the traditional industrial centers where proletarian consciousness had long been educated by the Socialist party, the VdU escaped the humiliation of absolute rejection by simply not running a list of candidates for office.

A third socio-economic group the VdU aimed its economic program at was that segment of the peasantry bound by strong nationalist and anticlerical sentiments. VdU Deputy-Chairman Karl Hartleb used the prestige he had acquired as a *Landbund* leader and vice-chancellor during the First Republic to lead the league's campaign for rural support. The VdU's agrarian program was not significantly different from that of the OeVP, but the People's party suffered from a considerable stigma among many peasants because of its association with the unpopular agrarian policies adopted by the coalition to deal with the severe food shortages in the immediate postwar years. The league was able to exploit peasant dissatisfaction over past confiscation of crops and rigid price controls and pandered to the unrealistic fear that a continuation of the OeVP association with the SPOe would mean nationalization of the land. As a result the VdU became a rallying point not only for the traditionally German nationalist and anticlerical peasantry, but also won a sizable defection of traditionally Christian Socialist peasants from the People's party.

To modernize and make respectable the German nationalist appeal in the wake of the universal horror of the German nationalism run rampant under National Socialism, the VdU was forced to reconcile the ambivalence resulting from an avowal of the membership of Austrians in the German *Volk,* who also swore patriotic allegiance to the Austrian state. In trying to find a solution to this apparent ambiguity, the nationally conscious Austro-Germans were again returned to the schizophrenic emotions which accompanied the collapse of *grossdeutsch* dreams of the nineteenth century.

Following World War I, the rupture of the multinational Austrian empire offered *Anschluss* as the obvious solution to end the division of the German *Volk*. But the Allied and Associated Powers in 1919 forbade union with Germany. Few Austrians had doubted that the division of the organic nation, politically expedient to Bismarck in the nineteenth century and to the victorious Big Four powers in the twentieth century, could long be maintained. German nationalism, whether a basis for an active political program or simply a passive desire, became respectable rather than self-destructive.

The return of the national ambiguity was, however, not long in coming, due partially to the development of an Austrian patriotism, but more to a growing distrust of the potential partner after 1933. To those Austrians who placed political, economic and *völkisch* unity above all other considerations, the ambiguity did not become immediately apparent. But *Anschluss* sentiment, although high in 1938, had dropped considerably from the overwhelming plebiscites of 1919 and the seven year experience of *völkisch* unity under National Socialism destroyed all rational support for unification with Germany. But the definitive acceptance of a politically divided *Volk* restored the ambiguity of the concept of the organic unity of the German nation and the separate existence of an Austrian state. It was upon this contradiction that the League of Independents had to construct a policy to conform to the emotional dictates of its nationalist heritage that would also be realistic in postwar Europe.

An important component of nineteenth century European nationalism had been the powerful desire to eliminate external political control and to assert the nation-state as a Great Power in the European balance of power. To mitigate the ambivalence caused by its avowal of the unity of the German *Volk* and its allegiance to the Austrian Republic, the VdU sublimated the discredited nationalism in its political legacy and turned to Europeanism as a means of ending the political collapse of Europe and exerting a "third force" in the prevailing bipolar world. Europeanism thus became a substitute for the emotional nationalism of the past and the VdU tailored a new concept of an international *Volkstum* in which all nations of Europe would be bound together in a great power bloc, yet retain their separate *völkisch* identities. The VdU saw a collectively shared great power status returning to Europe as an effective substitute for the political power pretensions that former *grossdeutsch* nationalists had sought through a "Greater Germany." Within this supranational community of European peoples Austria would, however, remain a constituent part of the German *Volk*.[49]

Europeanism in 1949 had the advantage of a broad political appeal. To the Western Allies an integrated Europe offered the prospect of a western-oriented capitalist ally in the Cold War against Communism. To the remaining European nations it offered the golden dream of prosperity through economic integration, and in its ultimate application the world political significance unobtainable by any one nation. To many Austrians, the United States of Europe seemed a modernized realization of the idealistic aspect of the Austrian mission of Habsburg universalism. To the Socialists integration was the fulfillment of internationalism. To the middle classes a United Europe offered the clearest path for a return to prosperity.

No earlier generation of Austrian *Grossdeutschen* could have been significantly stirred by such a moderate statement of nationalist ideals. But in 1949, following the catastrophe of National Socialism, they had no viable alternative and behind the moderate avowal of German cultural unity within the United States of Europe ardent nationalists could see a respectable means for dissolving the border between Austria and Germany which they regarded as an artificial division of the *Volk*. To many Austrians this temperate cultural nationalism was a welcome relief from the absolute denial of their German *völkisch* identity which the Allied Council forced on the Austrian government in order to eradicate ". . . the after effects of the war and of Hitlerite misrule . . . [and to eliminate] German influence in the whole life of Austria."[50] The coalition government, largely composed of concentration camp alumni, had applied itself assiduously to this task, partially out of a desire to coax a state treaty out of the Allies, but also because of their own understandable desire for total alienation from Germany. In foreign policy this resulted in a strict anti-German posture, which by 1949 was seen by many Austrians as economic suicide. At home, the government went beyond the ill-conceived and ill-applied de-Nazification laws to absurd lengths to "de-Germanize" Austria. Typical of these measures was the elimination of German language classes in the schools in favor of classes in the *"Unterrichtssprache."*[51] In order to help legitimize this contrived distinction between the language spoken in Austria and the German language, Minister of Education Felix Hurdes commissioned the compilation of an Austrian dictionary. Although most Austrians were eager to identify themselves as Austrian citizens rather than as Germans, they publicly ridiculed the attempts to carry this distinction beyond political identification; the "new" tongue was promptly christened with the exotic name, *"Hurdestanisch,"* after its founder.

All these measures to eradicate the influence of Germany and to forge an Austrian nation were overreactions. Most Austrians had been disabused of the *Anschluss* concept and were unquestionably devoted to the building of their own independent state. Many were, however, not yet ready to accept the concept of a separate Austrian *Volk*. The only public opinion poll available on this question was conducted in 1956 and therefore does not directly reflect the political opinions of the election year of 1949. Nevertheless, eleven years after liberation and less than one year after the jubilantly celebrated state treaty ending the Allied Occupation, forty-six percent of the Austrians polled thought of themselves as members of the German *Volk,* while forty-nine percent identified a separate Austrian *Volk* and five percent were undecided. Summarizing the results of his findings according to age, sex, education, profession, party affiliation and region, pollster Dr. Walter Fessel concluded:

> The opinions whether the Austrians are a separate *Volk* or a group of the German *Volk* are approximately equal.... The younger and the higher the education, the higher is the opinion that the Austrian is a part of the German *Volk*. In Vienna is found the highest percentage of "Austrians," in Salzburg, Styria and Carinthia, the most "Germans."[52]

Thus, the VdU program that recognized cultural nationalism, while accepting political separatism, seems to have been consistent with the opinions of the young, middle-class, well-educated voters, to whom it was primarily directed.

A third area of the traditional national-liberal program was that of religion. As on the national question, the VdU adopted a moderate position which accepted Christianity as a moral code, but rejected political interference by the church in affairs of state.[53] Although this posture bore only a pale resemblance to the vigorous anticlerical programs of past national-liberal parties, it was predicated on the assumption that all middle-class, anticlerical votes would fall to the VdU under any circumstances and that a strident anticlerical statement would only alienate loyal Catholics who might be drawn to the league for other reasons. The temperate approach to the religious matter was clearly a retreat from the anticlerical legacy of the national-liberal camp in an effort to detach the Roman Catholic Church from the arsenal of the People's party and give the VdU an opportunity to end the solid grip which the OeVP had held on the middle class since 1945. But, as has been subsequently observed by Professor Walter B. Simon in his analysis of Austrian voting patterns, clericalism was no longer an important issue in Austria, because of the voluntary retreat by the church from open political activity.[54] Thus the historic anticlerical posture of the national-liberal camp was irrelevant to the political activity of the Second Republic and religion played only a minimal role in the program and propaganda of the VdU.

At least as important to the "attack" plan as the traditional national-liberal blandishments was the VdU's critical stance vis-a-vis the OeVP-SPOe coalition government. Initially, it was the antigovernment opposition of the *Salzburger Nachrichten* and *Berichte und Informationen* that had provided the impulse for the political realization of the "third force" and the most important single factor in its successful fruition was the issue of de-Nazification. Dr. Reimann clearly enunciated the VdU position on this question in a campaign speech in which he explained:

> ... as far as is known, I was the first one who publicly espoused the humane treatment of our former National Socialists and Dr. Kraus the first who took a strong position against the National Socialist Law. At first it was not easy for me after four-and-a-half years of imprisonment at hard labor, from which I barely emerged with my life and which have left in me some bitterness still. I hate National Socialism, but never people.... we have again and again emphasized our rejection of National Socialism as a Weltanschauung. We have however espoused the liquidation of the National Socialist Law ... only because the National Socialist Law represents an injustice, because it is inhumane and undemocratic and because there can never be peace in our country as long as it exists.[55]

The VdU tried to shift the focus of de-Nazification from an issue of narrow concern influencing only a segment of the Austrian population into a universal question of justice and humanity which threatened the reintegration of Austrian society. In its propaganda, the league consistently rejected any introduction of National Socialist principles, and in the summer of 1949 Dr. Kraus forbade any negotiation with former Nazi leaders for political support.[56] But if the league was extremely sensitive to allegations of neo-Nazism and vehemently denied such charges by the People's party, it eagerly accepted the image of the party of ex-Nazis. United by a sense of injustice in response to the indiscriminate severity of de-Nazification, the newly enfranchised, former *Minderbelasteten* flocked to the support of their protector. Some twenty years later, in reflecting on the impulses which consolidated the League of Independents in 1949, co-founder Viktor Reimann cautioned against overemphasizing the presence of former Nazis in the VdU. To place Nazism in its historical context he argued:

> ... National Socialism in Austria was only a transitory phenomenon. One does not know how strong the NSDAP was in Austria before 1938. At the time of *Anschluss,* many of the old *Grossdeutschen* and *Landbündler* might have voted against National Socialism, but nevertheless turned Nazi because their *grossdeutsch* sentiments coincided with those of National Socialism. This didn't mean however, that these fellow travelers shared all of the radicalism of the National Socialist movement. Austria has a long tradition of liberal, middle-class, nationalist third parties whose ideals roughly coincided with those of National Socialism.[57]

In order to translate the momentary political power of the third-party movement in 1949 into a realistic "third force," a legitimate heir to the pre-Nazi national-liberal tradition, the VdU needed to establish a positive *raison d'etre*. For the moment however, the bitter hostility against the de-Nazification laws of the OeVP-SPOe coalition was adequate as a unifying force.

A second faction the negative, anti-government stance of the VdU appealed to was composed of almost 500,000 war veterans who, when considered with their wives and families, comprised approximately one quarter of the entire Austrian electorate. The possibility of a bloc vote had already been carefully noted by the leaders of the VdU in 1947, when a public opinion poll by Dr. Kraus's Research Institute for Economics and Politics revealed that two-thirds of the veterans in a scientifically selected cross-section of the Austrian population favored the establishment of a new party, compared with only forty-nine percent of the sample of the general population. Of these, 46.7 percent favored a party of the right, while 31.1 percent supported a middle line and 4.4 percent a leftist direction.[58] The bulk of those veterans could be expected to vote according to family political traditions and economic class considerations once they had been successfully integrated into civilian life. Nevertheless, a sizable number of these former soldiers fit into the general category of the politically dissatisfied, and it was to these that the VdU directed its appeal. The problem of adjusting from a battlefield to a civilian mentality is difficult under any circumstances. For the Austrian soldier returning home to a government that denied his efforts as essentially traitorous and failed to adequately care for him and to indemnify him for his disabilities, the disillusionment was bitter. To further exacerbate the irritation, thousands of men returned home from the detention camps of the victorious Allies after the choice positions in both public and private enterprise had been filled. These late-returning prisoners of war either had to accept undesirable jobs or join the large pool of unemployed. If the veteran happened to have been a member of one of the military units designated as political by the National Socialist Law, he suffered further discrimination. Among the veterans, as among the former Nazis, the distinction which the VdU made between condemning the system of National Socialism while demanding justice for its individual adherents found enthusiastic support.

A third group to which the VdU's negative assault appealed was the youth. Here also, the league's policy on National Socialism was decisive. In 1949, virtually every Austrian voter under the age of thirty had been subject to the intensive indoctrination of Nazism during some of his formative years, and most males in this group had served in the military. Consequently, the journalistic campaign conducted by

Kraus and Reimann against the de-Nazification laws and for an early amnesty for young people had won a broad following among the youth of Austria several years before their decision to actively participate in politics.

Neither Kraus nor Reimann, born in 1911 and 1915 respectively, were significantly older than the generation at which they aimed their anti-establishment appeal. They recalled that the rigid dictates of socio-economic class, religion and ideology in the past had begotten political chaos, then dictatorship. The Austrian Republic had not been reestablished to again embrace dictatorship even if guised as democracy behind the trappings of the two party coalition. Instead the youthful founders of the VdU appealed to their contemporaries to reject the corrupt, scheming heirs of the bankrupt political parties of the past and to pursue an independent course ". . . in the center, for youth is too sober to see a solution for the problems of life in extreme ideologies."[59] To replace the fanaticism of Nazism, the VdU offered a new idealism based on the desire of young people for ". . . a democracy free from the inequities of the NS laws, in short a new start for Austria and the Austrians. This body formed the electorate of the VdU. The VdU was a movement of the young generation."[60] The new ideal? — A United Europe which ". . . can only be accomplished by the entire strength of the youth of Europe."[61]

A final major group the VdU antigovernment stance appealed to was the so-called *Volksdeutschen,* ethnic Germans of the succession states of the old Habsburg Empire, who were driven into exile after the war by the bitter anti-German policies of the East European governments.[62] Traditionally the German enclaves and borderlands had been strongly nationalist even under the monarchy and many of these *Volksdeutschen* had been enthusiastic supporters of National Socialism with the *Anschluss* sentiment that dominated the national-liberal camp in the First Austrian Republic. When forced into exile in 1945, tens of thousands of these refugees along with many from the Soviet-occupied zone of the old German Reich fled to Austria.[63] But Austria after 1945 proved inhospitable to many of these ethnic German refugees. The *Volksdeutschen* who carried the stigma of former party membership suffered even more than the Austrian former Nazis under de-Nazification, without friends or family to help ease the burdens. The process of obtaining citizenship was long and complicated; it was not until 1954 that these refugees were naturalized as a group. In the meantime, without political rights or champions these new Austrian residents lagged far behind the general population in the return to peacetime normalcy. Wherever *Volksdeutschen* gathered, whether in the industrial complexes of Upper Austria or in the electric power construction sites high in remote Alpine regions, they formed a concentrated pool of dissatisfied and unrepresented people. The individuals who had obtained citizenship since 1945 voted Socialist out of working-class loyalty. But in 1949, they formed a solid bloc behind their new champion, the VdU.[64]

As a whole, the VdU electorate was a large, enthusiastic constituency built on established political traditions as well as current issues. From these elements alone, however, the VdU could not have been formed, for they could have been absorbed by the two major parties. In 1949, the cohesion for this temporary but dynamic political movement was the deep sense of frustration with the existing government and its policies. The reasons for disillusionment among the various elements of the third party movement were by no means common. For some the VdU signified a new alternative for Austria, an opportunity to sweep away past stigmas and create a new democracy with equality for all, regardless of party membership, present or past. These idealists turned to the goal of a United Europe to replace the old narrow-minded nationalism which had sent them to the front to fight a lost cause. For others, and above all the lower leadership of the VdU, the league offered a haven for men who did not want to recognize the evil of the Third Reich. These men were seldom neo-Nazis, but they did look with fond memories on the glory, the sense of purpose, the camaraderie and the distorted sense of freedom they had enjoyed under National Socialism. For these, the VdU's strong distinction between the individual and the system provided a political alternative which did not force them to accept humiliating self-denigration. For still others, the VdU was the natural extension of a long tradition of nationalist, anticlerical, middle-class opposition to the major parties, both black and red. In short, the VdU was a crucible of heterogeneous and to a degree even mutually opposed elements. The possibility in 1949 of forging these elements into one political party was destroyed by the reduction of the severity of the National Socialist Law, by the end to occupation and above all by increasing prosperity.

In the long run, third-party movements require more than dissatisfaction and demands of the moment to justify a move from transitory pressure groups into durable political parties. They must present positive, clear and appealing alternatives to the established parties. Without a viable rationale for existence, a third party is condemned to dissolve into its component parts, to be absorbed by the major parties or to remain splintered in a variety of political factions with no more significance than that of an eternal complainer. The VdU suffered both these fates. But in 1949, the future looked bright and the election campaign seemed only to confirm the power and future of the "third force."

The campaign strategy of the two major parties vis-a-vis the League of Independents was dominated by two issues: 1) the potential of the VdU to split the middle-class front previously controlled by the OeVP, and 2) the question of neo-Nazism.

With regard to the former, the SPOe adopted the pious attitude that the three-party system imposed by the Allied Council in 1945 was artificial and undemocratic, permitting the split of the working class into two parties while preserving a monopoly by the OeVP over the non-Marxist population. Since 1948, Socialist Minister of Interior Oskar Helmer had argued that the Allied restrictions on the founding of new political parties were unconstitutional and this remained the SPOe posture throughout the campaign.

On the matter of National Socialism, as long as the VdU avoided any overt appeal to Nazi instincts, the Socialist leadership dictated a policy of strict, objective and proper criticism of the social and economic programs of the league. Only on the lower levels where *Betriebsrat*[65] election campaigns were being conducted simultaneously with those for the *Nationalrat* was there any significant deviation from this posture.

In circumstances where the SPOe was confronted with a significant challenge to its past, almost monolithic superiority among the workers, it reacted with some of the hysteria characteristic of the OeVP campaign. Typical of these smear tactics was a campaign flyer with a drawing of the Iron Cross, upon which was inscribed a swastika. This was surrounded by a number of crosses representing plain wooden gravemarkers. The text read:

> For every one Iron Cross there are 10,000 plain black wooden crosses, 100,000 cripples, widows and orphans. Whoever is for the Iron Cross votes VdU. Watch out! Votes for the *Wahlpartei der Unabhängigen* guarantee Iron Crosses and increase the wooden crosses, the widows, the cripples and the orphans.[66]

On the whole however, the Socialist attitude was one of toleration and on occasion open protection. Whenever local OeVP authorities threatened to confiscate *Die Neue Front* for alleged neo-Nazi publicity, all editor Reimann had to do was to telephone Minister of Interior

Helmer to prevent the action.[67] Without this protection VdU publicity would have been severely restricted and an important source of campaign revenue blocked. In response to continued accusations by the OeVP that the league was engaging in National Socialist agitation, Helmer used the resources of the Ministry of Interior to investigate and publicly repudiate the charges.[68]

For the SPOe, the campaign provided no serious contradictions with regard to the ex-Nazi vote, since it expected little support from this overwhelmingly middle-class group. For the People's party, however, the League of Independents presented the alternative of a middle-class party with a socio-economic posture not significantly different from its own. If the OeVP wanted to maintain the majority position it had enjoyed in the parliament since 1945, it had to win a sizable percentage of the newly enfranchised ex-National Socialists. This congruity of potential constituency with the VdU forced the People's party to resort to emotional attacks, for lack of substantive issues vis-a-vis this intruder into the middle-class electorate.

Naturally, the most emotionally charged issue in the campaign was that of Nazism, but in seizing upon it, the OeVP created a serious ambiguity in its own tactics. It was a simple matter to label the VdU a neo-Nazi party since the term, as defined by the Allied Council in 1945, applied not only to attempts to revitalize the Nazi spirit, but also to anyone who did not carry out an "... active, sustained and determined struggle against the remnants of Nazism and its supporters in all spheres of the political, cultural and economic life of the country."[69] Thus even though men such as VdU leaders Kraus and Reimann had been vigorous opponents of National Socialism in its day, they were labeled neo-Nazi for their "soft" attitude on de-Nazification. Other VdU leaders, such as Stüber, Gollob and Pfeifer, edged closer to what might legitimately be called neo-Nazism with their emotional *völkisch* rantings; viewed objectively even these tended to be more nationalist oratory in the traditional rather than the neo-Nazi sense. Lacking any substantive evidence of neo-Nazism within the VdU, the OeVP mounted an emotional smear campaign based on political expediency that was widely perceived as such.

Furthermore, the emphasis placed by the People's party on the National Socialist question seriously compromised its own attempt to capture the votes of the ex-Nazis. While the VdU specifically forbade negotiation for any bloc support from former National Socialists, the OeVP openly courted former Nazis and secretly bargained for their political patronage. The first of several meetings took place in the

Upper Austrian lake resort of Oberweis, where the future Chancellor, Julius Raab, met with former SS and SA leaders. According to a *New York Times* exposé of these proceedings, incriminated ex-Nazis, personally still barred from political activity, promised to deliver the greater part of 700,000 ex-Nazi voters to the OeVP in return for the power to name the OeVP candidates for twenty-five secure seats in Parliament as well as the post of *Landeshauptmann*[70] in Styria.[71] On August 22, a second meeting took place in Leoben, where the OeVP again entered into negotiation with former Nazi leaders in order to create a common front against the Marxist parties.[72] The ambiguity of the OeVP position on the question of National Socialism was clearly revealed in its own press release which on the one hand admitted that it had ". . . negotiated with representatives of various circles of National Socialists. . . ," while in virtually the same breath it declared strongly against the creation of a neo-Nazi party.[73] For the OeVP it was clearly acceptable to campaign for the votes of ex-Nazis, but not to establish a party which represented their interests.

The second emotional tactic which the People's party used against the VdU was to conjure up the specter of a Communist takeover in the wake of a loss of the parliamentary majority by the OeVP. While simultaneously accusing the League of Independents of neo-fascism and itself appealing for the ex-Nazi vote, by some rather tortured logic, the OeVP concluded that "every vote for a 'fourth party' means support for the power lust of the Communists."[74] But in attempting to prevent the dreaded breach in the middle-class bloc and create an "anti-Marxist and Austrian national united front," the People's party seriously compromised itself by unjustifiably casting its government partner of the past four years into the same political pot with the Communists. In its frenzied attempt to substantiate an imagined anti-OeVP conspiracy among the VdU, the SPOe and the KPOe, the People's party commissioned an agent to steal some correspondence from the league offices in Vienna. The first of these letters published by the OeVP attempted to establish that Vienna VdU leader Fritz Stüber was pro-Soviet because he had requested *Die Neue Front* to stop ridiculing the Russian contentions that they had invented fire, because: "They are sensitive and are making things difficult for us here."[75] With continuing inconsistency the OeVP press attacked Dr. Kraus a month later for an excessively hostile article against the Soviet Union.[76]

A second letter from the stolen correspondence quoted Dr. Stüber:

In my talk of yesterday in the Ministry, H. (no one in the world could guess, that with this Helmer was meant! Ed.) informed me that he would immediately take care of our requests for permission for the provincial organizations in Vienna, Lower Austria and Burgenland, so that we can figure on acceptance in the next few days.[77]

With this "sensational exchange"[78] of letters the OeVP hoped to fix the VdU-SPOe-KPOe conspiracy in the minds of the voters. But the supposed Communist connection was farcical and the tacit support of Helmer for the VdU was neither startling nor scandalous to anyone who had been watching the development of the movement.

In the final week of the campaign, the OeVP hysteria against the League of Independents reached a fever pitch. In one single article published in the central organ of the People's party it was implied that the VdU was receiving political support from all four Allied occupation forces as well as financial donations from mysterious German sources. Another letter from the stolen VdU correspondence was published, this time addressed to Dr. Kraus and written under the letterhead of a Salzburg "Jewish Committee" indicating substantial, continuing financial contributions to the league.[79] Only three days after this attempt to discredit the VdU among its ex-Nazi followers by exposing Jewish financial support, the OeVP returned to its earlier attack on the league as a neo-Nazi party by spinning a tale of espionage and intrigue which alleged that an ex-SS officer who had escaped from an American detention camp had set up a secret organization under the code name "Spider" which was ". . . the real core and head of the League of Independents."[80] The OeVP "revelation" connected the "Spider" with the likewise mysterious "Brown House" centered in Munich and together were reputed to have access to vast amounts of gold which Hitler allegedly had smuggled into the mountainous Salzkammergut lake region near Salzburg.[81]

At the eleventh hour before the election, the People's party tried to avoid the inevitable split in the middle-class vote which its campaign propaganda had failed to forestall by approaching Dr. Kraus with an offer of several ministerial posts in an OeVP government in return for a last minute withdrawal from the election.[82] When this final maneuver failed, on the very day of the election, the OeVP central organ published a special Sunday edition as a final effort to dissuade the voters from casting their ballots for the VdU. Among the last salvos from the People's party's journalistic arsenal was an alleged interview with an unidentified VdU central committee member who speculated that the Allies might nullify the election of individual VdU candidates on the grounds of neo-Nazism.[83]

Finally, after months of intensive political party activity, the political stage was surrendered for one day to the Austrian voters. They spoke with a sense of involvement that brought ninety-seven percent of all registered voters to the polls, more than in any election since the beginning of the First Republic. If public participation in the election was decisive however, the results were not:[84]

PARTY	VOTES	SEATS WON
OeVP	1,846,581	77
SPOe	1,623,542	67
Left Bloc	213,066	5
VdU	489,273	16
6 Other Parties	21,289	0

The press of each of the major parties could claim a victory of sorts. The People's party had again emerged with the largest number of popular votes. But the Socialists could be satisfied with the results which saw an increase of 186,000 votes over the 1945 total. Even the Communists could trumpet an absolute gain in total votes as well as seats in Parliament as a result of its fusion with the Radical Socialists who had defected from the SPOe to form the left bloc.

But what every party had to admit in smaller print was that the VdU, with its infant organization, scant financial resources and minimum means of propaganda, had won a stunning victory. It was particularly costly for the OeVP which lost eight seats in Parliament and with them an absolute majority. For the Socialists, the election was described as a "fruitful disappointment."[85] The SPOe lost nine seats in all, eight to the VdU and one to the left bloc. Viktor Reimann's prognosis in his discussion the previous May with SPOe Chairman Schärf had proven correct. The SPOe had suffered just as much from the presence of the VdU on the ballot as the People's party. No longer could the Socialists maintain their detached, objective attitude toward the new party. In order to draw attention from the fact that large numbers of workers, above all in the industrial centers of western Austria, had voted for the candidates of the league, the SPOe now joined the OeVP in resurrecting the issue of National Socialism. In an effort to explain this worker defection from the SPOe to the VdU, the Socialist press pointed out that the roughly 450,000 votes which the VdU received coincide almost exactly with the number of formerly registered Nazis in Austria. That is, the remaining part of the new voters divided themselves between the two major parties (about 240,000 for the People's party, 180,000 for the Socialists); seen statistically, the former National Socialists voted for the VdU.[86]

The VdU not only vigorously denied this charge, but contended that "the election results have indisputably shown that the VdU is not only not neo-Nazi, but that it did not even win the greater part of the former National Socialists' vote."[87] Reflecting almost twenty years later on the results of the 1949 election and the VdU constituency and voting behavior, Dr. Kraus maintained that although the league was greatly colored by the presence of former Nazis there was no consistent pattern throughout the country.

> In Vienna, where the total percentage of the National Socialist element in the general population was the smallest, the VdU was undoubtedly dominated by ex-Nazis. In Carinthia, the VdU was totally a peasant party, in Vorarlberg, a liberal party with nationalist overtones. In Salzburg and Tyrol it was dominated by the middle-class veterans, in Styria, predominantly by those nationalists who had been absorbed by the Nazis. In Upper Austria it was largely a *volksdeutsch* and *grossdeutsch* workers party.[88]

Although a statistical tabulation of the votes of former *Minderbelasteten* with the VdU vote cannot sufficiently define the voter profile to corroborate Chairman Kraus's analysis of the league's electoral constituency, it does clearly discredit the superficial conclusion drawn by the Socialists that "seen statistically, the former National Socialists voted for the VdU."[89] (See Tables I and II)

Although there is unquestionably a definite correlation between the strength of the VdU and the incidence of newly enfranchised *minderbelastete* National Socialists, within the general population, and more dramatically within the newly enfranchised electorate, there appear such significant deviations as to indicate that previous sympathy for Nazism was by no means the sole factor binding the new electoral bloc.

Statistical analysis and graphic representation do not yield sufficient information to judge precisely the degree to which the VdU was voted by former *minderbelastete* National Socialists, but the overall pattern seems to sustain Drs. Kraus and Reimann in their estimates that the constituency of their electoral party was approximately sixty percent former Nazis.[90] The remainder seems to have defected to the

VdU out of dissatisfaction with either of the coalition parties, with wide regional variations. But this speculation masks another important factor; despite fascism, both black and brown, despite war and occupation, the class-political structure of Austria had survived. Throughout the First Republic, the presence of a strong German national-liberal political bloc had consistently wooed between twelve and twenty percent of the electorate from the major parties, thereby denying any single party a parliamentary majority. In the final democratically administered Austrian election in 1930, the so-called Schober Bloc *(Nationaler Wirtschaftsblock und Landbund)* drew virtually the same total number of votes as did the VdU in 1949. Relieved of the artificial restrictions imposed on the exercise of party politics by the Allied Council in 1945, Austrians returned to their traditional practice of entrusting the task of government to no single party.

With the election campaign over, the VdU hoped to be rid of the neo-Nazi label and looked to its future in Parliament fully aware of the legacy of the national-liberal parties of the First Republic as a balance on the political scale between right and left. Based on the party configuration in the new Parliament, the VdU appeared capable of being a decisive force between the two major parties. As *Die Neue Front* triumphantly trumpeted:

> We have reached our goal: the black majority has been broken and the red blocked. The *Nationalrat* consists of one hundred sixty-five members, so when Parliament gathers, a group of eighty-three has the absolute majority; this time the People's party received only seventy-seven seats and as a result lost its position of power. But the Socialist party with sixty-seven cannot take over this position. We, therefore, have conquered the key position which we had intended to achieve. We always have the possibility of supporting the group that makes the most reasonable suggestion to pass a law.[91]

One basic difference separated the VdU from the national-liberal "third force" of the First Republic, however: National Socialism. As a consequence of this unhappy period, the national-liberal camp had been severely compromised. To erase this stigma, Dr. Kraus issued an "Appeal to State-Political Reason":

> Certain elements not only want to label us Nazis, but even want that we become neo-Nazi.... Now, when we have achieved a certain influence in Parliament, it is our first step to formally declare that we have nothing to do with neo-Nazism or Pan-Germanism....
>
> We want to become a party of the center and to prevent a majority dictatorship.[92]

Table I

Comparison of the Number of VdU Votes Cast with the Number of Former *Minderbelastete* National Socialists Reenfranchised by the Amnesty Law of April 22, 1949

Province	Former *minderbelastete* National Socialists*	VdU Votes Cast**	Ratio of NS/VdU
Vienna	112,945	79,149	1.4/1
Lower Austria	77,196	38,385	2.0/1
Burgenland	14,343	6,398	2.2/1
Upper Austria	75,225	124,520	.6/1
Styria	89,441	94,991	.9/1
Salzburg	29,190	31,919	.9/1
Carinthia	39,326	51,247	.8/1
Tyrol	42,762	38,377	1.1/1
Vorarlberg	16,225	22,287	.7/1
Total	497,693	489,273	1.0/1

*"Die Durchführung des NS Gesetzes," pp. 139–145 in *Österreichisches Jahrbuch 1949 nach ämtlichen Quellen*, ed. Bundespressedienst, einundzwanzigste Folge (Vienna: Druck und Verlag der Österreichischen Staatsdruckerei, 1950), p. 141.
** *Wahlstatistik* (Vol. III of *Wahlhandbuch*), p. B127.

Table II

Comparison of the Numbers of *Minderbelastete* National Socialists Admitted to the 1949 *Nationalrat* Elections with the Number of Votes Cast for the Various Parties*

Province		Valid Ballots 1. 1949 2. 1945 3. difference	Number of Votes per 100 Votes cast for the various parties 1. 1949 2. 1945 3. gain or loss				Number of Votes divided according to party 1. 1949 2. 1945 3. gain or loss			
			OeVP	SPOe	KPOe	VdU	OeVP	SPOe	KPOe	VdU
Vienna	1.	1,142,160	35	49	8	7	401,854	565,440	89,710	79,149
1-7	2.	889,324	35	57	8	-	310,803	508,214	70,307	-
Bezirk	3.	252,836	0	-8	0	+7	91,051	56,226	19,403	+79,149
Lower	1.	886,095	53	37	6	4	464,854	330,631	48,459	39,385
Austria	2.	704,878	55	40	5	-	384,214	284,430	36,234	-
8-11	3.	181,217	-2	-3	+1	+4	80,640	46,201	12,225	+39,385
Upper	1.	597,523	45	31	3	21	268,578	184,042	18,574	124,520
Austria	2.	469,027	59	38	3	-	276,676	179,975	12,376	-
12-16	3.	128,496	-14	-7	0	+21	-8,098	4,067	6,198	+124,520
Salzburg	1.	172,060	44	34	3	18	75,212	57,752	5,759	31,919
17	2.	126,390	57	39	4	-	71,631	49,965	4,794	-
	3.	45,670	-13	-5	-1	+18	3,581	7,787	965	+31,919
Tyrol	1.	226,497	56	24	2	17	127,528	53,820	3,705	39,377
18	2.	153,571	71	27	2	-	109,360	40,857	3,354	-
	3.	72,926	-15	-3	0	+17	18,168	12,963	351	+39,377
Vorarl-	1.	101,837	56	19	2	22	57,402	19,262	2,435	22,287
berg	2.	69,707	70	28	2	-	48,812	19,189	1,706	-
19 Bzk.	3.	32,130	-14	-9	0	+22	8,590	93	729	+22,287
Styria	1.	653,755	43	37	5	14	280,719	244,482	29,617	94,991
20-23	2.	493,861	53	42	5	-	261,358	205,779	26,724	-
	3.	159,894	-10	-5	0	+14	19,361	38,703	2,893	+94,991
Carin-	1.	248,834	34	41	4	20	83,801	101,356	10,002	51,247
thia	2.	179,260	40	49	8	-	71,265	87,572	14,451	-
24	3.	69,574	-6	-8	-4	+20	12,536	13,782	-4,449	+51,247
Burgen-	1.	164,972	53	40	3	4	86,700	66,739	4,805	6,398
land	2.	131,336	52	45	3	-	68,108	58,917	4,311	-
25	3.	33,636	+1	-5	0	+4	18,592	7,822	494	+6,398
All	1.	4,193,733	44	39	5	12	1,846,581	1,623,524	213,066	489,273
Austria	2.	3,217,354	50	45	5	-	1,602,227	1,434,898	174,257	-
1-25	3.	976,379	-6	-6	0	+12	244,354	188,626	38,809	+489,273

Province		New Voters Total Minderbelasteten Non-NS	Percent NS in total electorate		New Voters percent NS percent non-Nazi		1. Ballots of new voters per party 2. Percent of new voters per party			
							OeVP	SPOe	KPOe	VdU
Vienna 1-7 Bezirk	1. 2. 3.	252,836 112,945 139,891	9.9		44.7 55.3		91,051 36.0	56,226 22.2	19,403 7.7	79,149 31.1
Lower Austria 8-11	1. 2. 3.	181,217 77,196 104,021	8.7		42.6 57.4		80,640 44.4	46,201 25.5	12,225 6.7	39,385 21.7
Upper Austria 12-16	1. 2. 3.	128,496 76,225 52,271	12.8		59.3 40.7		-8,098 -6.5	4,067 .3	6,198 .5	124,520 96.9
Salzburg 17	1. 2. 3.	45,670 29,190 16,480	17.0		63.9 36.1		3,581 7.8	7,787 17.1	965 2.1	31,919 69.9
Tyrol 18	1. 2. 3.	72,926 42,762 30,164	18.9		58.6 41.4		18,168 24.9	12,963 17.8	351 .5	39,377 54.0
Vorarl- berg 19 Bzk.	1. 2. 3.	32,130 16,225 15,905	15.9		50.5 49.5		8,590 26.7	93 .3	729 2.7	22,287 69.4
Styria 20-23	1. 2. 3.	159,894 89,441 70,453	13.7		55.9 44.1		19,361 12.11	38,703 24.2	2,893 1.8	94,991 59.4
Carin- thia 24	1. 2. 3.	69,574 39,326 30,248	15.8		56.5 43.5		12,536 18.0	13,782 19.8	-4,449 -6.4	51,247 73.7
Burgen- land 25	1. 2. 3.	33,636 14,343 19,293	8.7		42.6 57.4		18,592 55.3	7,822 23.3	494 1.5	6,398 19.0
All Austria 1-25	1. 2. 3.	976,379 497,653 478,726	11.7		51.0 49.0		244,354 25.0	188,626 19.3	38,809 4.0	489,273 50.1

* For ease of calculation and considerations of space I have omitted the statistics for the five additional parties which ran for the *Nationalrat* in 1949. Based on the assumption that strong party discipline hinders any significant shift in voting patterns, the relative differences between 1949 and 1945 can largely be attributed to the weight of the newly enfranchised voters. The statistics may be found in "Die Durchführung des NS Gesetzes," and in *Wahlstatistik*, p. B 127.

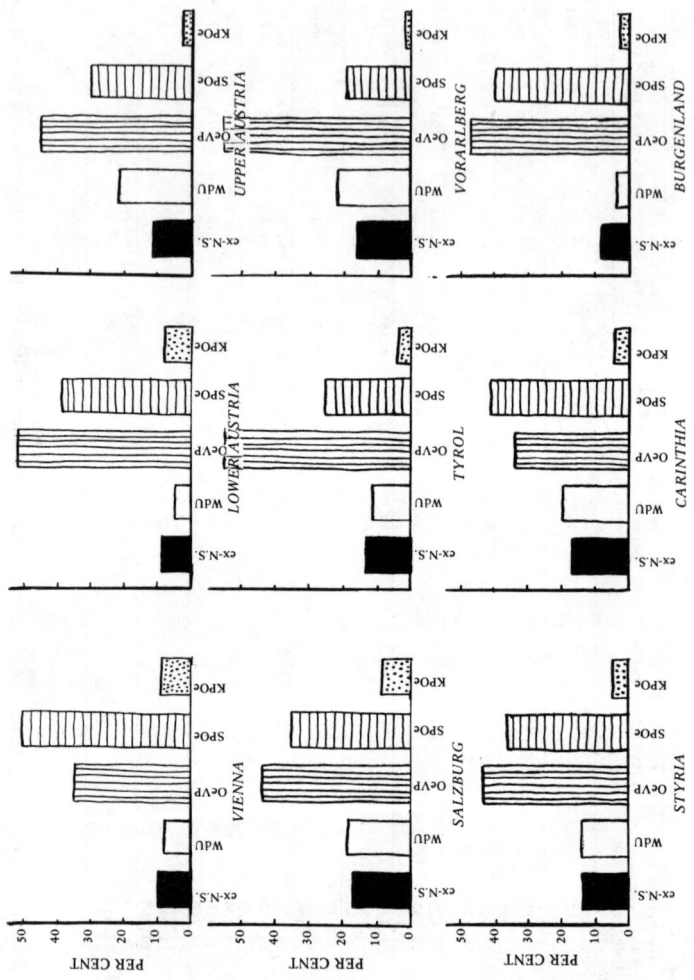

Figure 1
Comparison of the Percent of the Vote for the Various Parties with the Percent of *Minderbelastete* Nazis according to Province

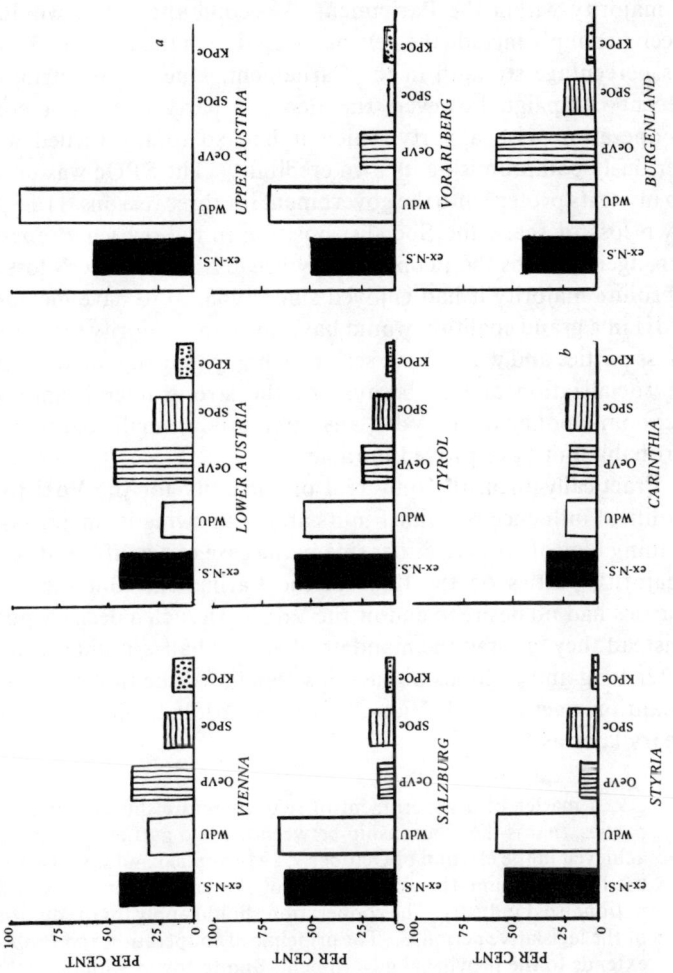

Figure 2
Comparison of the Percent of New Voters Voting the Various Parties with the Percent of New Voters Who Were *Minderbelastete* Nazis according to Province

Technically, it would have been possible for the VdU to join forces with either of the major parties and form a small coalition to command a majority within the Parliament. A second alternative would have been to simply include the new party faction in the *Proporz* relative to its percentage strength in the Parliament. Due to the vitriol of the recent campaign however, the People's party could not consider cooperation with a party which it had so totally reviled without seriously compromising its own credibility. The SPOe was unwilling to invite its protegé into the government for three reasons: 1) despite its own loss of seats, the Socialist position in the revised *Proporz* was stronger vis-a-vis the People's party because of the latter's loss of the absolute majority it had enjoyed since 1945, 2) to have included the VdU in a grand coalition would have given the majority to the middle-class parties and would have seriously hampered any further attempts at socialization and 3) because of the strong liberal, antisocialist economic policy of the VdU, any attempt at a small coalition would probably not have proved durable.

Practically then, the only real opportunity for the VdU to exert political influence remained in its ability to swing its majority-determining bloc of votes to either side in the case of a confrontation of the majority parties on the floor of the Parliament. But the majority parties had no desire to endow the VdU with such a decisive position. Instead they ignored the mandate of almost half-a-million voters and after long and arduous discussions concluded the first of the written coalition pacts, which Vice-Chancellor Adolf Schärf described six years later as

> ... a matter of a government of two, therefore shutting out third parties; that is the relationship between the two parties, the *Proporz* achieved in the election of October 9, 1949 applied and was also to be used to determine the appointment of the leading functions in the nationalized industry. The cooperation should apply for the duration of the legislative period.... The principle of cooperation and *Proporz* extends to the provincial governments and to towns with more than 10,000 inhabitants. Special coordinating committees for the purpose of negotiating between the two parties were to be considered.[93]

Based on the slight OeVP plurality in the Parliament, Figil again became chancellor with his Socialist opposite number Schärf again as vice-chancellor. The new government included in addition five OeVP and four SPOe ministers with one state secretary from each party. The new *Proporz* was OeVP: seven, SPOe: six.[94]

V

Isolation, Impotence and Renewed Hope

With the exception of the Communist party, which had been ignored since 1947 as a mouthpiece of the Soviet Union, meaningful parliamentary opposition had been unknown in Austrian political life. This the VdU intended to change with its sixteen man parliamentary delegation, registered as the *Klub děr Unabhängigen* [KdU]: Club of the Independents. In his response to Chancellor Figil's "Declaration of Government" VdU Chairman and parliamentary faction leader Kraus put the government on notice that the KdU generally supported the policies enunciated, but that on certain matters it would follow a policy of "... constructive opposition ... as a regulator for the interests of the state against party interests."[1] Furthermore the Club would seek

1) a one-third budget and income tax reduction subject to public sanction via plebiscite as provided for in the Constitution.
2) a reversal of the trend towards nationalization of industry, a shift of the superfluous and wasteful bureaucracy to the more efficient control of private enterprise and a vigorous program of housing, road and power plant construction by the state as well as by private enterprise encouraged by generous credit terms as a means of stimulating production and reducing unemployment.
3) an increase of foreign trade so as to equalize the balance of imports and exports by the 1952 expiration of the Marshall Plan. Specifically this was to include reestablishment of trade and tourism with the Federal Republic of Germany.
4) the reestablishment of the *Rechtsstaat,* by ending party influence on all areas of justice and an end to the inequality of former National Socialists before the law.[2]

The refusal of the coalition parties to accept the Independents as a meaningful legislative partner became apparent in the opening session of the new Parliament when by mutual consent they shunted the KdU into the isolation of the extreme right bank of benches in the assembly hall.[3] When Dr. Kraus rose from this position to deliver his faction's response to the chancellor's "Declaration of Government," his statement of goals was repeatedly interrupted with catcalls and accusations of Pan-Germanism.[4] That the KdU could not accomplish any of its goals with its sixteen vote bloc was clear. What it wanted, however, was expressed in a speech by former *Landbund* President Karl Hartleb who had once served as minister of interior and vice-chancellor during the First Republic. Hartleb demanded that the majority parties make room for the KdU ". . . in the center of the house, not only in one sector, but in both."[5] This was not just petty hair splitting, but rather symbolized the desire of the VdU to assume a centrist position from which it hoped to loosen the rigid two-party *"Demokratur."* In this manner the VdU proposed to establish an area within which Parliament could pass legislation on the basis of the sympathies of a majority of the delegates on the floor rather than simply rubber stamp predetermined government proposals.

To a degree, Hartleb's protest against the extreme rightist label was justified. If the members of the KdU had been seated according to their individual political orientations, they would have ranged from the right wing of the Socialist sector where Vice-Chairman and co-founder Reimann would have been politically comfortable, to the left-wing of the OeVP benches where Kraus would have been seated, and finally to the far right where former Nazis Drs. Stüber and Pfeifer would have found company with a number of representatives of the People's party. But the stamp of right-wing extremism was a convenient label with which the VdU could be stigmatized, isolated and ignored. That several members of the KdU deserved this label provided the other parties with a continuing basis for defamation. In contrast to Kraus and Reimann who bore no trace of Nazism in their past or present attitudes and even to Hartleb who, with so many *Landbündler,* had enthusiastically welcomed the coming of National Socialism but direly regretted his actions, Dr. Stüber and a segment of the VdU constituency looked back on the Nazi era with fond memories and bitterly resented the stigma which they bore. When baited on the floor of the *Nationalrat* they overreacted with defensive outbursts that seemed to lend credence to the accusations. In many cases the sessions became so stormy that meetings were suspended, and on one occasion Reimann actually became involved in a fist fight on the floor of the Parliament with a socialist delegate.[6] This stigmatization of the VdU as a neo-Nazi organization combined with the political impotence of the KdU in the *Nationalrat* to produce a public image of the Independents as a faceless party of which ". . . the average voter knows very little, but which is identified very strongly with the banned NSDAP."[7]

In Parliament, as a consequence of the secret coalition pact, bills came to a vote only after they had been accepted in the closed meetings of the two government parties.[8] Any proposal from one party that was not followed by a similar proposal from the other was understood to be a political demonstration for publicity purposes and never discussed any further. As a result, Parliament became little more than a debating society, or a "voting machine" as the VdU preferred. The KdU, isolated on the far right, with neither representation in the government nor the means to force a vote on its own numerous legislative proposals, was quickly disabused of its idea to exert a "balance on the scale" between the two major parties and transform the *Nationalrat* into a true democratic parliament with open debate and free voting procedures. Instead, its "constructive opposition" and positive programs were rendered meaningless by the coalition pact and the KdU became merely a baiter of the majority parties with no more importance than that of a chained watchdog. Its fractious presence did, however, serve to publicize what the league saw as the most glaring errors and injustices of the administration. Its continual complaints received automatic publicity in government publications and where these protests reflected genuine public sympathy the independent press expanded the scrutiny of the government. Thus, in lively, if ineffective speeches in Parliament and in indirectly influencing public opinion, the VdU was able to force some of its demands on the major parties. The most notable of these successes was the reduction of the severity of the National Socialist Law. This struggle for the easing of de-Nazification which had initially been made respectable by the independent press was adopted as the goal of the KdU parliamentary program.[9] It was under the pressure of the KdU in Parliament and the pressure of aroused public opinion that this unfortunate chapter of postwar history came to a conclusion.

On the provincial level, the opportunity for VdU influence at first seemed greater because, unlike the national government, the provincial constitutions dictated that provincial governments be formed with party representation in proportion to the number of seats held in the *Landtag*. In Salzburg, Carinthia and Styria, where the major parties were equally balanced, the VdU representatives could really hope to be the "balance on the scale." But due to the extension of the coalition pact downwards to the provincial and local assemblies,[10] the VdU was rendered impotent even where it was significantly represented.

The one area where the VdU was able to force its way into positions of responsibility was in the political representative bodies for individual businesses and industries as well as in the provincial workers' and employees' boards in western Austria. In its approach to the blue and white collar workers, the VdU was selective, choosing to campaign only where significant support was indicated, usually in areas with a strong *grossdeutsch* tradition or with a large *volksdeutsch* concentration. In such areas, the VdU had a significant advantage over the Socialists who were traditionally weaker in the west than in the older industrial areas of Vienna and Lower Austria. Furthermore, in a number of the western industries there were many politically sophisticated ex-Nazis who had been forbidden to return to their former middle-class professions under the restrictions of the National Socialist Law. These workers eagerly supported the VdU and generally had greater leadership ability than opposite numbers in the SPOe. In the relatively nonclass-conscious west, the VdU organizational efforts paid handsome rewards.[11] In virtually every local industry and business council election where it chose to campaign, the VdU became at least the second largest party and in many western concerns even outpolled the SPOe. Particularly stunning and alarming to the Socialist party were the VdU victories in several major industrial complexes of Upper Austria and Salzburg. At the enormous hydroelectric construction site of Kaprun located high in the Hohe Tauern mountain range of Salzburg, the VdU polled 911 votes to 699 for the SPOe, 271 for the Communists and 44 for the People's party. At Grossraming the results were just as decisive: VdU: 285, SPOe: 161, KPOe: 60, OeVP: 8.[12] The crowning victory however, came with the industrial council election in the giant, nationalized VOeST (United Austrian Iron and Steel) Works in Upper Austria, where the VdU received a majority of 3,233 to the SPOe: 3,056, KPOe: 72 and the OeVP: 56.[13] Fourteen and a half percent of all blue and white collar workers voted VdU in the industrial council elections of the fall of 1949.[14]

The Socialist labor leaders were alarmed, but for the most part sought explanations for their defeats in their own failures, not in heated tirades against alleged neo-Nazism of the VdU.

> The excuse of former Nazis and *Volksdeutschen* does not apply. First of all, these people voted our Socialist lists two years ago and secondly, these people have been workers for almost four years now and we must strive to win them for our democratic socialist *Weltanschauung*. We have had time enough. We just have not used it, or have used it poorly.[15]

To be sure, these victories were in areas of relatively new industrial development where the Socialist party was weak. But this was of little consolation to a party which prided itself on its programmatic appeal to the working class. To correct this situation, the SPOe analyzed the reasons for the defeats and outlined its tasks:

> It has been correctly indicated that among these new working classes, class-consciousness and class-solidarity must be lacking.... It is here a matter of a not yet established class and a not yet firm proletariat, partially *Volksdeutschen,* partially displaced persons and in all cases unschooled [in socialism] workers who occupy a special position in the Austrian working class. With these groups we will have to very seriously concern ourselves.[16]

This analysis was accurate. In the next several years, the SPOe worked to dam this breach in its ranks. This was accomplished by strong-arm tactics in some cases and in others by diluting strong VdU contingencies by forcing transfers or dismissals or key personnel. More important however, was the fact that the VdU was basically a middle-class party and was really not attuned to the interests of the average worker. Moreover, because of its impotence at the governmental level and because of the monolithic position which the Socialists occupied overall in the industrial councils, the trade unions and the workers' and employees' boards, even sympathetic workers came to the realization that the VdU was an unrealistic vehicle for expressing their interests. As a consequence, the league steadily lost its support among the workers.

In the long run, the political impotence of the VdU at all levels condemned the movement to an existence of vocal opposition with little real opportunity to influence government. As a consequence, the heterogeneous elements which constituted the movement gradually lost their optimism, and the cohesion provided by the dissatisfaction of 1949 was gradually eroded by increasing prosperity and by rapidly fading memories of postwar alienation. In the years following its promising initial success, the VdU failed to develop a positive *raison d'etre* and its subsequent course became what political journalist Alexander Vodopevic has described as ". . . the history of the alienation of groups and interests which never belonged together."[17]

Because of the intentionally vague nature of the program and the loose democracy of its organization, each of the many varied factions contained within the league believed its own particular orientation to be the most important and struggled to win control so as to more completely commit the VdU to its policy. As a result, the leadership was constantly confronted by challenges to its policies from below. The remaining history of the League of Independents is therefore the narrative of the attempts and ultimate failure of this leadership to provide the common base for unified action necessary to ward off these challenges. The result was disintegration of the league in three directions: 1) the defection of individuals to the two major parties out of disillusionment with the league's program or feelings of futility from its political impotence and isolation, 2) resignations from the VdU and the creation of new political groups by people whose personal aspirations or political goals had been frustrated by the relatively moderate policy of the Kraus-Reimann leadership, and 3) the attempts of dissidents to overthrow the moderate leadership and raise new men to power for the purpose of reorienting the league's program and policy. This resulted in a continual purging of the party, further straining its political credibility.

The process of disintegration had already begun, even before the formal announcement of the founding of the league in February of 1949, but was momentarily stayed during the summer by enthusiasm and optimism surrounding the establishment of the program and the excitement of the election campaign. But once the electricity of the campaign had died away, the loose, nonmembership structure of the league made it difficult to sustain the movement beyond the impulses of the moment. Mass meetings which had proven so successful during the campaign[18] now drew only a handful of the faithful. The party organ, *Die Neue Front,* which had been a modest source of revenue for the movement before the election, became a drain on the treasury. It became evident that the *Verband der Unabhängigen* was indeed an "association of independents," who were willing to vote for the league's electoral party, but who were unwilling to lend their money, their time or their energies to its perpetuation.

In February of 1950, the first important resignation since the preceding spring touched off an organizational crisis which seriously threatened the existence of the provincial organization in Upper Austria. This emergency was stimulated by the resignation of the charismatic, if somewhat schizophrenic,[19] working-class leader, Oskar Hümer. In explaining his action to the *Salzburger Nachrichten* Hümer complained

> ... that forces were tolerated in the VdU which he did not consider consistent with his social and positive Austrian orientation. According to his opinion, workers did not exist to simply vote. He had promised the workers that he would sound the alarm if the VdU

should ever cease to represent the workers. Now he has fulfilled this responsibility. The VdU has strayed so far from its original program, that he can no longer encourage workers to remain in the VdU any longer.[20]

As the crisis developed, it became apparent that the Hümer resignation was not merely an individual action, but the result of a severe split in the Upper Austrian organization, reflecting the dissatisfaction of one faction with the federal leadership. In order to halt this disintegration of the Upper Austrian League which would have detached thousands of workers from the party, Deputy Chairman Reimann went to Linz to personally work out a solution to the problem. At this point however, the crisis expanded to divide the entire league into two factions, one headed by Drs. Reimann and Kraus supporting the existing leadership in Upper Austria and the other mobilized behind General Secretary Gordon Gollob who supported the dissidents.[21] Representatives of the provincial organizations of Styria, Tyrol and a part of the Carinthian organization entered into discussions with the insurgent Upper Austrian group in order to strengthen the position of the German nationalists headed by Gollob against the Kraus-Reimann leadership.[22]

To ameliorate the differences between the warring factions, Dr. Reimann, on behalf of the federal leadership, proposed a compromise which expelled a number of the dissidents including the previous head of the provincial league. But to promote closer relations throughout the entire league, Reimann proposed the establishment of a standing committee of representatives from all levels of the provincial organization as well as specific representation from the peasant and working classes.[23] In this committee the representation of the latter group was to be twice as strong as that of any other, emphasizing the importance that the VdU leadership placed on retaining the support of the Upper Austrian working class.

On March 20, the executive committee of the league approved the compromise and took a further step to placate the Upper Austrian workers by reaffirming its dedication to the ". . . broad expansion of the social and trade union policy."[24] Although the immediate crisis was ended and the VdU could claim that the numerous resignations that had followed in its wake (not only in Upper Austria, but throughout the entire organization) had "cleansed, not weakened" the league, the portents for the future were threatening. Despite the attempts to woo the workers, Upper Austria was the only province in the entire country that failed the next year to return as many votes for the very popular VdU candidate for the presidency as had been cast in the 1949 *Nationalrat* elections. The Hümer Affair and the ensuing crisis combined with redoubled Socialist education, propaganda and recruiting efforts to produce a massive defection of workers from the VdU.

A second characteristic of the disintegration of the VdU that had become apparent in the Upper Austrian turmoil was the tendency of the league's diverse constituency to split into its component parts along ideological lines. The wave of resignations throughout Austria that followed in the wake of the Hümer Affair psychologically weakened confidence in the entire organization and stimulated the defection of groups, vaguely referred to as "nationalist-Bolshevik," into separate splinter parties.

The first of these splits occurred when the Lower Austrian provincial chairman, Josef Heger, resigned to form the *Nationaldemokratischer Verband*.[25] In the recent *Nationalrat* election, Heger had embarrassed the league by boasts of "connections direct to the center of an Occupying Power."[26] The OeVP seized on this to imply a connection between the VdU and the "international Communist conspiracy" threatening to compromise the league's strict anti-Communist posture. When the VdU leadership sought to discipline Heger for his indiscretion, he withdrew his membership and led a radical right faction out of the Viennese league. The new splinter group was composed mostly of former SS officers who mingled a fanatic German nationalism with totalitarian Communism, similar to elements of the postwar Communist party in the German Democratic Republic.

Less than a month later there was another defection from the Vienna league by former SS members and unreconstructed Nazis who had joined the VdU in hopes of finding a resurrected NSDAP. When this hope failed to materialize they shifted to the *Nationale Liga — Bund der Schaffende Österreicher* forming under former SS Öbersturmführer Dr. Felix Slavik.[27]

These defections and consolidations of rivals for the third-party vote left the Vienna and Lower Austrian league in shambles and threatened total subversion by the radical right; responding to these challenges, the VdU executive council suspended recognition of the provincial organization and placed League Chairman Kraus in temporary control until the membership could be purged and a new leadership installed.[28]

In view of the total numbers involved, the defections to these "nationalist-Bolshevik" organizations were insignificant and had the positive effect of ridding the VdU of undesirable elements, but the publicity gleefully accorded these difficulties by the party press further damaged the credibility of the league. Demonstrative of this growing lack of confidence was the defection of a number of prominent functionaries in the Tyrolean league to the OeVP out of fears that "... within the VdU, forces were at work which are striving towards cooperation with the Communists."[29] The VdU press de-emphasized the importance of these events and again wrote of the cleansing effect on the organization as a whole. Evaluating the numerical influence of these defections and expulsions, this was a fair analysis, but psychologically the effect was much greater, for these continuing upheavals seemed to substantiate suspicions about the long-range viability of the league.

Much more serious for the stability of the organization than the developments in Vienna and Lower Austria was the simultaneous challenge mounted by General Secretary Gordon Gollob, who used his strongly *grossdeutsch* Styrian league as a power base to demand a dramatic increase in the German-nationalist emphasis of the VdU program and policy. In the summer of 1949, Dr. Kraus' ban on any direct negotiations with former Nazis had begun to alienate Gollob from the VdU leadership, and by 1950 he led the consolidation of an anti-Kraus-Reimann constellation which aimed at seizing control of the league and establishing a more outspokenly nationalist program. The first hint of this movement had been revealed in the Hümer Affair. Before those difficulties were fully resolved, the Styrian leadership attempted to *putsch* the central leadership by issuing a sharply worded "resolution" expressing no confidence in the VdU federal leadership and demanding a general assembly for the purpose of electing new leaders.[30] The occasion for this move of the Styrian league was the hope of preventive retaliation against what they feared would be the imminent expulsion of Gollob from the Executive Committee in punishment for his role in the organizational struggle in Upper Austria.

This certainly was the design of the general leadership, and the opportunity to begin the maneuver against the ambitious General Secretary presented itself early in the summer of 1950. At the staging of the traditional, ancient, Germanic, *völkisch* ceremonies celebrating the arrival of the summer solstice, Gollob and his lieutenants undertook a vigorous round of speaking engagements to recruit new members sympathetic to their orientation. In traditionally Germanic settings with blazing torches, roaring bonfires and folk costumes, reminiscent of German-nationalist and Nazi meetings of the past,

Gollob and his colleagues spoke to large crowds of enthusiastic and responsive German nationalists. These meetings came under the close scrutiny of the Minister of Interior and as a consequence of speeches by Gollob and Styrian VdU *Landtag* Club Chairman Elsnitz in Graz, the provincial league was dissolved for "agitation forbidden by the constitution," i.e. neo-Nazism.[31] In this action Minister of Interior Helmer unconsciously served the needs of the Kraus-Reimann faction in the Executive Committee of the VdU. Using this move by the Minister of Interior to justify its own action, on July 10 the Executive Committee announced its intention of conducting an investigation of the accusations against the Styrian league. As a means of disassociating itself from the *grossdeutsch* nationalists the Kraus-Reimann leadership faction innocently proclaimed that it had

> ... shown the Allies that we ourselves shy away from real neo-National Socialist tendencies. Because they [the Styrian league] have indicated a connection with certain people, we ourselves will conduct an investigation against them, firm in the conviction that the greatest part of all accusations will be revealed as lies. However, whoever is actually recognized as guilty and through his actions has brought the VdU into the most dangerous situation since its founding, must bear the consequences.[32]

Thus, using the power of the Ministry of Interior to ban allegedly neo-Nazi activity, the Kraus-Reimann group issued a clear warning to Gollob and his "dissidents" to either desist in their efforts to undermine the leadership or be expelled from the league. In this way, the moderates did not have to raise the ticklish issue of nationalism, which was taken care of by Helmer's action. Instead, the Kraus-Reimann group could criticize the Ministry of Interior for acting arbitrarily, while concentrating itself on the disruptive efforts of Gollob. But the threat against Gollob was ineffective and on July 20, the Kraus-Reimann-Hartleb-dominated federal leadership decided to expel the general secretary, but avoided the issue of excessive nationalist agitation and instead justified its action on the grounds that

> ... Herr Gollob has gone against the interests of the VdU in the worst way, because he instigated the defection of several provincial leagues from the federal league and because he disseminated incorrect and distorted reports to the opposition press about leading VdU functionaries.[33]

At the same time, the federal leadership expelled several members of the Salzburg league, including provincial Secretary Gustav Zeillinger, who, although opposing the extreme nationalism of Gollob, felt that the expulsion of so many nationalists would only lead to further disintegration of the VdU.[34] In an effort to provide a vehicle for the reestablishment of unity in the seriously shattered organization, the federal leadership decided to call a general assembly to sanction the recent developments and for the first time to select the league's leadership in a democratic election by convention delegates.

The intent of this decision had been to "clear the air" of the "poison" which for months had threatened the very life of the league. Instead it touched off another organizational crisis which threatened a struggle to the death. Gollob personally refused to accept his expulsion and demanded that his case and numerous other matters, which, he charged, had been arbitrarily dictated by the Kraus-Reimann-Hartleb clique, be brought before a general assembly.[35]

Anticipating the convening of a general assembly, members of both factions traveled throughout Austria seeking support for their respective positions and in the process essentially split the league into pro- and anti-Gollob factions. The Styrian organization, although prohibited from open activity, lobbied its neighbor league in Carinthia into a resolution condemning the Gollob expulsion and calling for his rehabilitation until the matter could be definitively settled by a general assembly.[36] The Salzburg league openly defied the federal leadership, reinstated its expelled functionaries and rejected the contention that it had ever endangered the unity of the VdU. To win support for this position the Salzburg leadership called a meeting of league representatives from Upper Austria, Tyrol, Vorarlberg, Styria and Carinthia in Salzburg to discuss the crisis within the organization. Both factions were represented and vehemently argued their respective positions, but in the end were able to collectively agree on a resolution to be communicated to Dr. Kraus:

> The provincial representatives hold firmly to the unity of the VdU, but want the position of the provincial leagues to exist as individual corporate bodies; it is emphatically demanded that all announced suspensions and expulsions since the Graz incidents immediately be cancelled, that all investigations of all those responsible for the strained relations be immediately carried out, and that a general assembly be held in at least eight weeks for the purpose of a new election of the federal leadership and the rectification of all pressing problems.[37]

With the increasing polarization of the league and the threat of total fragmentation, the federal leadership agreed to schedule a general assembly for October 1, and requested the election of delegates by the provincial leagues.[38]

In the meantime, a "Committee of Three" in Graz took the task of "settling the crisis in the VdU" and through its chairman, the Graz *Nationalrat* Dr. Scheuch, had obtained the rehabilitation of Gollob at least until the meeting of the general assembly.[39] In the weeks immediately prior to the convening of the general assembly, the "dissidents" mounted a vicious attack on the existing league federal leadership, accusing Kraus and Reimann in particular of being in the pay of Jews and of being traitors to the *grossdeutsch* nationalist tradition.[40]

On October 1, the power struggle that had been gathering since the beginning of the year climaxed in the opening session of the First Annual General Assembly. In an exhausting thirteen hour session the two feuding factions came into open confrontation in the election of the league chairman. The dissidents consolidated around Dr. Scheuch in opposition to the league founder, Dr. Herbert Kraus. In contrast to the typical voice vote of other Austrian parties, the polling was by secret ballot so as to eliminate pressure from the two factions on the uncommitted delegates. Of the one hundred forty-four votes cast, Dr. Kraus received a slim seventy-seven vote majority, clearly illustrating the need to ameliorate the differences within the organization. Drawing the necessary conclusion from the election, Kraus delivered a conciliatory speech to the assembly, while former deputy-chairmen, Dr. Reimann and Professor Miltschinsky, who had been under strong attack by the "dissidents," declined to run for reelection. With the way thus cleared, Dr. Scheuch and Colonel Gollob were elected along with Karl Hartleb and Thomas Neuwirth to the Executive Committee. Along with Kraus and the four deputy-chairmen, a twenty-six man leadership council was made up of the chairmen from each of the nine provinces and thirteen at-large representatives elected from the floor of the convention to lead special study committees on specific social, economic and political problems.[41]

The impact of the general assembly was significant in reorienting the league's federal leadership and in establishing precedents that radically altered and ultimately destroyed the initial coalition of 1949. First, the preeminence of co-founders Kraus and Reimann in the federal leadership had been successfully challenged by the provincial organizations using the innate revulsion of the independents to central control at the federal level and the league's emphasis on internal democracy to shift power to the provinces. Second, the provincial organizations were more dominated by nationalist sentiment than the founding leadership had been and the inclusion of Scheuch and Gollob in the executive committee and the exclusion of Reimann severely diluted the previously strong commitment to social reform. In the general federal leadership however, eight of the thirteen at-large members represented worker or social reform groups, reaffirming the strong desire of the general assembly to continue recruitment from the working class.[42] The result was approximately a sixty percent to forty percent predominance of the moderate orientation over the nationalists in the federal leadership council,[43] despite a probable edge to the nationalists among the general membership.[44]

This same proportion also held in the Executive Committee where despite the 2:2 ratio of Kraus-Neuwirth: Scheuch-Gollob groups, the balance shifted away from the nationalists by the tendency of Deputy Chairman Hartleb to support the strongest group. Hartleb saw himself as the same kind of force within the league as he hoped the VdU would be in the general political scene, i.e. "the balance on the political scale." In assessing the mood of 1950, Hartleb decided for the Kraus direction in hopes of moderating the public image of the VdU, thereby making it possible for the league to play a real parliamentary role in the political life of Austria.[45] This hope, Reimann feels, was unrealistic, since given the existence of the Occupation, neither of the two parties could accept a coalition with a party stigmatized as a party of ex-Nazis for fear that it would endanger the prospects for the state treaty.[46] The impossibility of a coalition was, however, not yet apparent in 1950 and as long as the prospect remained, the liberal-social reform element was able to maintain its dominance against the nationalist-dominated lower organization.

Even while the organizational splits in the VdU were being patched together, the league was confronted by a serious crisis of a totally different nature. Since 1945, the Austrian Communists had tried through both legal and illegal means to gain control of the government and pull at least the Russian-occupied sector into the Soviet Union's network of satellite People's Republics. In the first years following the end of the war, extreme shortages and severe inflation threatened to provide the fuel of discontent that could guise a Communist *putsch* in the garb of a people's revolution. In 1947, in order to stabilize the economy, the government parties negotiated the first wage-price agreement. The Communists feared that economic stability would diminish their political leverage and therefore sought to obstruct the agreement by making unrealistic demands on the agreement, allegedly on behalf of the working class; when these were not met the Communists called for protests and demonstrations in hopes of generating the appearance of a popular revolution. Minister of Interior Helmer had been able to prevent a Communist attempt to infiltrate the police force and therefore could rely on loyal security forces to quell the revolt. In the next two years, additional wage-price agreements followed which kept pace with the recovery and expansion of the economy.

Late in the summer of 1950, government control over foodstuffs ended and the trade unions and the various worker and employees' councils began negotiations to fully normalize the economy and end the black market through a fourth and presumably final wage-price agreement. Involved in the plan was a devaluation of the schilling to make Austrian products more competitive on the world market and a commensurate increase in domestic wages and prices to adjust to the new exchange rate. Although the intent of the agreement was to stimulate production and employment by increasing foreign trade, there was widespread fear that the devaluation would touch off a wild inflationary spiral that would quickly wipe out the wage increases. Consumers, fearing a reduction in their buying power, rushed to the shops to stockpile goods, while shopkeepers quickly cleared their display windows and shelves to store goods for future sale at inflated prices. In this moment of economic instability, the Communists perceived their perhaps last chance to ease Austria into the Soviet bloc of People's Democracies, before the imminent onset of an Austrian "economic wonder."

Since the SPOe was party to the proposed fourth wage-price agreement, the Communists saw an ideal opportunity to exploit workers' fears and seize control of the trade unions from the Socialists. The VdU, unaware of the portentous plans of the Communists and optimistic of its own future in the trade unions in the light of its recent industrial election victories, likewise saw the widespread dissatisfaction over the wage-price pact as a means of increasing its own influence among the workers at the expense of the Socialists. Furthermore, since 1947 Herbert Kraus, in line with his own traditional liberal economic convictions, had been a vociferous critic of the wage-price agreements as violations of the natural and beneficent operation of a market economy. The VdU at its founding had accepted this precept and loudly demanded an end to artificial controls over the market economy. Therefore, it was ideologically consistent that in 1950 the VdU should attempt to exploit public dissatisfaction with the proposed new pact to its own advantage. In this maneuver however, the VdU unwittingly played into the hands of the Communists.[47]

The *putsch* attempt began on September 26, when the Communists organized 16,000 workers from the Russian controlled USIA industries in the south of Vienna, proclaimed a general strike and marched on the center of the city in protest against the wage-price agreement. This touched off a wave of sympathy strikes in most major industries in the Soviet zone and extended far to the west where the iron and steel workers of the VOeST, the Linz street car employees and workers in five other Upper Austrian industrial enterprises walked off their jobs. Even in the western zones of occupation, Communist party agitators were able to rouse antigovernment demonstrations in Salzburg and Innsbruck. For the next ten days Austria seemed on the verge of civil war and in the Soviet sector private armies of Socialist and Communist workers clashed in open street battles. Austrian efforts to restore order were severely hindered by the obstructionism and tacit support given Communist rioters by the Red Army.[48]

Confronted with the serious threat of a Communist seizure of power and prevented from effectively employing its own security forces, the government authorized Foreign Minister Gruber to appeal to the three western Occupying Powers to at least break through the Communist barricades on the interzonal access routes to Vienna. The Allied forces refused, maintaining that their troops were neither equipped nor trained for police action. If they were to act, it could only be militarily, and at this point, during the early phases of the Korean War, the Western Allies were unwilling to risk an open confrontation with the U.S.S.R. over what appeared to them to be purely an internal matter.[49]

In the meantime, the VdU which had real power among the workers only in Upper Austria, was placed in a highly compromising position. On September 26, when the general strike was called by the Communists in the Soviet zone, the VdU, although excoriating the demagogy of the KPOe, nevertheless supported a one hour wildcat strike of the previous day as a "vote of no confidence" against the Socialist controlled League of Trade Unions.[50] By September 28, the VdU representatives of the VOeST strike committee in Linz ordered their fellow workers back to work to protect the giant factory from attacks by Communist paramilitary forces from Lower Austria as well as from sabotage from within.[51]

Meanwhile, in the Soviet zone, the government was gradually restoring control. The Socialist party, through its influence in the trade unions, was able to mobilize its members and convince the bulk of the population that support of the strike would benefit only the Communists. Responding to the appeal to save Austria from a Communist *putsch,* Socialist workers made their way through the barricaded, rubble-strewn streets back to their factories where they threw up cordons to protect against the motorized Communist commandos. By September 27 calm had been restored and most industries in Vienna and Lower Austria were back to partial production.[52]

In an effort to exploit the anger of the unionized workers and win their support for the KPOe, the Communists issued a call to all Austrian Industrial Council representatives to meet on September 30 in a locomotive factory in the Viennese industrial suburb of Floridsdorf to discuss action against the wage-price agreement. But the SPOe-controlled Federation of Unions branded the meeting a pure "communist-fascist matter" and urged Socialist Industrial Council members to boycott the meeting. When the conference met it was almost all Communist functionaries who decided on an ultimatum demanding either a retraction of the price increases or a tax-free doubling of all forms of compensation, a price freeze and a commitment that no further devaluation would occur. Finally, if these demands were not met the conference threatened: "ON WEDNESDAY STRIKES IN ALL INDUSTRIES!"[53] Both sides mobilized their forces to meet the crisis and Vienna and its environs braced for what appeared to be civil war.

Open Soviet aid was given to Communist demonstrators; in one particularly blatant action in the suburb of Wiener Neustadt the Soviet commanding officer obstructed an attempt by Austrian police officials to clear the post office of Communist demonstrators through threats of action by Red Army troops.[54] When the Austrian Police President Holaubeck received no satisfaction to his October 3 protest to Deputy Commandant Col. Pankratev about Soviet obstructionism, Federal Chancellor Leopold Figil appealed directly to the Allied Council. The Soviet response was to assert that restrictions of Austrian police activity and the admitted intervention in Wiener Neustadt had occurred wholly in the Soviet zone of occupation and therefore was not subject to the control agreement on occupation.[55] At this point, the key to the Viennese revolution was the posture of the Soviet Army. Until October 4 Soviet troops had given tacit, but isolated aid to the Communist rioters; if the Red Army could be prevented from openly supporting the *putschists,* the government felt the revolution could be aborted. Convinced that the Soviets were unwilling to risk an open confrontation with the Western Allies, Foreign Minister Gruber directed identical notes to the foreign ministries of all four occupying powers describing the situation in Vienna as well as the aid which Soviet troops had been lending to the insurrection.[56]

Before the diplomatic wheels had had a chance to turn, however, the Communists escalated their sporadic demonstrations into an open grasp at power through the vehicle of the general strike. As announced, on the morning of October 4, the Communists mobilized the workers of the Soviet-controlled USIA industries who thronged into downtown Vienna and assembled in front of the Rathaus. By this time it had become apparent to the Communists that their call for a general strike had been answered by only a small percentage of the population of Vienna and Lower Austria. A popular, peaceful transfer of power was clearly not in the making, and so they turned to violence as a means of paralyzing the economy and gaining access to the reins of power. The demonstrators turned to the tactics of open revolution and began to tear up cobblestones, overturn streetcars, trucks and automobiles in order to barricade the streets. But the non-Communist Viennese led by Socialist trade unionists resisted the *putsch*. It quickly became apparent that the people of eastern Austria would not allow themselves to be detached from the west and absorbed into Soviet Eastern Europe. Armed with the strength of the anti-Communist resistance and with the expressions of outrage registered by the foreign offices of the three occupying powers, Foreign Minister Gruber personally confronted the Soviet representative in Vienna, General Kopetelow. Although the Soviet government declined a formal response to Gruber's earlier protest, Kopetelow had apparently been authorized to back down in case of resistance; he personally claimed innocence in the matter and promised Gruber that there would be no further violation of the terms of the Control Agreement.[57] With neither popular support nor the continued aid of the Red Army the Communists abandoned the strike and the last serious threat of internal revolution against the Second Republic was at an end.

The political residue from this attempt at revolution was, however, significant for the future. The SPOe emerged from the crisis with the well-justified image of the savior of Austria for its heroic defense of the streets against the Communists. Even the most conservative Austrians were forced to admit that their fears of Socialist-Communist collusion to convert the country into a People's Republic were grossly unfounded and that the Socialists were committed to a democratic, albeit socialist Austria. The VdU through its opportunistic attempt to gain strength in the trade unions at the expense of the Socialists clearly lost stature in the eyes of both its middle-class and proletarian adherents. Although Socialist accusations of VdU complicity with the Communists were clearly exaggerated as evidenced by the early return of the VOeST "Independents" to work and the general attempt of VdU workers to protect against Communist sabotage, the league had nevertheless chosen a dangerous course of opposition to governmental policy. Although the similarity of VdU policy and that of the KPOe was purely accidental, the guilt by association did nothing to polish the already tarnished image of the league.

As the second, dissension-riddled year of VdU existence drew to a close, all Austria was shaken by the sudden death of its esteemed president, Dr. Karl Renner, who first as provisional state chancellor and then as president had served as a non-partisan symbol of the unity and cooperation that the country so direly needed in the difficult first years following the end of the war.

The task of finding a suitable replacement for this venerable statesman whose prestige reached far beyond the narrow borders of Austria was not an easy one. Furthermore, precedents for electing a president were ambiguous. According to Article 60, Paragraph 1 of the 1929 constitutional revision, the president was to be elected by the people in a direct and secret election.[58] But this article was set aside in the crisis year of 1931 before the reelection of Wilhelm Miklas and no Austrian president had ever been elected under this provision. Although the 1929 version of the Constitution generally had been put back into effect, Dr. Renner, as the first and only president of the Second Republic, had been elected by joint session of the *Nationalrat* and the *Bundesrat* under a special law invoking Article 60 of the 1920 Constitution.[59]

In 1948, an amendment to Article 64 of the 1929 version of the Constitution was passed, providing for the election of a person or persons to fill the functions of the president in case of temporary incapacitation, further specifying "the immediate election of a president" in case of permanent incapacitation.[60] According to Article 60 of the constitution to which this amendment applied, this would be a popular election. But since there was neither precedent for such an election nor a specific statement implementing Article 60, the issue was open to interpretation.

In the fall of 1948 secret discussions between the OeVP and the SPOe had already begun in anticipation of the necessity of a presidential election. According to Dr. Schärf, chairman of the SPOe, a tentative agreement was reached to continue the practice of electing the president in a joint session of the *Nationalrat* and the *Bundesrat* and accordingly, he worked out the Initiative Bill (165/A) for legislative approval. Suddenly the People's party reversed its position and began a lively press campaign for a popular election. The reason for this renege on the prior agreement Schärf saw as the result of changed perception based on

> ... the presumption that a middle-class candidate would be elected to the presidency [and] they wanted to supply his honor and his office with the great weight of a popular election in disagreement with the Socialists. As a consequence the bill was rejected by the OeVP and it appeared that a popular election was ensured.[61]

But with the emergence of the VdU in 1949 competing for the middle-class vote, the People's party returned to its earlier unity with the SPOe on the manner of presidential election. In the 1949 coalition pact with the Socialists, it was understood that ". . . as Renner's successor, a delegate of the People's party would be elected in the *Bundesversammlung* [joint session of the *Nationalrat* and *Bundesrat*] with the votes of the Socialists."[62]

But by 1951 the political winds had shifted and the major parties again split on the issue of presidential election. Thus, as Austrians awakened to the news of the death of their beloved president on New Years Day, they were also confronted with the controversy of how his successor should be chosen. There was no precedent for a popular election, but neither was there a legal basis for a *Bundesversammlung* election, since the law authorizing the 1945 election had stipulated that this procedure should apply for the "first time." But in a long analysis of the history of the presidential election law, the official *Wiener Zeitung* concluded that the ". . . stipulation of Article V of the Constitutional Law of 13 December 1945 might be extended to the impending election, that is, that the possibility of the *Bundesversammlung*, again being entrusted with the election of the President, is not shut out."[63]

For the next two weeks, the election law became the prime topic of political discussion. The People's party conducted a vigorous campaign to keep the election in the *Bundesversammlung*, confident that even if the coalition were destroyed as a result, the VdU would eagerly grasp at the opportunity to replace the SPOe in the coalition.[64] The Socialists, despite their long-standing demands for direct democracy, might have been willing to cooperate along the lines specified in the

1949 pact in order to avoid a disastrous breach in the coalition, had the OeVP not chosen Dr. Heinrich Gleissner as its candidate for the presidency. But the SPOe would not tolerate this "former clerical-fascist." Instead the Socialists selected their popular former mayor of Vienna and former imperial general, Dr. Theodor Körner and raised the cry for a popular election,[65] thereby joining the VdU which had assumed this stand in the first issue of their party organ following the death of Dr. Renner.[66]

Confronted with the united SPOe-VdU front, as well as strong public support agitated by a virtually unanimous independent press, the OeVP acceded to the demand for a popular election, and the political parties unanimously passed the new election law.[67]

As a result of the political history of the past two years, the position of the VdU in the election was favorable, not because of its own actions, but due to the virtually equal balance of political power between the two major parties. In the 1949 elections, the People's party had won a plurality of votes, but if the same voting pattern occurred in 1951, it could not command the majority necessary to elect its candidate to the presidency. Furthermore, due to the increased prestige with which the Socialists had emerged from the upheaval of the previous fall and the non-ideological moderation of its candidate, the SPOe threatened to attract some of the progressive and restive middle-class voters of the OeVP and VdU.

For the OeVP, the dictate was clear. As Gruber recalls, "It was necessary to seek allies. As such only the moderate wing of the Independents came into question."[68] The VdU eagerly accepted the opportunity to discuss cooperation with the People's party in hopes that this would bring an end to their isolation and perhaps even prepare the way for inclusion in the next coalition. In order to make itself available to either party and yet not preclude the possibility of running its own candidate, the league's federal leadership enunciated a neutral position and promised a decision later on behalf of a candidate "... who will maintain a strict nonpartisan position according to the meaning and spirit of the constitution."[69] This was a popular stance, based not only on the implied intent of the constitution, but also upon the recent historical precedent of Dr. Karl Renner who had proved that even a man of strong party background could stand above party. This appeal quickly found its echo in the independent press, led by the *Salzburger Nachrichten,* which mounted a vigorous campaign to publicize the advantage of a nonpartisan or above-party president.

At this point, the VdU suspended publication of *Die Neue Front* for two months in order to conduct negotiations with the OeVP without being forced by public pressure to make premature press releases. In these negotiations, the VdU was clearly trying to exploit the promise of delivering approximately half-a-million votes and therewith the election to the OeVP in return for political favors. But, according to Gruber, when the SPOe learned of the discussions they ". . . kicked up a great row. This so intimidated our people that they advised a retreat. . . . The discussions were broken off without result."[70] Suddenly the VdU, like the Socialists before them, "discovered" the unacceptable "clerical-fascist" background of the OeVP candidate and moved to nominate a candidate of their own.

Realizing that its greatest impact on the public mind had been during the political enthusiasm of the 1949 election campaign, the VdU went about the selection of a candidate with extreme care. In the light of its own demands for an above-party presidency and the widespread public and press support for this principle, the league moved to consolidate all available forces to support a nonpartisan candidate. One source of support for this movement was found in the Youth Front, a wing of the OeVP which by admission of the OeVP leadership

> . . . was only permitted to be founded in 1949 because the election stood before the door and it had the effect of making the generation between twenty and thirty-five politically active and hindered them from drifting into extreme camps, which was particularly necessary due to the rise of the VdU and the first participation of tens of thousands of former National Socialists.[71]

If the established OeVP leadership saw the Youth Front as merely a tool to undercut the appeal of the VdU, its leaders perceived the situation quite differently. Though lacking the magnetic force of journalistic charisma that had attracted many ex-National Socialists to the VdU, the Youth Front attracted a similar constituency. Appealing to the youthful idealism of the war generation that had been alienated from the OeVP for many of the same reasons that had forged the VdU, the Youth Front posed the hope of reforming the People's party from within and ending what they regarded as the "sell out" to socialism.

Organizationally, the Youth Front did not build a large youth movement for the OeVP, but rather sought to act as a pressure group for internal reform within the party apparatus. Ultimately it hoped to replace the old leadership predominantly inherited from the Christian Socialist party of the interwar years with representatives of the younger generation. The Youth Front enunciated its intention to renew "... the OeVP with regard to its correct, yet distinctly theoretical program." In order to end the era in which the OeVP had so seriously compromised its principles and restore purity to the party it was necessary to bring about

1. ... the termination of the general, and to a large degree understandable, escape from all politics and to awaken the consciousness of each and every part of society to its coresponsibility for the destiny of the community.
2. Education for a living democracy. ...
3. ... the solidarity which must necessarily come from an honest and correctly understood avowal of Austriandom [which] must produce the realization that *all men are brothers.*

   Let everyone, but above all he who by his involvement in politics bears primary responsibility, first make peace with himself. Then let us bring our families, the nucleus of our society, into order and achieve national security and carry this spirit of sincere, human unity into the greater community of the *Volk!* Only in this way, and not in the legalistic and insufficiently ethnically based confederation established by one *Volk,* will Pan-Europe and ultimately the United Nations as the ultimate family, be able to become a reality.[72]

Although in this statement of goals, the Youth Front did not go even as far as the VdU's moderate statement of cultural German nationalism, its leadership was dominated by nationalists who held much in common with the right wing of the League of Independents.

By the end of 1950, the refusal of the OeVP leadership to significantly recognize the demands of the Youth Front or to admit its members to responsible positions within the party totally alienated the executive council of the faction. As a consequence, at the beginning of the 1951 convention of the People's party held in Salzburg to confirm the leadership's selection of Gleissner as the party's candidate for the presidency, *Nationalrat* Dr. Strachwitz declared the Front's inability to continue within the existing structure of the party.[73] Although not all Youth Front delegates followed Strachwitz out of the convention,[74] the defection left those who remained without power or future influence in the party. In a press release explaining the dramatic exit of the bulk of the Youth Front from the convention Strachwitz explained that their desire for reform of the party had been dependent upon a change in the personal composition of its leadership. In the face of the absolute intransigence of the OeVP "establishment" the Youth Front was forced "... to continue to work for reform against the present leadership of the OeVP. It reserves to itself freedom of decision in all political questions."[75] Although the Youth Front never formally joined its political sibling, the VdU, it supported the independent presidential candidate and played an important role in the subsequent evolution of the independent party movement.

In the meantime, the VdU was busy drawing together independent forces for the purpose of generating a viable third-party presidential candidacy. On March 15, forty-four such independents gathered in Salzburg's Cafe Bazar to announce the formation of the "Committee of Above-Party Unity." Although the VdU had provided the initiative and formed the nucleus of the coalition, the league, in accordance with its propaganda demands for a truly non-party president,[76] was not numerically dominant in the committee. Dr. Burghard Breitner, the Innsbruck surgeon whom the committee selected as its presidential candidate, ideally personified this spirit of "Above-Party Unity." Breitner was a man of immense personal prestige who was widely known as the "Angel of Siberia" for his humanitarian efforts there in the prison camps of World War I, and remained in the public eye as a highly respected president of the Austrian Red Cross. In January, while the VdU was still negotiating with the OeVP, the *Salzburger Nachrichten* raised its standard for an above-party presidency and identified Breitner as the logical, prominent and politically neutral candidate for the nomination.[77]

Although technically Breitner was a candidate of the "Committee of Above-Party Unity" and was personally unaffiliated with the VdU, a natural association was drawn in many people's minds that did much to dilute the negative image of the league, thus severely handicapping the customary defamatory tactics of the major parties.

News of Breitner's candidacy was received with wild enthusiasm by the VdU members in Salzburg, who literally painted the town red with the BB initials of the candidate.[78] For purposes of form, the VdU had renounced any intention of running its own candidate several days before and it therefore came as no surprise when Dr. Kraus announced the league's endorsement of Dr. Breitner's candidacy to a news conference of the Vienna press.[79]

In the next two months, numerous additional groups and non-politically affiliated committees joined the Breitner campaign, both out of great respect for his person as well as a firm belief in the validity of the principle of an above-party presidency. Although it was primarily the VdU organization that coordinated and financed the campaign, the league carefully avoided any suspicion that Dr. Breitner was associated with any political group. There was no attempt to establish a campaign program and indeed had one been constructed it could only have torn the fragile web of alliances that had been spun by the BB committee. Nor was there any need for a program. The office of the president of Austria possesses virtually no positive political power. By the nature of the office, the president's strength rests primarily on his power to serve as a popularly elected check on the actions of the parliament, in addition to his various ceremonial functions. Therefore, the success of a legislative program is to almost no degree dependent upon having a president of the same party as the government. Thus, Austrians have consistently looked to their president as a possible means of checking the policies of the parliament and it was not until 1970 that the Austrian electorate entrusted the position of chancellor and president to men of the same party. In 1951 this pattern had not yet been established as a precedent, but with a black-red coalition in power, the demand for a president beholden to neither of the ruling parties held considerable appeal.

Breitner's posture throughout the campaign was not only "above-party" but above politics, to the consternation of his supporters throughout the country who vainly appealed to him to attend their rallies on his behalf. But Breitner steadfastly refused to campaign actively and asked the indulgence of his more politically conscious supporters maintaining:

> It is against my concept of propriety that I, in my capacity as an above-party candidate, campaign for myself. A professional politician can, yes, should campaign for himself and for his party. For me the rules are different. Please do not be angry with me. Believe me. The people will understand my position. If the desire is really as great for an above-party candidacy as you believe, then the success will not be dependent upon whether I make a lot of ballyhoo or not. The people should not decide in a narcosis of propaganda, but in all peace and quiet.[80]

Accordingly, Dr. Breitner limited his participation in the campaign to rare weekend appearances and the remainder of the time devoted himself to his responsibilities as a surgeon and a professor of medicine. He refused to be identified with any party or program,[81] declaring only that he would ". . . do everything to fulfill [the] tasks, whose range is given by the Constitution and whose nature can be characterized by justice, law and a willingness to be helpful."[82] When questioned about his lack of preparation for these tasks, he responded: "I am convinced that decisions are not merely juridically based, but must also be morally indisputable."[83] The necessary juridical expertise was readily obtainable through competent advisors,[84] the more important moral bases for decision-making would come from his love of country and his willingness to follow the wishes of its people.[85]

In virtually all respects, the BB campaign was amateurish. Lacking the funds for the flood of campaign posters with which the major parties plastered every available wall and fence, the Committee resorted to painting the initials BB on every conspicuous surface. In compliance with Breitner's wishes, there was no specific program. Instead, Breitner artlessly appealed to the Austrian voters to elect a nonpolitical, ordinary citizen whose exemplary moral character would assure a proper execution of the office of President. Politically the campaign was naive. But because of its simplicity and apolitical nature, the Breitner plea for morality free from political artifice struck a responsive chord in many Austrians who were alienated by the highly politicized character of public life.

In marked contrast to the low key approach of the BB campaign, the propaganda machinery of both major parties operated in high gear. Again the People's party tried to bludgeon the electorate into electing its candidate by personal smear tactics and innuendo. Rumors were circulated implying that the elderly SPOe candidate, the venerable Theodor Körner, was ". . . almost a living corpse and if elected, one would only have to pay for a state funeral in a short time."[86] The OeVP unleashed its anti-Nazi propaganda guns from the 1949 campaign against Breitner. In an attempt to compromise the morality approach of the Breitner campaign, the OeVP always identified Dr. Breitner as the "VdU candidate" and therefore with the alleged neo-Nazi stigma that it had tried to attach to the league since its inception. In this way the People's party strove to detach the Breitner supporters who had been attracted by the above-party concept, but who would not vote for the VdU. The OeVP further implied guilt by association by "revealing" that twenty-five of the members of the "Committee of Above-Party Unity" were former Nazis[87] (eighteen of these had supported the OeVP candidates in October 1949).[88] The OeVP press agency further defamed Breitner by lifting passages out of context from one of his books to portray him as a proponent of war, class hatred, and brutality, and as a believer in racial superiority.[89] This approach was significantly less successful than in 1949 because there was only one man involved. In the parliamentary election the VdU, although campaigning on a strict rejection of National Socialism, nevertheless ran several ex-

Nazis as candidates. Some of these were indeed immoderate and extreme nationalists who in unguarded moments had made untoward statements which lent considerable credence to the OeVP allegations of neo-Nazism in the VdU. But Dr. Breitner was a man of high personal character with no ex- or neo-Nazi taint, whose achievements in medicine and involvement with international humanitarian endeavors corresponded in no way with the image which the OeVP tried to paint of the VdU and the above-party candidate it supported.

The Socialists' posture vis-a-vis Dr. Breitner was similar to their stance of 1949. The SPOe made no attempt to defame the character of the above-party candidate, but rather concentrated on his political naivete and strongly questioned whether in fact any candidate could truly be above party.

One significant difference between the campaigns of 1949 and 1951 was the attitude of the independent press. In 1949, Dr. Canaval and his *Salzburger Nachrichten* had set the tone for the other Austrian independent newspapers in attacking the VdU and its candidates as vigorously as had any of the OeVP party organs. In 1951 however, the *Salzburger Nachrichten* led the campaign for an above-party presidency and was among the first to publicly endorse the candidacy of Breitner. Initially, Dr. Canaval saw the Breitner candidacy as of strictly nuisance value by which both major parties could be denied the majority necessary to elect a president. In the anticipated run off with Breitner excluded from the ballot, the BB voters would prove the decisive force, probably shifting as a bloc to OeVP candidate Gleissner out of middle-class socio-economic sensitivities. An alternative existed, however, that would see a VdU-SPOe agreement that would remove Körner from the ballot to be replaced by Breitner as a coalition candidate.[90]

As the campaign continued, however, the slogan "above-party" caught the public imagination and even the OeVP moved to organize an "Above-Party Committee for Gleissner." Traditional party discipline seemed to play a less important role in a parliamentary election such that a *Salzburger Nachrichten* editor could speculate about a significant shift in the dynamics of presidential elections:

> The President of the people on the face of this election will become an above-party president. . . . For why should not a supporter of the OeVP vote for Theodor if he has been impressed by this venerable old gentleman? Or why should Socialists not vote for Heinrich Gleissner, the successful "provincial father of Upper Austria?" Not to mention a movement of voters to Burghard Breitner. Who knows how many

otherwise party-bound people will vote for the Innsbruck surgeon and university teacher, because he personally has not become involved in the campaign, as have his two political opponents, because he has another profession which his conscience forbids him to neglect until he is elected. Men stand for election and not political programs.[91]

This optimism for a softening rigid party discipline proved too idealistic. Although Breitner won an impressive number of votes for a third-party candidate, party loyalties proved stronger than the above-party appeal. The results showed:[92]

CANDIDATE	VOTES	PER CENT
Gleissner (OeVP)	1,725,451	39.48
Körner (SPOe)	1,682,881	38.51
Breitner (VdU)	662,501	15.16
Fila (KPOe)	219,969	5.03
Hainisch	2,132	0.05
Ude	5,413	0.12
Invalid	72,227	1.65

Nevertheless, neither of the major party candidates had achieved a majority. In Salzburg, Breitner had polled more votes than any other candidate and in Vorarlberg and Tyrol, he trailed only Gleissner. Only in the Soviet-occupied zone and in Upper Austria did Breitner poll less than 20 per cent of the total vote cast. The VdU central organ could justifiably trumpet: "The Opposition the Only Winner." In the public runoff election to follow, the rigid two-party coalition could not be used to shut out expression of the "third force." The VdU and its ally, the BB committee, had finally achieved the position of the balance on the scale. The implications of this position for the runoff election were portentous. The VdU was at the zenith of its influence. Although Breitner was eliminated from contention, his supporters would determine the outcome.[93]

According to the terms of the election law, either or both parties could substitute a candidate for the runoff. If either of the major parties had done so and placed Breitner or another above-party candidate on its ballot, it would have undoubtedly won the support of the vast bulk of the Breitner voters and with them certain victory. This prospect had already been discussed in the press prior to the first election[94] and would have brought complete triumph to the VdU-BB committee's campaign. But despite the distinct advantage of such a tactic, the possibility was never seriously contemplated by either party. The OeVP's continuing defamation of the VdU and its candidate Breitner precluded any eleventh hour reconciliation and the SPOe likewise refused to desert its candidate. The possibility of an above-party candidate was excluded and negotiations for support went underground. Again, as in January, OeVP functionaries sought the support of the Independents, but the feeling was so strong within the People's party that the Breitner voters would follow their middle-class sympathies in any case that the discussions were broken off without result.[95]

While the major parties geared up for the new campaign, the VdU intoxication of May 6 gradually sobered to the realization that its momentary prestige and prominence was totally eclipsed by the two party runoff election. To try and salvage some political leverage from the situation, the VdU overtly seized the leadership of the "Committee for an Above-Party Unity." A joint meeting of the VdU parliamentary delegation and the league's federal leadership was held to discuss strategy for the runoff election. In a day-long, passionate debate it was decided that the league would make no formal endorsement of either candidate, thereby leaving the decision to each individual BB voter to determine personally.[96] This decision was probably the most realistic that could have been made, since, given the independent nature of the League of Independents as well as the "Committee for an Above-Party Unity," the VdU leadership could probably not have delivered the Breitner voters as a bloc to either candidate and massive failure would have only further revealed the lack of unity in the organization. Instead, the VdU leadership skirted the issue, avoiding any responsibility for electing the future president. But to retain some degree of involvement with the election and thereby maintain at least the illusion of political significance, the VdU laid down guidelines for its voters by putting ten rather embarrassing questions to each of the two candidates. The questions, which dealt not with the presidency but rather with parliamentary party politics, were delivered as an ultimatum to the coalition parties to publicly declare a reform of their past abuses or risk forfeiting the vital "Independent" votes.[97] Neither of the two major parties chose to jeopardize its position in the coalition by directly answering the questions, thereby criticizing its coalition partner. As a result, the VdU leadership remained mute and "Independents" went to the polls with no guidelines other than those of individual preference.

The "Committee for an Above-Party Unity," whose affiliation with the VdU had ended with the defeat of Breitner, was confronted with a similar quandry. Unlike the VdU, it had no party-political status to maintain. It had been founded with the sole intention of electing a nonpartisan president. With the election over, its *raison d'etre* disappeared. The "Committee," without the pressure on the VdU to maintain its image for future elections, might have disbanded after its failure to move Breitner into the runoff. But when the left bloc (KPOe and Socialist Workers party) announced its support of Körner, the specter of a reunified Marxist front eliminated any possibility of an endorsement by the overwhelmingly middle-class "BB committee" for the SPOe. But the alternative was scarcely more attractive. The vast majority of the members of the "BB committee" had defected from the OeVP only five months before and the continuing defamation by the OeVP of the "committee" and its candidate during the campaign had only served to deepen this disaffection. Although the decision was painful, the committee really had no choice. Despite ". . . a far-reaching exasperation and rage over the unfounded defamation and vituperation and false accusations which were carried out above all by the KPOe and the OeVP against the personal integrity of Professor Breitner," the committee declared that

> . . . after careful and deep consideration without any pressure and without direct recommendation, due to the fact of the unification of the left bloc with the Socialists for the election [it] does not demand that its voters cast their ballots against the candidate, Dr. Heinrich Gleissner.[98]

This endorsement was, however, not to be construed as any kind of support for the policies of the OeVP against which the committee promised to continue the fight:

> The Committee hastens to add that after the election it will enter into discussions to maintain the unity of the vote reservoir which it has just won to oppose the interest clique . . . which until now has shown that it can neither renew the state, nor the individual parties in personnel or objective respects, nor free them from the prevailing corruption.[99]

Although the SPOe declared that it had not sought the support of the left bloc nor would it in any way compromise its stance against the Communist party,[100] the BB committee chose to adopt a hard-line, antileftist stance against an imagined Socialist-Communist conspiracy. In rejecting the statement of good intentions by the Socialists as well as the proof of its anti-Communist record, the "BB committee" staked out a position to the right of the VdU and in doing so presaged a future trend of the third-party movement.

For the majority parties, the runoff campaign was the most vicious that either had waged against the other during the Second Republic. Both competed shamelessly for the Breitner votes, with the OeVP again raising the specter of a People's Democracy along East European lines, and the SPOe appealing to the middle-class ex-Nazi voters by revealing the duplicity of the OeVP ". . . with regard to their promises for the former nationalists."[101] "Better," the Socialists argued with an inverted sense of logic, "an honest enemy . . . whom you can trust, than a false friend who has already betrayed you several times."[102]

As election day neared, no visible trend towards either of the candidates had become apparent. The 220,000 Communist voters were almost certain either to vote for Körner or to cast a blank ballot, but the 662,000 Breitner voters were an unknown quantity. The sizable working-class contingency that had produced the stunning VdU victories in the selected Industrial Council elections of 1949 and 1950 could fairly safely be assumed to vote Socialist, while the additional voters mobilized for the "third force" by the "Committee for an Above-Party Unity" would vote their anti-Marxist convictions despite their alienation from the People's party. Thus the decision rested in the hands of the remnants and heirs of the traditional national-liberal camp who were largely middle-class, but strongly anticlerical independents, who were, incidentally, largely ex-National Socialists. In evaluating the electoral behavior of its constituents, the VdU estimated that the Breitner voters would split three ways, with one-third tolerating Gleissner, while another third shifted to Körner; the remainder would simply refuse to compromise their principles and would cast blank ballots. Including the 220,000 Communist votes for the Socialist candidate, this would bring a 52.5 majority to Körner.[103] But, in an obvious effort to wring concessions from the OeVP, the VdU suggested that

> . . . any really credible reform of the OeVP could very easily occasion the turning in of a blank ballot by that embittered third currently oriented towards Körner and could moreover turn that second third that without recommendation would vote "neither black nor red" into votes for Gleissner, which would give a 52 per cent victory to the OeVP.[104]

Neither of the major parties made any significant concessions to win a VdU endorsement, nor took a satisfactory position on the ten VdU questions. As May 27 neared, the election appeared to be a photo finish with Körner holding a slight lead. Although the VdU as an organization made no recommendations, VdU functionaries became active in the campaigns of the candidates who most nearly represented their ideals. According to Socialist reports, several members of the VdU actively worked in the Körner campaign[105] and co-founder Viktor Reimann privately expressed his support for Körner in meetings of the Federal Leadership Council.[106] Dr. Kraus however, feared that the election of Körner would reverse the orientation of the SPOe towards the political center and would create a new Marxist Front. This he felt would end any further possibility of compromise between the middle class and the proletarian parties and would ultimately lead to a split into two hostile camps from which only civil war and absorption into the Communist bloc could result.[107]

Deeply disturbed by this threat, Dr. Kraus decided to violate the VdU leadership decision to make no recommendation on the election. In response to many individual requests from Breitner voters for a personal endorsement, Dr. Kraus published an article in the independent Vienna daily, *Die Presse,* explaining his fears and stating his reasons for supporting Gleissner.[108] In taking this position, Kraus took pains to emphasize that his statement was neither to be construed as VdU policy nor as an attempt ". . . to help this internally rent, practically leaderless and so often failing party in its greatest need"; rather, he hoped

> to force it into a position where there is not only one alternative; either a complete change of course, or the rise of a new electoral group which will cost it the greatest part of its voters. . . .
> However, this personal decision of mine in no way signifies an absolute position against the SPOe. On the contrary, I am ready at any time to vote with the SPOe when its position more closely represents the VdU program than that of the OeVP.[109]

But Kraus's personal attempt to influence the independent vote at the eleventh hour misfired. When the votes were tallied the results read:[110]

CANDIDATE	RUNOFF ELECTION VOTES	PER CENT OF TOTAL	FIRST ELECTION VOTES	PER CENT OF TOTAL
Körner	2,178,631	49.82	1,682,881	38.51
Gleissner	2,006,322	45.88	1,725,451	39.48
Invalid	188,241	4.30	72,227	1.65

It is difficult to precisely determine the electoral behavior of the over 890,000 voters who had cast their ballots for the four minor party candidates in the first election. On the basis of an analysis by electoral district, *Salzburger Nachrichten* editor Gustav Canaval speculated that the Breitner votes divided almost evenly between the candidates with 43.7 per cent for Körner and 42.4 per cent for Gleissner, while a substantial 13.9 per cent rejected both candidates and showed their displeasure by casting a blank ballot.[111] Viktor Reimann, writing for the VdU organ, *Die Neue Front,* estimated that somewhat less than 40 per cent of the Breitner voters had decided in favor of Gleissner, and somewhat more than 40 per cent for Körner, with the remaining 20 per cent invalidating their ballots.[112] Regardless of the precise division, it appears that the "better red than black" motto voiced by the nationalist-liberal parties of the First Republic applied for many independent voters, if for different reasons. The refusal of the Breitner voters to move as a bloc to Gleissner despite the endorsement of the BB committee and the personal recommendation of VdU Chairman Kraus clearly revealed the "third force" to be exactly what the title of its only significant political body expressed; it was clearly a "League of Independents."

VI

Broadening the Basis?

The League of Independents had never been a real political party, but was rather a movement of diverse political forces which had been compressed into an organizational structure by common dissatisfaction and the lack of viable alternatives. The electoral success of 1949 had deceived the leaders of this movement into believing that their coalition of frustration had become, in fact, a political party. After a period of drifting and crisis in 1950, the presidential elections of 1951 provided a vehicle for the expansion of the "third force" by attaching additional dissatisfied elements, thereby increasing the numerical impact of the movement; the importance of this bloc in determining the election of the new president significantly escalated the aspirations of the independents and stimulated the VdU as the only representative body of the "third force" to take the next logical step that would ally all Breitner supporters. This conclusion was clearly drawn by Dr. Reimann in his analysis of the runoff election:

> The election result of May 6 revealed that notwithstanding the great personality of Professor Breitner himself, the primary success is to be accredited to the VdU organization. Although the Breitner Committee with its journalistic agent, the *Salzburger Nachrichten,* in contrast to the VdU Executive Committee, published a clear Gleissner recommendation, sixty percent of the Breitner votes did not follow this suggestion and on the basis of the composition of the VdU, it would be dubious to accept that the other forty percent voted Gleissner because of this recommendation. The lack of success of the Breitner Committee's declaration is to be attributed to the neutrality of the VdU. The realization which has to be drawn by everyone is this: an organization which has been set up in two years of difficult work is the basic pillar and strongest guarantee for success. Only then come all other means, the first of which is journalistic. A newspaper which has no organization behind it can produce no decision as is proven in Salzburg. However, all forces together can bring in a result that is sensational and portentous, as again Salzburg proved in the first election.[1]

In order to develop and expand the "third force" between the two major parties into a meaningful political party, the VdU began a campaign to "broaden the basis" as had already been promised by the Breitner Committee in its statement of reluctant support for Gleissner in the runoff election.[2] To try and consolidate the available elements, the VdU emphasized its posture as a "true synthesis between the fronts"[3] representing "neither limited profit possibilities nor wage leveling,"[4] and charted a course of social reform based on

> ... a just distribution according to the achievement principle, which with one blow will nullify the laughable reproaches of past resentments ... and will achieve victory, not only in Austria but will bear fruit far beyond our borders.[5]

To achieve these goals, the VdU announced that in the interest of "... broadening the basis which strives towards a reformation and renewal of political life," it would not stand in the way.[6] The appeal for the merger of the Breitner alliance on a firmer organizational level did not go long unheeded. On July 9, the VdU together with the BB committee and representatives of other groups met "... to work out principles under which the consolidation will take place."[7]

In the meantime, another crisis in the league's leadership had developed. As a consequence of his negotiation with the OeVP immediately after the first presidential election, Dr. Kraus had earned considerable animosity from the nationalists and anticlerics among the VdU functionaries. After his personal recommendation for Gleissner, this resentment built to such a point that only the total efforts of Reimann, who had argued against an endorsement of Gleissner, were successful in saving Kraus from being removed as league chairman.[8] The whole episode nevertheless served to considerably weaken the control of the Kraus-Reimann faction at a time when new elements of a much more strongly nationalist character were gaining strength.

In a considerable escalation beyond the moderate statement regarding German nationalism in the 1949 program, former Nazi journalist and member of the league's federal leadership, Dr. Fritz Stüber, published a series of articles in *Die Neue Front* strongly condemning the idea of "... the so-called 'Austrian Nation' that has never existed and which never will exist."[9] This fallacy, Stüber maintained, had its origin in the western political concept of the state imposed on the Germans by the Allies. In contrast, he contended:

> The German remains true to the original sense of the word. The German ties the concept 'nation' even today, to be sure emotionally,

with the togetherness of peoples of the same *völkisch* origin, of the same narrow blood descent, of the same speech, historical unity and tradition. To the German, the nation is a higher category of thought and feeling, standing above the transitory state form of community life, the biological and intellectual unity of its being, above and beyond state boundaries and millennia. The German too derives political consequences from his concept of nationality, but not exclusively.... In the sound of the word 'nation' there is included the great relationships of history, culture, language and the unity of the *Volk* by blood.

This means no contradiction to the state. State and nation according to the German concept are two different levels. The broader concept, that the entire nation must be together within one state, can not and must not be pursued today.... We must however energetically stipulate that the recognition of the Austrian state does not have the least to do with clear recognition of the German nation and the unity of the German character.[10]

Stüber, in order to survive in the postwar world as a *grossdeutsch* anachronism, had to deny the final conclusion of a century and a half of *völkisch* thinking: that is, that nation, *Volk* and state must coincide. In reconciling the disparity between state and nation, Stüber was amenable to the vague VdU concept of an international *Volkstum*[11] and defined this as a "... brotherly community of all nations, not in a conglomerate of nationally uprooted human individuals."[12] But despite his cautious treatment of potentially incendiary ideas, the social-progressive wing of the VdU was deeply concerned that Stüber's efforts in this regard might stimulate an over-zealous reaction from the unreconstructed *grossdeutsch* nationalists and thereby so seriously compromise the league as to forever preclude it from sharing in political responsibility with the majority parties.

The shift in the ideological center of gravity of the VdU implied by Stüber's new departure was borne out even in the articles of the moderates who began to flavor their writings with nationalist phrases so as not to lose control of this constituency. Even the arch anti-Nazi Reimann tied his appeal for social reform to "... the National Socialist idea of the *Volksgemeinschaft*, which has become one of the basic principles of VdU social opinion."[13]

The reason for the nervousness of the moderate faction vis-a-vis the nationalists became apparent when the Second General Assembly of the VdU gathered in Salzburg on December 1, 1951. In a lead editorial in *Die Neue Front* published on the morning of the opening session, Viktor Reimann pleaded for an end to the personality conflicts within the league and exhorted the delegates to rededicate themselves to the cause of reform on behalf of justice, and political and economic honesty which had united them in 1949.[14] In his opening remarks to the assembly, Chairman Kraus reported on the activities of the federal leadership and particularly praised the favorable trend towards the inclusion of additional independent elements since the presidential election. In conclusion he particularly emphasized the need for the league to remain ideologically catholic and to reject any tendencies that could lead to centrifugal disintegration. Finally Kraus moved to allay fears awakened by his close relationship with the OeVP during the past year. In answer to rumors circulated by the SPOe that Kraus was going to lead the VdU into the coalition as an OeVP puppet to bolster the middle-class front,[15] the chairman reaffirmed the league's commitment to a policy of opposition as long as the government parties remained resistant to reform.[16]

When the floor of the assembly was opened to discussion, the anti-Kraus faction headed by Dr. Stüber and Deputy-Chairman Karl Hartleb severely attacked the chairman for his negotiations with the OeVP and particularly for his *Presse* article in support of Gleissner. The reason for this onslaught became clear when the opposition nominated Hartleb for the position of chairman against Dr. Kraus. Again, for the second successive year, the balance in the assembly remained with the moderate, social-progressive wing of the league and Kraus was reelected with eighty-five votes to sixty for Hartleb. In protest, thirty-four representatives from the Viennese, Carinthian, Upper Austrian, Salzburg and Styrian delegations left the hall.[17] Headed by Hartleb, Scheuch and Gollob, this minority faction created a second locus of leadership in the league, which although lacking any power nevertheless held the sympathy of many in the provincial organizations. In an interview with the *Salzburger Nachrichten* the dissidents denied that this action represented their resignation from the league; rather Hartleb and Gollob signaled a power struggle by rejecting any cooperation with the federal executive committee until Kraus was removed from control and the process of "broadening the basis" had been completed.[18]

After the exodus of the Hartleb-Scheuch-Gollob group the remaining membership of the federal leadership was elected with large majorities and essentially the 3:2 moderate:nationalist ratio of the previous year was retained with ex-Colonel Max Stendebach and Jörg Kandutsch filling, somewhat more moderately, the vacancies left by Scheuch and Gollob.

The next day, the unpleasantries of the election were smoothed over by the appearance of two officials of the German Free Democratic Party whose appeal for a *freiheitlich* political, economic and social order and a "German cultural circle" for the new ordering of Europe sounded a responsive chord among the assembled VdU functionaries.[19] This speech expressing the unity of the totally respectable FDP with the VdU as a kind of sister party did much to end the mood of hostility at the convention. The applause which the delegates accorded to the visitors also reflected favorably on Chairman Kraus whose personal connections in Germany had drawn this tie.[20]

Thus the VdU Assembly was able to again plaster over the deep fissures in its organization and in a mood of amity concluded a bold, optimistic resolution that requested the occupying powers to renounce their tight control over Austrian public life, reaffirmed the league's appeal for a unification of Europe and demanded early elections for the *Nationalrat*.[21]

As its third year of political activity drew to a close, the VdU could look with both satisfaction and concern at the events of 1951. On the one hand, the presidential election had raised the league, through its association with Burghard Breitner, to a degree of political respectability. Although the accusations of neo-Nazism were still heard, they had lost their emotional impact through overuse, through the accusers' readiness to negotiate with the alleged neo-Nazis and through the VdU's own diligent avoidance of any overt actions that could in any way justify the label. Although the VdU continued to be identified as a party of ex-Nazis in the public mind, there was increasingly less anxiety about the existence of such a party. Organizationally, the independent elements that had united with the VdU behind the Breitner candidacy seemed to offer a significant potential for increasing the scope of the league beyond its already heterogeneous ranks. Finally, the firm association established with the German FDP lent further respectability to the VdU and seemed to be a possible first step towards the normalization of party-political relations with the Federal Republic of Germany, towards the ultimate goal of European unity shared by both parties. On the negative side however, the Kraus leadership had only barely survived a challenge from the nationalist wing of the league and an internal split was opened that seriously endangered the continued unity of the organization.

In his New Year's message stating the league's goals for 1952, Dr. Kraus drew the necessary conclusions from both positive and negative factors. For the coming year, Kraus presented three major tasks confronting the VdU. The first was to continue the efforts already underway to broaden the basis of the movement; but, he cautioned,

> there should however be no broadening of the basis of the political goals. . . . The task of the movement is the opposite, to more precisely define and more clearly formulate. . . . For this reason, the task of assembling is a task of an even more constructive programmatic orientation. For this reason it does not mean to add political forces or to patch them together, but to consolidate.[22]

What Kraus failed to realize, or refused to accept at this point, was that as a result of the "broadening of the basis," a number of small, individually weak groups which would probably have found their home under the OeVP umbrella of the middle-class front had been attached to the league. This only further weakened the cohesion of the organization and the control of the federal leadership. With such a conglomerate membership, any defining of program and goals beyond the vague statements of 1949 could lead only to further defections.

The second task which Dr. Kraus enumerated was that of

> . . . cultivating connections with foreign countries, particularly Germany. Here we take up a good Austrian tradition: to feel ourselves German and through our greater world openmindedness create a sincere relationship of the heart between the great German nation and the *Völker* of a Europe that belongs together.[23]

Here Kraus was clearly expressing his own idealistic hope for an economically and ultimately, politically united Europe as a viable "third force" between East and West, in rhetoric sympathetic to the nationalists who saw in the United States of Europe an acceptable means of dissolving the border between Germany and Austria and bringing about the long-desired unity of the German *Volk*.

The third and final task confronting the league that Kraus inferred from the recent events was the necessity of bringing an end to the petty internal power struggles so as to avoid the erosion of voter trust and the deterioration of the idealism of the functionaries.

Throughout 1952 these three objectives became interrelated. The goal of European unity and a closer association with Germany emerged as the main ideal of the movement for political renewal and succeeded in broadening the basis of the organization, but ultimately weakened its cohesion.

In Parliament, the Independents remained an impotent, but vocal force of opposition. Their frequent proposals for additional amnesties for certain groups of *belastete* Nazis were ignored, just as were their protests against further wage-price agreements, income taxes and the "empire" of SPOe Minister of Commerce and Nationalized Industry Waldbrunner, who exercised what they alleged was a virtual dictatorship over the Postal Service, the Ministry of Energy and the entire nationalized sector of industry. The public forum remained the league's only hope for political influence. With the prospect of new elections within the next year, the VdU accelerated its attempts to "broaden the basis," hoping for an increase in parliamentary representation that would force the major parties to accept it into the coalition.

The most important group with which the VdU had to negotiate for this expansion was "Action for Political Renewal." Action emerged out of the Youth Front which had split with the OeVP and had supported Breitner in the presidential election of 1951.[24] In the runoff, however, it had returned to the People's party, and in the drastic internal reorganization after the loss to the Socialists sought the reforms it had been demanding since its inception. When their hopes were again dashed, Youth Front leaders Ernst Strachwitz and Wilfred Gredler declared their independence from the OeVP.[25] Throughout the summer of 1951 Strachwitz and his supporters reestablished the contacts they had made with other independent elements during the Breitner campaign and on October 21 announced the founding of Action based on the principles of

> . . . justice for all, *Rechtsstaat,* elimination of the exceptional laws [regarding former National Socialists], humanization of the state, organic instead of party democracy, a social order of capitalism in contrast to Marxism and finally, the entrance of Austria into the future European *Grossraum.*[26]

Action's leaders invited cooperation with other groups interested in the reform of Austrian political life and opened discussion with the VdU for a fusion into a more broadly based movement for political renewal. But despite the obvious similarity of the stated objectives of the two groups, Action shared another characteristic with the VdU that repeatedly thwarted attempts at amalgamation: a personally ambitious leadership. The VdU leaders were willing to incorporate Action and any other compatible group but were unwilling to expand the leadership to include the new elements. Action, however, demanded the creation of a new organization with a new name and new leadership and criticized the VdU for considering itself the only exponent of political renewal.[27]

This impasse produced a hiatus in the negotiations until the prospects of an approaching parliamentary election and the seductive memories of the success that cooperative action had produced in the Breitner campaign overcame, at least momentarily, the ambition of the two leadership groups. On June 13, 1952, the press agencies of the VdU and Action announced the creation of a joint committee to work out the arrangements for a fusion of the two organizations and to carry out the recruitment of additional like-minded elements. Drawing from the trend towards a more overt expression of nationalism, the fusion statement emphasized that

> the new movement will, in a greater degree than was previously possible for either of the two organizations, overcome the false developments in Austrian politics since 1945, and, proceeding from the obvious membership in the German *Volkstum,* will place the traditional ability of Austria to unify peoples in the service of European integration. As a precondition for a true *Volksgemeinschaft,* the new movement will represent a social-progressive program. One of the most important tasks it sees is the elimination of the prejudice of the recent past and the conquest of obsolete political contradictions that today still burden our political life.[28]

Several weeks later Dr. Kraus and Dr. Strachwitz announced that their respective organizations had agreed to run a common list of candidates in the next *Nationalrat* election and that the final, formal fusion would be accomplished in the fall.[29]

The response to this apparent consolidation was varied. The Socialists, hopeful that their success in the presidential election of the previous year presaged a shift of independent sentiment in their direction, found themselves in a defensive position vis-a-vis the VdU-Action consolidation. Realizing that it was in competition with the Independents for electoral support, the SPOe, like the OeVP in 1949 and 1951, turned from a policy of permissive toleration to one of aggressive attack on the agency of the "third force." In an effort to drive a wedge between the new partners, the Socialist press published an account of friction in the joint committee between Kraus and Strachwitz and concluded that the supposedly warm relationship between the factions was in fact "somewhat frosty." The report closed in a manner reminiscent of OeVP sensationalism of the past, referring to the financial contributions from the Jewish Committee of Salzburg and labeling the new group a ". . . nationalist mélange, topped with a monarchist frosting."[30]

In a similar reversal, the OeVP, which had consistently and bitterly attacked the VdU, now adopted a non-committal attitude towards the new formation. Rudely disappointed by its defeat of the previous year, the OeVP was undoubtedly contemplating the possibility of cooperating with the middle-class competition to maintain its accustomed dominant position in the *Nationalrat*. Dr. Kraus further encouraged this line of reasoning when in an interview with the OeVP's Salzburg organ he speculated that while he did not foresee the possibility, it would not be ruled out.[31]

But despite these favorable prospects for the increased influence of the "third force," the movement was still plagued by its own internal contradictions. Kraus's attempt to conclude a final fusion agreement with Action ran aground on the opposition of his everpresent enemies in the extreme nationalist wing of the league. Although Action also favored a strong stance on the national question, it supported a traditional liberal approach to economic questions, and as an offshoot of the People's party was in no way hostile to the Catholic Church. Cooperation with such a group was abhorrent to radical and anti-clerical ex-Nazis who feared that in a truly fused party the Kraus faction would be strengthened, paving the way for increased cooperation with the OeVP. Viennese provincial Chairman Fritz Stüber warned against cooperation with ". . . persons whose uniformity of ideas cannot be guaranteed," and demanded that "the great broadening of the opposition take place under national and social principles."[32] Stüber and Hartleb both carried their anti-Kraus campaign to the convention of the Salzburg Provincial League prior to the 1952 general assembly where they were received with such wild enthusiasm that the independent Viennese *Presse* speculated that there was a strong trend in the VdU towards the political right, jeopardizing the efforts of Dr. Kraus to complete the fusion agreement with Action.

What threatened to be another major assault on Chairman Kraus and his policies by the nationalist wing of the league was stopped halfway by the October 23 collapse of the government coalition. When the OeVP and the SPOe failed to reach the necessary agreement on the budget for the coming year Chancellor Figil and Vice-Chancellor Schärf tendered their resignations to President Körner.[33] Körner accepted the resignations, but asked the government to continue on in a caretaker capacity until parliamentary elections provided for a new government.[34]

For the VdU, these events not only offered the hotly demanded *Nationalrat* elections, but presented the distinct possibility of either an end to coalition government or VdU inclusion within either a small or grand coalition. In either case, the absolute necessity of the appearance of unity was imposed on the VdU delegates as they assembled in Graz on October 25 for their third general assembly. A prime function of the convention was to sanction the plan for fusion with Action which Kraus and Strachwitz had finally agreed upon after three months of tedious negotiations. But the plan which called for total integration of the two organizations met with vigorous opposition from the floor of the convention and after fourteen hours of heated debate was defeated. In its place the assembly substituted a compromise proposal by which the two groups would cooperate in the coming elections, but would submit the question of fusion to further discussions in the future.

Thoroughly repudiated by this vote, Kraus acknowledged his defeat and withdrew his name from candidacy for the chairmanship of the league. In his place, the German born former Colonel Max Stendebach was elected with 84 of the 142 votes cast. Dr. Kraus was elected as deputy chairman as were Fritz Stüber and Jörg Kandutsch.[35] The internal rents in the organization had taken their toll and the liberal-progressive wing of the league which had retained control by virtue of its initial leadership in the movement was forced to relinquish power to the nationalists.

The reaction of Action to this renege on the part of the VdU was one of surprise and anger. But at its general assembly two weeks later, Action accepted the offer of cooperation and announced that the two organizations had agreed to campaign as the VdU-Action coalition under the title "Movement for Social Renewal." Otherwise the two associations were to remain independent, joined only by an executive council chaired by the VdU with three deputy chairmen from each organization.[36] In a joint press conference a month later Stendebach and Strachwitz, as leaders of their respective groups, announced that the symbol for the coming election would be the capital letter E for *Einigung, Erneuerung, Europa* (Unity, Renewal, Europe).[37] Due to the confusion that could arise from campaigning under either the letter E or the name "Movement for Social Renewal" (VdU-Action), it was announced that Action had agreed to accept the label *Wahlpartei der Unabhängigen* under which the VdU had run in the past.[38]

In its political program, the VdU tried to capitalize on the above-party image of the 1951 presidential election and emphasized that "The ideal of unity symbolized by a large E would go far beyond the coalescence of the VdU and Action."[39] In the economic sphere the VdU supported the principle of laissez faire and where possible demanded either an end to the nationalization of industry or at the very least the application of sound commercial principles.⁴⁰ In parliamentary matters, Kraus, as faction leader of the Independents in the *Nationalrat,* announced his intention to vote with the SPOe on some issues and the OeVP on other issues so as hopefully to become the long-desired "balance on the political scale." In the light of the recent rupture of the government coalition, the obvious question arose regarding the Independents' willingness to participate in an expanded *Proporz.* To this, Stendebach replied that if the government parties' program included important points required for social renewal, then the KdU would consider sharing responsibility in the government rather than maintaining opposition at any price.⁴¹ Thus coordinated, if not completely united, the "third force" optimistically entered the *Nationalrat* election campaign of 1953.

Election day was set for February 22, 1953. A winter election! This factor alone determined the main thrust of the campaign. In the eyes of the People's party the timing of the election gave an automatic advantage to parties of the left, for, as OeVP Foreign Minister Gruber explained: "An election campaign at the height of winter unemployment — at a time when school costs, heating and food burdened the little man with higher expenditures — could not work to the interests of a moderate party."⁴² Economics became the principal focus of campaign propaganda. At a time when recession was beginning to tarnish the "economic wonder" that had brought relative prosperity to Austria since 1949, the social welfare program of the SPOe was particularly attractive.

To counter this built-in handicap, the OeVP campaigned under the slogan: "Checkmate Inflation, Road to Freedom." Under this banner, the People's party published a twelve point program which laid the evils of unemployment, diminishing real wages and pensions, over-bureaucratization and high taxes at the door of the Socialists' economic policies.⁴³ But fiscal stability had little appeal to the man who had no savings to protect and the demand for efficiency in the bureaucracy and nationalized industry seemed only to carry the threat of a reduction in the work force and greater unemployment. Simple posters depicting starving pensioners posted by the SPOe next to OeVP placards demanding stability of the schilling carried a dramatic impact.

In marked contrast to the largely negative OeVP program which demanded the reduction of state influence in the economy and sought to educate the electorate on the beneficent operation of private, free enterprise, the SPOe proposed a program of positive social programs to bring about full employment, equal pay for equal work, increased pensions, stimulation of public housing, etc.[44]

For the VdU, the winter election posed a perplexing dilemma. On the one hand, its economic program was even less suited to the winter season than that of the People's party which at least had a record of social welfare legislation in cooperation with the SPOe. On the other hand, it had been demanding the earliest possible new elections since the beginning of the previous year, hoping that its apparently broadened basis would produce an even greater success than in the presidential election of 1951. Therefore the VdU was obliged to accept the election date with public enthusiasm, even though a later election would have better suited its purposes. In its campaign, the VdU chose not to attack the goals of the major parties which ". . . are to be supported and striven for." But it continued, these were the same goals that had been enunciated in 1949. "The VdU was the only party that fought for the government program in the Parliament, while the government parties opposed their own programs."[45] The reason for the lack of progress was that in order to preserve the coalition, each party had compromised itself. The appeal carried in this campaign was much the same as in 1949: end the *Proporz!* End the government of compromise and transform the "voting machine" in the *Nationalrat* into a true forum of peoples' representatives!

Symbolic of its positive program, the VdU campaigned under the capital letter E: for *Einigung, Erneuerung, Europa.* As evidence of the first E for unity, the VdU nominated a slate of candidates that reflected the above-party image of 1951. Twenty-five were members of the VdU, six of Action and sixteen had no previous affiliation with either group.[46] Under the second E for renewal, the VdU included its political and social-economic program. Politically the Movement for Social Renewal adopted the demands of both the VdU and the Youth Front for "the full equality of all citizens."[47] This nebulous demand was a code phrase that embodied all of the customary VdU and Youth Front appeals to the dissatisfaction of the ex-Nazis, the *Volksdeutschen* and the veterans upon whom both movements had been built.

More critical in the 1953 election campaign were, however, the economic and social issues so vigorously debated by the major parties. *Die Neue Front*'s headlines and heavy print carried seemingly progressive demands for "Unified Economic and Social Policy," "Social Achievement," "Higher Living Standard," "A Great Program of Creating Employment," etc. But behind the phrasemaking lay the basic principle that these goals could be achieved only through private enterprise and a free market economy. In small print, the VdU rejected the nationalization of industry, the extensive program of public health insurance and facilities, government control over wages, prices, imports, exports, etc. In this regard, the VdU program reflected even more than before the link of the "third force" with the traditional liberal economics of the past, an emphasis stemming primarily from internal changes in the VdU and its association with Action.

Under "social renewal," the VdU posited the reduction of the number of public employees and proposed a program for their transfer into the private sector. It agreed that this might cause momentary economic dislocation, but suggested that this could be mitigated by tax incentives and generous credit policies to encourage private enterprises to employ those terminated. Soon, the VdU reasoned, there would occur a tremendous upsurge in total production, which, if restrictions on imports and exports were eliminated, would make Austria industrially competitive within the future economic community of Europe. Profit-sharing programs based on the VdU's "achievement principle" would enable the working class to share in the general prosperity and the state would likewise benefit from a higher tax base which it could pass on to public officials in higher wages, to the aged, infirm and indigent in increased social benefits and to the general population in generous credit terms to stimulate private housing construction, new businesses and an expansion of agriculture. The key to this renewal was simply the release of the economy from the strictures of government planning and control.[48]

The third E of the Movement for Social Renewal was the goal of the revitalization of Europe as a united, third force in the prevailing bipolar world. European integration had always occupied an important place in VdU propaganda as a means by which the emotional reservoir of obsolete German nationalism could be sublimated to a popular, acceptable goal. This appeal received particular emphasis in the 1953 campaign and under the nationalist-oriented leadership of both the VdU and Action, the VdU expanded the Europe concept into the campaign slogan: "The WdU: For Austria, for the German Nation, for a United Europe."[49]

In this appeal to the German nationalists the VdU encountered significant competition from OeVP Foreign Minister Karl Gruber who could point to his own accomplishments in easing the anti-German policies of the immediate postwar years. In a speech in Salzburg Gruber declared:

> We want no artificial boundaries between these two countries. That would be just as idiotic as a new *Anschluss* policy. . . .
> On the other hand, we may permit ourselves no political adventures, for our relationship with Germany is too good for that. Germany will again take its rightful place in the community of peoples when it has been successful in winning back the trust of the world. If we Austrians pursue irresponsible *Anschluss* slogans, we would not only seriously compromise Germany, but even place the unification of Europe in serious question. . . .
> We hope that in the VdU those men will triumph with whom a reasonable policy can be made. We reject however, the adventure of individual speculators who want to conduct a transparent policy under the slogan Germany.[50]

In this statement Gruber was clearly trying to win the support of the moderate nationalists to his party. At the same time, however, he realized that the OeVP might want to form a small coalition with the Independent delegates in the *Nationalrat* and therefore tried to encourage the VdU into acceptable channels.

The appeal by Gruber was one against which only the most adamant German-nationalists took serious offense, forcing the VdU to artificial and obsolete protestations of distinction. For this purpose *Die Neue Front* editor Viktor Reimann exhumed OeVP support of government policy in the immediate postwar years which had supported ". . . a negative posture vis-a-vis Germany. . . . No German language classes, but a Language of Instruction . . . an Austrian dictionary . . . a press attaché in Bonn who wrote . . . that it was a misfortune that Austria has German as a mother tongue."[51] Against Gruber's contention that Germany had to earn its way back into the community of peoples, Reimann made the German "economic wonder" a VdU campaign issue stating that "only Germans have worked and have reestablished the prestige of the currency in the world, and Austrian tourism is borne almost forty percent by Germans. The first phase ended therefore with a brilliant German victory."[52] In contrast to this "proven" anti-German policy by the OeVP, Reimann argued that the VdU wanted ". . . a close economic and cultural relationship, because the economic as well as the cultural area will become sterile without close exchange with Germany."[53] There was little that the major parties could find fault with in these measured statements. Even in the ranting avowals of membership in the German *Volk* by nationalist orators such as Stüber, the distinction between the political and the organic nation was always made and any suggestion of *Anschluss* was assiduously avoided.

Accordingly, for the first time since the emergence of the VdU, accusations of neo-Nazism did not play a major role in the campaign. With the exception of a personal attack on VdU Chairman Stendebach for the "mass murder" of his troops in over-zealous military activity during the siege of Leningrad,[54] the campaign against the VdU was conducted with no more venom than was exchanged between the two major parties. By 1953, the issue of Nazism had so significantly paled that the OeVP, which in the past had so bitterly reviled the VdU on charges of neo-Nazism, went so far as to publish an appeal by the founder of the Austrian National Socialist party for former Nazis to shun their natural inclinations for the VdU and vote for the People's party.[55] This radical departure from past campaign practices by the OeVP was undoubtedly motivated by serious fears of a loss of control in the *Nationalrat*. In this case, the OeVP wanted to leave itself free to maneuver the inclusion of the other middle-class party in the coalition, should the Socialist presence be considerably increased.

The fears of the OeVP were well justified. When the votes were tallied, it became apparent that the OeVP had lost its position as the most popular party in Austria, but because of the method of alloting seats according to province, it still emerged with a one seat plurality in the new *Nationalrat*. The morning after the election the OeVP press could still boast: "OeVP the Strongest Party in the *Nationalrat* with 74 Mandates."[56] Justifiably, the Socialist press claimed: "SPOe — the Strongest Party."[57] Both claims were correct. The results were ambiguous. Only the VdU suffered defeat both in representation in the *Nationalrat* as well as in the total vote. In general these trends applied in the simultaneous *Landtag* elections in Styria, Carinthia and Burgenland as well. (See Tables III and IV.) In a bitter analysis of the results, Dr. Reimann sought a scapegoat for the VdU defeat and criticized the Austrian people for ". . . sinking to the level of voting cattle . . . following the path of least resistance. As it were, they wanted the famous Austrian *Ruah*."[58]

Ironically, however, the only party to suffer an absolute electoral loss emerged with the greatest potential for improving its position in the new government to convene in March. The OeVP viewed its loss of support among the masses as the result of popular disapproval of the concessions it had made to the Socialists in eight years of coalition government. Disenchantment with its partner on the left and fear that public despair might lead to a revival of right-radicalism suggested to the OeVP ". . . that the second middle-class party, the Independents, should participate in the government in order to balance the weight of the left on the governmental wagon."[59] Thus in its moment of defeat,

Table III

Results of the 1953 *Nationalrat* Election and the Difference for Each Party Relative to the 1949 *Nationalrat* Election and the 1951 Presidential Election*

Party	1953 Votes	1953 Mandates	1953 %	Difference from 1949 Votes	Difference from 1949 Mandates	Difference from 1949 %	Difference from 1951 Votes	Difference from 1951 %
SPOe	1,818,517	73	42	+194,993	+6	+3	+135,636	+3
OeVP	1,781,777	74	41	− 68,804	−3	−3	+ 56,326	−1
VdU	472,866	14	11	− 16,407	−3	−3	−189,634	−5
VO**	228,159	4	5	+ 15,093	−1	0	+ 8,190	0

*"Die Nationalratswahlen vom 22. Februar 1953," ed. Bundesministerium für Inneres: Österreichischen Statistischen Zentralamt (Vienna, 1953), pp. XIX–XXX, XXXII, reprinted in *Wahlstatistik*, pp. C 137, 139, 140, 146.
** Wahlgemeinschaft Österreichischer Volksopposition, ostensibly KPOe.

Table IV

Results of the 1953 Landtag Elections in Styria, Carinthia and Burgenland and the Difference for Each Party Relative to the *Landtag* Elections of 1949*

Party 1 Results 2 Difference	Styria Votes	Styria Mandates	Styria %	Carinthia Votes	Carinthia Mandates	Carinthia %	Burgenland Votes	Burgenland Mandates	Burgenland %
SPOe 1	271,162	20	41.1	122,245	18	48.2	74,934	14	44.6
2	+27,301	+2	+3.7	+21,009	+3	+7.4	+8,464	+1	+4.4
OeVP 1	268,546	21	40.7	79,093	11	31.9	81,138	16	48.4
2	-10,907	-1	1.2	-6,772	-1	-3.4	3,358	-2	-4.2
VdU 1	89,837	6	13.6	42,877	6	16.9	6,056	1	3.6
2	-4,861	-1	-1.0	-8,135	-2	-3.6	-271	0	-.3
VO 1	29,039	1	4.4	10,337	1	4.1	5,386	1	3.2
2	-489	0	-.1	+427	0	+.1	+602	+1	+.3

* *Die Wahlen in den Bundesländern seit 1945: Nationalrat und Landtage*, ed. Verbindungsstelle der österreichischen Bundesländer Vienna: Selbstverlag des Amtes der niederösterreichischen Landesregierung, 1962).

the independent party movement appeared to be in a position to exert its long-desired "third force."

Two days after the election, the caretaker government was dissolved and President Körner requested former Chancellor Leopold Figl, as chairman of the narrowly predominant OeVP, to form the new government. For Figl however, this task posed enormous difficulties. The Socialists, enjoying a majority in the popular vote and virtual parity in the *Nationalrat,* were certain to make their cooperation in a new coalition cost the OeVP dearly in acceptance of socialist programs. But it was precisely such concessions to the SPOe since 1945 that many in the OeVP leadership felt had led to the serious decline in the popularity of the party. The leadership of ex-Christian Socialists Figl and Hurdes became discredited in the eyes of the younger and predominantly non-Viennese functionaries. These second-line leaders saw a greater community of interest between the Vienna OeVP leaders and the Socialists than with their own party colleagues in the provinces. In 1951, after the OeVP defeat in the presidential election the emerging younger leaders in the party had stripped Figl and Hurdes of their party leadership, although leaving them in their government positions. In 1953 however, having suffered the third successive election disappointment, the "Young Turks" of the OeVP had had enough of the old guard and prepared their final assault. Chancellor-designate Figl, trying to form a government as charged by the president, was confronted by the Socialists with demands for increased power commensurate with their election victory and by intransigence from his own party colleagues against such concessions. The obvious way out of this dilemma was to include the VdU in the coalition. Although the Socialists could be expected to resist the inclusion of a second middle-class party in the government, it was reasoned that the alternative of leaving the government and taking up the opposition in the *Nationalrat* would be even less desirable. Accepting this alternative, Figl designated a negotiating committee to discuss arrangements with the VdU.

Anticipating the overture, the VdU leadership met in Vienna to discuss participation in the government. The anti-OeVP and largely nationalist faction led by Stüber vigorously opposed cooperation and was supported by Action representatives Strachwitz and Gredler. Kraus however, arguing that "without participation in politics we will starve," was able to win over his erstwhile enemy Karl Hartleb and with him a majority of the leadership. A communiqué was released to the press indicating a willingness to participate in the government, but subject to certain "demands."[60] These "demands" were understood to be the position of Minister of Trade in the new cabinet, the inclusion of a VdU representative in the presidium of the *Nationalrat,* and certain additional concessions with regard to the National Socialist Law.[61] These conditions were immediately accepted by the OeVP negotiating committee and a common policy was announced for the construction of the new government.[62]

Having apparently assured middle-class domination of the new government, Figil and OeVP Chairman Julius Raab opened negotiations with the Socialists about the new government. Figil, as a concentration camp alumnus and bitter enemy of National Socialism, had little enthusiasm for including the "browns" in the coalition, but went along with the plan in preference to admitting the victory of the Socialists and granting them appropriate equality of representation in the new government. In the negotiations with the Socialists it was Raab who became the chief proponent of the three-party coalition, demanding either the inclusion of the VdU or a return to the configuration of the 1949 pact.[63] Neither of these alternatives was acceptable to the SPOe, for inclusion of the VdU would certainly hinder realization of its campaign promises of more extensive social welfare benefits, while a restoration of the previous government would leave control with the OeVP and likewise thwart its designs. Negotiations quickly reached an impasse and were suspended.

The OeVP negotiators returned to their middle-class partner and worked out a joint parliamentary program based on their mutual ideals of economic conservatism.[64] This was an obvious attempt to force the SPOe into cooperation with the threat of exclusion from the government by a OeVP-VdU coalition. When the Socialists still proved intractable, the OeVP escalated the pressure by using its narrow, but adequate majority in coalition with the VdU to elect Independent Karl Hartleb as Third President of the *Nationalrat* over Socialist contender Dr. Bruno Pittermann.[65] The situation seemed ominous. Outside the government the SPOe would have no chance of putting through its programs. Its only weapon was the power that it held in the trade unions in calling strikes and street demonstrations to influence legislation by extra-parliamentary means. But this policy had brought Austria repeatedly to the brink of civil war in the First Republic and the Socialists were unwilling to risk this danger, particularly where such upheaval might be effectively exploited by the Communists.

For the same reasons, Figil began to have second thoughts about the

OeVP demands. Preferring a renewal of the black-red coalition to the possibility of civil war, the chancellor-designate began private discussions with the Socialists.[66] Before these negotiations had a chance to bear any fruit however, the OeVP withdrew support from Figil and named party-head Raab as the candidate for chancellor. The official reason given for this move was a request by Figil to be released because of his continuing inability to build a government.[67] Socialist Party Chairman Adolf Schärf however, who had been in telephone contact with Figil only minutes before the change was made, claims that this came as a total surprise to the chancellor.[68] Figil's failure to form a government could not have been the real reason for his removal, because the three-party coalition demand on which the negotiations with the Socialists had foundered had been Raab's. A more probable explanation is that Figil's inability to form a government was the final blow used by the dissidents in the OeVP to dislodge the chancellor from the dominant position he had held since 1945. But as long as the People's party insisted on the inclusion of the VdU in the government, Raab had no more success than Figil.

Concerned that the political impasse might encourage another Communist attempt to attach Austria to the Soviet bloc, the western powers exerted their influence on leaders of the OeVP to return to the stability of the black-red coalition. Meanwhile rumors were circulating to the effect that the Socialist President Körner would not recognize a coalition of the two middle-class parties.[69] In a speech on March 27 at the opening ceremonies of a UNESCO exhibition in Vienna, President Körner lent substance to these rumors in a sternly critical observation of the political proceedings:

> The people, the great mass of the electorate, has unmistakably recognized the achievement of a peaceful democracy. Eighty-four percent of the votes, more than in any previous election, fell to the two major parties which for years have borne the burden of responsibility for themselves. In accord with this clear election result, I called the representatives of the two major parties to me and requested them to again create a government, as previously, on the political basis which has shown itself firmer and stronger than in any other country.
> To broaden this basis and thereby make the cooperation of the parties in the government more difficult did not appear necessary to me. . . . I have seen that mere declarations and promises of an individual, as of a party, do not suffice to turn a negative criticizing force into a positive, state-avowing force over night.[70]

Using the threat of a small coalition as a lever, Raab continued to negotiate with the SPOe on the terms of a new coalition. When he had maneuvered the Socialists into accepting a revised *Proporz* moderately reflecting their increase in parliamentary power, yet still acceptable to the OeVP, Raab abandoned his demand for inclusion of the VdU. With these obstacles circumvented, a new coalition pact was sealed. Although the "voting machine" requiring obligatory acceptance by the party factions on all government bills was continued, on the surface the 1953 pact did not seem as rigid as its predecessor. Agreements between the two parties at the federal level did not apply to the provincial and local councils or cultural-political questions and there was a *"Koalitionsfreier Raum"* in which the pact did not apply.[71] This latter agreement was a sop which the OeVP had demanded to placate its rejected partner. The VdU gleefully received the concession proclaiming that the *"Demokratur"* of the past had been eliminated and predicting that where the coalition pact did apply, a truly free parliamentary system would develop in which the VdU would play a decisive role as a central balance between the right and the left.[72] Unknown to the VdU however, the specific terms of the secret pact rendered the publicly proclaimed *"Koalitionsfreier Raum"* meaningless. The OeVP had indeed negotiated for a means by which it could merge with the VdU on parliamentary votes on issues of mutual agreement.[73] But this was rejected by the SPOe on the grounds that it would seriously jeopardize the good faith necessary between coalition partners. But the OeVP negotiators were under such pressure that ". . . they were adamant that the expression *"Koalitionsfreier Raum"* be in the pact, even if it meant nothing." No objections were raised to this ruse and therefore it was agreed that "if . . . the '*Koalitionsfreier Raum*' is specifically stipulated, then its realization is dependent upon acceptance by the Socialists. It exists therefore only when it is not unacceptable to the Socialists."[74] At the federal level at least, the *Proporz* was again total!

Despite its failure to gain access to the chambers of the government, the VdU entered the new parliament full of optimism for the future. But the *"Koalitionsfreier Raum"* proved just as unproductive to the Independents as the isolation of their first parliamentary session. For a second time, the VdU was pressed into an impotent opposition with no real responsibility for the political course of Austria. The *Nationalrat* again became a kind of marionette theater in which the delegates moved on strings controlled by their party secretaries according to compromises worked out in secret negotiations. Parliamentary representatives were seen by the public as responsive to their parties rather than their constituencies. Austrians not mobilized for political action through their unions or employees' associations became apathetic and turned their attentions to enjoying the fruits of a resurgent economy after the stagnation of 1952. In this atmosphere of political lethargy, the mortar that had cemented the heterogeneous "third force" together in the early postwar years began to crumble. Deprived of the opportunity to seriously influence political life, the moderate elements lost interest in the seemingly hopeless struggle, and the nationalists moved into the vacuum. The emerging nationalist leadership failed, however, to realize that the electoral successes of 1949 and 1951 had not been the fruits of the movement's nominal nationalist posture; rather they were the expression of a people frustrated and disappointed by the failures and half-measures of a rigid, highly centralized government in Vienna, seemingly insensitive to the needs of its people.

Negativism alone however does not provide the kind of cohesion necessary to sustain a political movement. The nationalists within the VdU had always been able to draw the most enthusiastic crowds and were deceived into believing that their modernized nationalist appeal and the demand for a United Europe could provide the ideological common denominator necesary to coalesce the diverse elements of the movement into a unified political party. Thus the remaining history of the VdU as the only potentially significant representative of the "third force" was dominated by the struggle and ultimate success of the nationalists to capture control from the moderate, social-progressive faction. The result was the consolidation of a new leadership cadre, but with the defection of the moderate voters who had really comprised the bulk of the VdU constituency after all.

VII

The Fragmentation of the "Third Force"

In the three years following the second failure of the Independents to gain admittance to the government, the chaotic course of fate which seemed to turn good fortune to bad and bad to good continued to make the history of the independent party movement appear to be one long, breathless toboggan ride plunging from crisis to crisis on the way to oblivion.

Despite its reversal in the 1953 parliamentary elections, the VdU had risen to an illusory pinnacle of power on the threshold of real political responsibility. But even in this moment of euphoria, the internal clefts within the league threatened to burst the fragile bonds of cohesion. Even the decision to join in coalition with the OeVP had been won only with extreme difficulty from the league's right wing. Led by Drs. Stüber and Ursin of the Viennese League, this faction claimed a popular mandate for its strongly nationalist, anti-OeVP posture because of a general increase of VdU voting strength in the area under their jurisdiction. In the wake of a general decline in electoral support (which only Salzburg, the home of the movement, had escaped) this demand for a stronger nationalist policy and uncompromising opposition to the governing parties carried considerable weight.

Resisting this tack, Dr. Kraus argued that eternal opposition without any parliamentary accomplishments would enervate the movement; a partial compromise on program and goals was acceptable if it meant that the league could use the spotlight of government responsibility to create a new and positive image for the movement.

Between these two poles wavered a faction led by Hartleb and the Action leadership that feared cooperation in yoke with the OeVP would cost the Independents their freedom to oppose the black-red *"Demokratur"* and would reduce the movement to little more than a "less black" arm of the People's party. But when Kraus won the promise to include Independents in both the government cabinet and the Presidium of the *Nationalrat,* and gave the VdU leadership the power of approval over the legislative program, the lure of respectability and actual participation in government proved too strong. Hartleb and his supporters returned to the Kraus-Reimann faction full of ambitions for the VdU to assume the fallen mantle of "the balance on the scale" that the national-liberals had worn in the First Republic.[1]

Momentarily, the nationalist challenge within the league leadership was buried and in this spirit of cooperation, Dr. Kraus was reelected chairman of the VdU parliamentary faction. If the VdU had been included in the government, it is conceivable that the moderates could have recaptured control of the movement and employed their strength to breach the two-party coalition and play a balancing role between two freely operating majority parties. But the exclusion of the VdU from the government coalition due to SPOe intransigence and the OeVP readiness to "sell out" its middle-class ally, the purely oppositional forces in the nationalist wing of the movement were able to point out, with considerable credence, that neither of the major parties was really amenable towards granting any political responsibility to the Independents. Should a political "bone" be thrown to the VdU in the future, its influence would be negligible and cooperation would only lead to self-prostitution and the loss of what political significance it commanded as the only agency of critical surveillance. Thus, the right wing argued, only through strong, vocal opposition based on the firm ideals and logical principles of the unity of the German *Volk* and the supranational cooperation of all peoples in a United States of Europe could the cohesion come for a truly meaningful political movement.

But it was not only within the right-wing of the "third force" that dissatisfaction arose with the Kraus policy of a common course with the OeVP as the path to political responsibility. Even before the election the other wing of the VdU political conglomerate experienced a defection of worker elements in response to the VdU negotiations with the economically conservative, middle-class Action. Most notable among these deserters was the leader of the VdU trade union faction, former deputy chairman and parliamentary representative Thomas Neuwirth who expressed the fear that the merger with Action would ". . . shift the center of gravity to that wing for whom — carefully stated — the struggle for a new, up-to-date economic social order was not a major desire."[2] During the agonizing negotiations to form a new government, the SPOe made good propaganda use of the close relationship between the VdU and the OeVP to win over worker and other adamant anti-OeVP elements.

Once the new government had been formed and the Kraus policy of cooperation lay in shambles, the leadership struggle within the VdU flared anew. In many of the provincial leagues Kraus's cooperation with Action and negotiation with the OeVP had alienated many. In most cases this stemmed from a deeply ingrained anticlericalism which usually coincided with a strong nationalist orientation. The foremost proponent of this sentiment in the league was the ex-Nazi Dr. Fritz Stüber, VdU chairman in Vienna. After his overwhelming reelection as chairman by a provincial assembly held in April, 1953, Stüber won from the delegates a virtual declaration of war on the federal leadership in the unanimously accepted resolution which contended:

> ... the VdU policy of absolute rejection of the black-red coalition finds increasing support in all areas of the population. The effect of this force becomes stronger, the more decisively and uncompromisingly it represents the natural basic demands of a healthy *völkisch* life in the family and the state and also avoids even the appearance of unity with the dying parties of Marxist class struggle and capitalist profit economics. Momentary tactical political advantages notwithstanding, the realization of the VdU program is to be achieved only through intellectual battle with its opponents, not through compromises with them. We are and remain the Vienna VdU.[3]

This was an invitation to all sympathetic elements within the VdU to join the Vienna League in purging the federal leadership and instilling a new ideological purity into the movement. A dissident faction of the Carinthian League enthusiastically supported the Vienna League to protest against their own provincial leadership which had adopted the pro-OeVP policy of the federal leadership to cooperate with the People's party in resisting immoderate power demands by the SPOe in the newly elected *Landtag*.[4] This dispute led to a leadership crisis in the Carinthian League that was resolved only through the personal intervention of Dr. Kraus. In Styria, Tyrol, Salzburg and Lower Austria, resignations, expulsions and statements of provincial autonomy from the federal leadership indicated a strong undercurrent of dissatisfaction and portended another leadership crisis at the general assembly scheduled for Vienna on May 16 and 17.

But the convention did not result in further fragmentation as had been widely expected. The dissidents attempted to pass a censure resolution against the federal leadership, but only won twenty-seven of the one hundred and fifty-one votes cast.[5] Another test of the convictions of the delegates developed over the election of the leadership for the coming year. Chairman Stendebach, a moderate nationalist himself, had taken a firm stand in favor of the recent attempt to enter the government and, despite the failure of the effort, felt the publicity was favorable for the image of the league. In order to reaffirm the concept of the league as a movement committed to democratic reform, the moderates nominated Stendebach for another term as chairman. The dissidents nominated Dr. Fritz Ursin, vice-chairman of the Viennese League, to test the sentiment for a nationalist-oriented policy dedicated to uncompromising opposition to the government coalition. Thus the election of officers was also a referendum on the political policy of the league. The resulting victory of Stendebach with 102 votes to 38 for Ursin again confirmed that the dissident faction was well outside the mainstream of the movement. Realizing the futility of further opposition and mindful of the barely-averted disintegration of its own provincial organization, the Carinthian delegation called upon the assembly to elect Stüber along with Kraus and Jörg Kandutsch as deputy chairmen to illustrate the continued stability of the organization to the full membership and the general public. The suggestion was heeded, and on this note of unanimity the convention was prorogued for four weeks in order that a definitive proposal for the final fusion of the VdU with Action might be prepared.

Despite the defeat which the Stüber-Ursin faction had suffered at the Vienna general assembly, it nevertheless controlled the one-third bloc of votes necessary to block passage of the fusion proposal presented by the federal leadership at the second session of the assembly at Villach on July 5 and 6. All proposals that would have acceded to Action demands that the merger be an amalgamation rather than an absorption were rejected. Agreement could be reached only on a resolution that required Action to dissolve itself and give its members a period of three weeks to join the VdU. Although unable to gain any real power to positively determine VdU policy, the dissidents, with their ability to deny the necessary two-thirds majority for statutory amendment, were eminently successful in thwarting any changes in the league's program or constituency.

As expected, Action rejected this attempt at absorption, but without any real alternatives, declared its loyalty to the mutually shared goals of the VdU[6] and indicated that its *Nationalrat* delegates Gredler and Herzele would remain in the parliamentary club of the Independents.[7] Despite the understanding of the VdU and Action to cooperate where possible in the future, it was clear that the first of the three E's in the 1953 campaign slogan had been overly optimistic. Unity with Action had been a favorite and almost personal project of Dr. Kraus since the

Youth Front first gave evidence of disquiet in the People's party. It was ironic that the personality conflicts that had repeatedly prevented attempts at unification since 1951 should be ameliorated only as Dr. Kraus lost control of his own organization. Appropriately, when a VdU-Action fusion agreement was finally reached it came up against the internal power struggle within the VdU itself.

Renewal, the second goal of the E slogan, represented another longstanding desire of Dr. Kraus to reform the system that politically represented the middle-class segment of the population. He had first used independent, critical and analytic journalism to stimulate reform of the OeVP from within. When the OeVP proved impervious to the demands for change, Kraus founded the VdU with the hope of creating a "third force" as the vehicle for political renewal. In 1953 the chance for realization of these dreams in the inner sanctum of the government finally appeared. Kraus leaped at the opportunity and when it slipped through his fingers, he was left without purpose and only the stigma of defeat for his efforts.

Although Kraus's failure to achieve the first two goals of the three E program did not immediately shift the ideological orientation of the league, it did cause increasing stress on the third goal, Europe. European integration had always been an acknowledged goal of the VdU. In itself it would appear to be the absolute antithesis of nationalism, but the emphasis was couched in language designed to stimulate German national pride and as such signaled a shift in stress, if not in the program, of the VdU. Characteristic of this new campaign was the fullpage coverage given by *Die Neue Front* to a speech by the chairman of the "League of Countrymen Driven from Their Homes," which had organized the solid support of the *Volksdeutschen* behind the VdU in all elections since its inception. In this speech Chairman Lodgemann came dangerously close to Pan-German expressions, declaring that

> ... the fundamental political activity of all the many millions of German displaced persons is to be the vanguard of a European order, which is not limited to the West alone, but which seeks to solve the problem of homeless refugees by the recovery of their homeland in the framework of the concept of a United Europe.
>
> No one who has seen the creative power of the Germans after their catastrophic defeat can believe that the end of the Germans in history has come and no one who follows the activity of Germans who have been driven from their homes in political, economic and cultural spheres will believe that by banishment, an irreversible fact has been established and that the East has been lost for Germandom.

> The liberation of Central and Eastern Europe from Bolshevism is vital. . . . This community of peoples could then reestablish, in cooperation with Germany and with the East, the lost European balance. . . . The reestablishment of the connection to the neighboring states is the European task of the Germans.
> In Austria, this international idea still lives. . . . On this ideal of the past, we must build a new multinational Europe of the future.[8]

Although this extreme nationalist vision of European integration reminiscent of nineteenth century dreams of an Austrian-German dominated *Mitteleuropa* did not directly represent the ideology of the increasingly nationalist-dominated VdU leadership and membership, the fact that this speech by a leader of a significant bloc of VdU voters was extensively covered the VdU press is a significant indicator of the programmatic trend of the league.

Several weeks later this drift was further revealed in the emphasis given by speakers of the VdU leadership to the principle of *Volksgemeinschaft* at the Villach session of the general assembly. The concept, which had been absorbed into the rich, if vague vocabulary of National Socialism, was generally understood to mean that only through the unity of the *Volk* and not through the *Volk*-destroying class-struggle could any real social and economic progress be achieved. League Chairman Stendebach also addressed himself to the principle by defining the traditional terms national and *freiheitlich* which were basic to the movement for the *Volksgemeinschaft*:

> *Freiheitlich* is no longer to be equated with anticlerical as in the past, since today, anticlericalism is no longer a reality. Much more, *freiheitlich* means the struggle for the rights of the individual, threatened with being trampled down by increasing collectivization. Just the same, the concept "national" means something different in its present definition from what it has meant in the past. No longer as a contradiction to other nations, but as the consciousness of the moral value of one's own *Volk,* as the maintenance of its biological substance and finally from the contribution which it has to make for the achievement of Europe.[9]

Clearly, the importance of some kind of modernized and sanitized version of German nationalism had emerged as the first priority of the new leadership with the purely political appeal for a "third force" receding into the background. This shift was based on tactical considerations as well as a sincere modification of program. Since its founding the VdU had relied upon nationalist elements for at least half its total support. Because of the hostility of ex-Nazis to the de-Nazification policy of the major parties in the immediate postwar years, the VdU did not have to woo the nationalist vote because there was simply no viable competition. But with the crystallization of a nationalist wing of the VdU itself threatening a seizure of power from within or a defection to a new party, the VdU leadership was forced to take a more emphatic stand in support of German nationalism.

As the fall session of the *Nationalrat* opened, all parties looked to the *Gemeinderat* elections in the cities of Salzburg and the *Landtag* election in Tyrol for a mandate on their respective parliamentary policies. For the Socialists the elections offered an opportunity to confirm the image of the SPOe as Austria's fastest growing party. The OeVP campaigned on Raab's record as chancellor. The VdU ran on its customary appeal for a "third force" as an alternative and a balance to the black-red coalition. Although the campaign aimed at local issues, the widely used slogan "Salzburg [Tyrol, Villach] is worth a second consideration," had obvious implications for the federal government as well.

The results of these elections were mixed and offered successes for both major parties. While not catastrophic, the results in these former bastions of VdU strength confirmed the trend of apathy that had marked the Independent turn-out in the February *Nationalrat* elections. Although political lethargy is a serious problem for any party, for a new, small one it is a matter of survival or extinction, and it cast ominous doubts on the future of the VdU. In the Salzburg *Gemeinderat* the election reduced the VdU from parity with the OeVP, while the SPOe increased its position as the strongest party. (See Table V.) In Villach, the pattern was similar. (See Table VI.) Here even *Die Neue Front* admitted a "debacle" which it blamed on the "splitting and false ambition,"[10] which led the Carinthian opposition faction to split away from the VdU to form its own "homeland list" in combination with the Vienna-based *National Liga*. As a result the anticlerical, nationalist bloc which had been the backbone of the Carinthian League was seriously divided. In the Tyrol, the *Landtag* elections were less damaging. (See Table VII.) Although the VdU lost almost 8,000 votes from the February total and won only half the votes received in the 1949 *Landtag* election, it had nevertheless been able to retain its four-man representation in the provincial assembly. But even here it was apparent that the "third force" had been splintered by former BB committee leader Ludwig Canal who, with no organization and little financial support, was able to attract one quarter of the VdU's

Table V

Comparison of the Results in the *Gemeinderat* and *Nationalrat* Elections of 1949 and 1953 in the City of Salzburg

Party	1953 Gemeinderat Votes	%	Mandates	1953 Nationalrat Votes	%	1949 Gemeinderat Votes	%	Mandates	1949 Nationalrat Votes	%
OeVP	18,502	33.8	14	19,545	32.4	13,623	28.8	12	18,019	32.9
SPOe	20,884	38.1	15	22,225	36.9	17,760	37.5	15	20,088	36.7
VdU	13,968	25.5	10	16,237	26.9	14,281	30.02	12	13,739	25.1
KPOe	1,470	2.68	1	1,984	3.3	1,666	3.5	1	2,012	3.7

Table VI

Comparison of the Villach *Gemeinderat* Election Results of 1953 with Those of 1949

Party	1953		1949	
	Votes	Mandates	Votes	Mandates
OeVP	4,937	9	4,191	8
SPOe	8,641	17	7,401	14
VdU	1,335	2	3,971	8
KPOe	1,092	2	1,457	2
Heimatliste	981	2	-	-
Nation Liga	447	0	-	-

Table VII

Comparison of the Results in the *Landtag* and *Nationalrat* Elections of 1949 and 1953 in Tyrol

Party	1953 Landtag Votes	1953 Landtag %	1953 Nationalrat Mandates	1953 Nationalrat Votes	1953 Nationalrat %	1949 Landtag Votes	1949 Landtag %	1949 Nationalrat Mandates	1949 Nationalrat Votes	1949 Nationalrat %
OeVP	134,169	57.7	23	132,655	55.1	126,510	56.4	24	127,528	56
SPOe	63,628	27.4	9	70,473	29.3	53,801	24.6	8	53,820	24
VdU	23,104	9.9	4	31,650	13.3	39,092	17.4	4	39,377	17
VO	3,707	1.6	0	5,716	2.4	3,667	1.6	0	3,705	2
List of Those without a Party	7,888	3.4	0	-	-	-	-	-	-	-

February total to his own list. The collective implication of the results of the three elections was that the apparent trend of support away from the VdU evidenced in February had not been reversed as hoped, but confirmed. Change appeared necessary to breathe life into the dying third-party movement.

For the second time within the year the electorate had revealed its increasing disinterest in the VdU as a "third force." Only in Vienna had the generally dismal election picture been somewhat brighter. Drawing the conclusion that his nationalist interpretation of the "third force" was the only salvation, Dr. Stüber stepped up the campaign to build his own power base within the league in order to support a future grasp at leadership. Although the VdU leadership had taken on an increasingly nationalist hue since Kraus had been forced out of the chairmanship, it remained adamant in its avowal of the Austrian state concept, while arguing for the cultural and economic unity of the German *Volk* to be realized within the framework of a United States of Europe. Since the February election debacle however, Stüber had moved far to the right of the measured nationalism of the VdU leadership and used his highly emotional brand of fanatic nationalism to build a small, but enthusiastic cadre with which he hoped to either *putsch* the existing leadership or to build a new party.

As a measure of self-protection, late in 1953 the league federal leadership conducted an investigation of Stüber's activities and expelled him from the organization. But because some degree of German national consciousness was held by the vast majority of the VdU constituency, the leadership took pains to emphasize that Stüber had not been expelled for his nationalist line, but rather because of his factionalizing activities within the league. The leadership then expressed the hope that this action would achieve "... the purification of the last internal differences," and reaffirmed its commitment to "continue undaunted its national-*freiheitlich,* state-avowing policy."[11]

Stüber's supporters in the Vienna League attempted to retaliate by purging their provincial organization of all members who supported the federal leadership, hoping to create a united front for an attempt to seize control at the next general assembly. In order to head off a seizure of control, the federal leadership dissolved the entire Viennese League until such time as a new leadership could be installed and control solidified over the membership.[12]

Thwarted in his attempts to reorient the league to his liking, Stüber led colleagues Deputy Chairman Fritz Ursin and federal leadership member Schyster out of the VdU to form a new party, the *Freiheitliche*

Sammlung Österreichs (FSOe).[13] Although the FSOe was unable to win any significant support from the VdU membership outside Vienna, the whole Stüber affair again revealed the continued inability of the federal leadership to control the organization. As in the Gollob affair of 1950, both the Salzburg and Carinthian organizations publicly disapproved of the expulsion of Stüber and the Salzburg organization even recommended fusion with the FSOe. In Styria the nationalist faction split with the federal leadership and decided to enter into discussions with the National Bloc which was then forming.[14]

In an effort to contain this disintegration, the VdU leadership began a vigorous redefinition of the program and goals of the league. Frequent ideological articles were published in *Die Neue Front* and mass meetings were held throughout the country to assess the opinion of the rank and file. As a consequence of this programmatic reassessment two basic points were made clear: 1) the necessity of bolstering the nationalist image of the league against competitors from the right, and 2) the need to develop a social program to win back the working-class element lost to the SPOe.

To burnish the nationalist image, VdU functionaries escalated this aspect of the program in their mass meetings. Dr. Kraus spoke of "the German task" which Austria had to fulfill[15] and even social-reformist and anti-Nazi Reimann demanded that "... in Austria, no policy may be followed that in any way endangers German interests. We will resist all tendencies against the German *Volk.*"[16] Even more emphatically, Deputy Chairman Jörg Kandutsch proclaimed:

> We must create a *new social order*. Within our *Volk* the fronts must be torn down and the people must again be led to one another. The great task of the VdU must be to stand firmly on the basis of its *national* and *social* convictions. We are *national* because we are *social* and because we are *social,* we are *national.*[17]

Although Kandutsch had been a Nazi during the war, his contrition and support of reparation for Jews in the postwar era had proven his rejection of the excesses of National Socialism.[18] Nevertheless his choice of word juxtaposition leaves little doubt as to the nature of the constituency which he sought to deny to the FSOe. Increasingly the VdU identified itself as "the only national and social movement in Austria" in an attempt to supply an ideological cement for a movement whose binding power of frustration and dissatisfaction had been sapped by political apathy and economic prosperity.

Paralleling the intensified nationalist emphasis, the VdU also broadened its social program. The league remained committed to the principle that what was good for private enterprise served the best interests of all Austrians. Nevertheless it incorporated within its social-economic program demands for improved social measures such as housing, pensions, tax reduction, etc. The hope was to attract those workers not locked into a mass production system who could see mutual benefit with their employers in the profit-sharing aspect of the "achievement principle."[19]

Hopeful that the recent purification of the membership and clarification of program had led to a revitalization of the organization, in the spring of 1954 the VdU leadership called for a general assembly to confirm the new directions. The threat of a mass exodus of the nationalist element behind Stüber resulted in a redefinition of the VdU program that was a significant reorientation in the nationalist direction. One by one, the provincial leagues held their conventions to elect delegates to the assembly and to prepare statements on the new policy. Uniformly they expressed regret at the expulsion of Stüber, but issued statements which enthusiastically supported the intensified nationalist emphasis and implied mass defections if the policy were not followed.

The fifth annual general assembly of the VdU gathered at Bad Aussee on May 15, 1954 apparently more united in program and goals than at any time since the founding of the movement. The shift from an emphasis on the political activity of the league as a "third force" in Parliament to an emphasis on the nationalist character of the organization was enthusiastically welcomed by the provincial representatives. Untroubled by the dissension that had marked previous conventions, the assembly proceeded to reelect Chairman Stendebach with an overwhelming majority. Similarly, Kandutsch, Scheuch and Kraus were given wide margins in the elections for deputy chairmen. Kraus declined the office citing his heavy duties as parliamentary club leader as justification. Both Kraus and Reimann were elected to the federal leadership, but for the first time since the inception of the VdU, neither of its two founders was represented on the Executive Council. The moderate: nationalist ratio now stood at 0:3. The programmatic trend of the past year had been confirmed in the makeup of the leadership and for the remaining two years of VdU existence, Drs. Kraus and Reimann were increasingly pushed into the background of the movement they had founded. Only in their parliamentary activities did they perform important league functions; policy rested in the hands of the ascendant leadership.[20]

To fulfill its promise of a new statement of goals, the VdU leadership presented the assembly with a new program based on a consensus of the opinion expressed in the mass meetings of the past months.[21] In its social aspects, the new program differed little from that of 1949, emphasizing the necessity of freedom from collectivism of any kind so as to ensure every individual the greatest possible opportunity to realize his personal potential to the fullest extent of his abilities. It emphasized that it was the joint responsibility of capital and labor to create a social market economy under a rational, systematic, but not planned economic policy in which private property, freedom of labor, profession and commerce were guaranteed. Finally, in a retreat from its earlier attack on socialized medical benefits, the VdU demanded the principle of social security for all individuals against sickness, accident and the poverty of old age.[22]

Concerning civil rights, the VdU reiterated its avowal of the *Rechtsstaat* and demanded equality of all citizens before the law and an end to party favoritism in administrative decisions regarding employment, housing, licensing, etc. There were no new departures from 1949, but rather the elimination or revision of the specific statements of that program into a more general statement of policy.[23]

The significant statements of the *Ausseer Programm* were contained in Paragraphs II and II, which defined the national and *freiheitlich* goals of the VdU. In a marked expansion of the modest 1949 avowal of membership in the German *Volkstum*,[24] the new program proclaimed:

> Austria is a German state. Its policy must never be directed against another German state and must serve the entire German Volk.
> ....
> The VdU pursues a national policy, that is it espouses the strengthening of the German *Volk* in the Austrian area and with it, its material and spiritual well-being.[25]

This policy was not pursued to its logical national conclusion, but leaped over the discredited goal of a politically united German nation to appeal to those who desired the position of a world power combined with the accomplishment of a united *Volk*. The solution to this incongruity had been suggested in the 1949 demand for a United States of Europe,[26] but the new program specifically spelled out the idea of a multinational superstate:

> The year 1945 was not only a German, but also a European tragedy.

As a result, the recognition that the fate of the European continent and that of the European nations can only be mastered in common was obscured. . . . Not only economic and national defense policies press towards the *Grossraum,* but also the preservation of the European way of life against every foreign influence requires the common effort of all Europe- and nationally-minded men. The freedom and the existence of every European nation in accordance with its particular racial character are ensured only within the framework of a European community.

Therefore, the VdU in this serious hour avows with particular emphasis the unification of Europe on the basis of the sovereign and equal rights of all *Völker.*

....

The European idea and the avowal of nations are not contradictions, but rather concepts of order which naturally complement each other. The true national ideal is a building block of the United Europe.[27]

With this proud statement on behalf of German nationalism, the VdU tried to reestablish its image as the only ". . . collecting basin of all national forces," against the threatened inroads of the FSOe and other nationally oriented groups, yet attempted to avoid the stigma of such a posture by embracing Europeanism.

Parallelling this appeal to the imagined national-liberal constituency of the VdU, the *Ausseer Programm* attempted to use anticlericalism as a weapon against the OeVP by demanding the application of *freiheitlich* principles devoid of any sectarian favoritism.[28] But this was an anachronistic remnant of the national-liberal ideology in the Second Republic where the Catholic Church has generally remained officially apolitical.

The intent of the increased national-*freiheitlich* emphasis in the *Ausseer Programm* was to ". . . provide the intellectual weapons for the *Landtag* and *Gemeinderat* elections in Vienna the coming fall."[29] What the proponents of this course failed to realize was that the election successes of 1949 and 1951 had not been the product of an electoral bloc unified behind the VdU as the reincarnation of the national-liberal parties of the past. Rather, the significant drawing power of the VdU was based on hostility of independent voters towards the partisan policies of the *Proporz* that controlled all levels of Austrian political existence from Vienna. The founders of the VdU had realized this and had sought to move from this negative *raison d'etre* to a positive role of governmental responsibility. When this policy failed and the nationalists eased the moderates from leadership to purify the VdU under a stronger, more clearly defined ideology, they misunderstood the motivation of the movement. It is true that the VdU organization appeared revitalized at the Bad Aussee general assembly by this new direction. But as former National Socialist Professor of Law and VdU functionary and parliamentary delegate Dr. Helfried Pfeifer has correctly noted, the VdU founders did not come out of the old nationalist camp, whereas the provincial leadership generally did.[30] It was natural that the delegates should applaud *Ausseer Programm* as the fruition of their programmatic efforts, but this was the enthusiasm of a relatively small group of registered members and officials. The VdU was primarily an electoral party without a strong membership base, and the opinions of functionaries, even though widely and enthusiastically accepted at all levels of the organization, did not necessarily reflect those of the independents who had voted the VdU lists. This fact was not realized by the buoyant VdU leadership fresh from the acclaim of Bad Aussee. Thus the league approached the elections in Vienna, Lower Austria, Salzburg and Vorarlberg confident of a reawakening of the "third force."

As promised at Bad Aussee, the new program formed the basis of the VdU campaign propaganda. Although some attention was given to its social policy, the overwhelming emphasis was on the national and *freiheitlich* aspects of the *Ausseer Programm*. In an attempt to eliminate competition for the nationalist vote the VdU announced its desire to cooperate ". . . with other *freiheitlich* associations in order to establish a unity of all *völkisch* and *freiheitlich* forces."[31] In Vienna and Salzburg this led to negotiations with Stüber's FSOe, which refused to be coopted and offered the nationalists an alternative to the VdU. Pressured by this potential split in the nationalist voting bloc, the VdU adopted an even more aggressive nationalist campaign than had been foreseen by the *Ausseer Programm*. In the final days before the elections the shrill propaganda reached a climax with the appeal:

> NATIONALISTS, vote VdU!
> The nationalist- and *freiheitlich*-oriented individual will not even have to contemplate how he will vote on the 17th of October. His ideals alone, which are based on respectability, forbid him to vote those who have for years portrayed him as morally inferior. His contemplation however, forbids him to vote splinter groups, which can not help the national cause as a whole, but rather hurt it because they weaken the force and in so doing directly and indirectly serve the interests of the governmental parties.[32]

Even more stridently, in the most open appeal to ex-Nazis since its founding, the VdU called upon

Former National Socialists!

You have been promised by the OeVP and by the SPOe before every election since 1945, equalization with all other citizens. Neither of these two parties has approached delivering these election promises. Only the VdU has demanded since the first day, the reestablishment of constitutional conditions, that is the equal rights of all citizens before the law and the elimination of unjust legislation.

The OeVP has limited itself to winning individuals from the nationalist camp. . . . These people go out and explain that they were nationalists and consider it consistent with their honor to vote OeVP today. What they do not say is that they have deserted the comradeship of the nationalists for personal advantage.

Nationalists! There is no solution for the National Socialist problem through the OeVP or SPOe. They recognize only those "ex's" who remain criminals to them. The whole problem is immediately solved when the nationalists assemble and create a united front against the OeVP and the SPOe.[33]

The plea for a strong party united on the nationalist principle was unmistakable. But as *Die Presse* concluded in its analysis of the election results: "The time for this kind of 'national' politics appears to be past."[34] In every province the defeat of the VdU was overwhelming and stunning.

In Salzburg, the home of the movement since 1945 and always at its head in membership, organization and voter support, the results showed a continuation of the trend away from the VdU. (See Table VIII.) In the remaining provinces the defeat was almost as decisive; in Vienna and Lower Austria the VdU did not even receive the necessary number of votes to be represented in the *Landtag*, and in Vorarlberg its presence was halved. (See Table VIII.)

Both major parties could view the elections as a success. In stark contrast Dr. Reimann wrote: "The 17th of October was not only a black day for the VdU, but for all *freiheitlich* and nationally oriented people in Austria."[35] With some justice, he placed blame on the chronic shortage of money for campaign propaganda, on Russian and Communist terror tactics and on unfair electoral arithmetic which worked to the disadvantage of the smaller parties. But all these factors had existed in previous elections and had been overcome.

The real reasons for the crushing defeat of the VdU lay within the league itself. The constantly recurring leadership crises of the movement since its inception had certainly weakened its image in the eyes of its former voters. In the early years, resignations and expulsions could be justified as the necessary consolidation of a young organization. But ultimately this purification should have ended in a stable organi-

Table VIII

Comparison of the 1954 *Landtag* Elections in 1) Salzburg, 2), Vorarlberg, 3) Vienna and 4) Lower Austria with Previous *Nationalrat* and *Landtag* Elections*

Party		1954 Votes	LT %	Mandates	1953 NR Votes	%	1949 LT Votes	%	1949 NR Mandates	Votes	%
OeVP	1	79,391	45.9	15	79,128	42.5	74,257	43.6	12	75,215	43.7
	2	61,105	58.0	16	24,531	55.5	56,960	56.4	16	57,402	56.4
	3	357,944	33.2	35	362,148	30.7	399,044	34.9	35	401,854	35.0
	4	436,686	50.7	30	438,348	48.5	464,785	52.5	31	300,067	34.5
SPOe	1	66,019	38.2	13	65,871	35.4	57,139	33.6	9	57,752	33.6
	2	27,357	26.0	7	24,531	22.7	19,293	19.1	4	19,262	18.9
	3	568,266	52.7	59	590,532	50.2	569,354	49.9	52	565,440	49.5
	4	353,070	40.9	23	360,791	39.9	329,549	37.3	22	330,631	37.3
VdU	1	22,789	13.2	4	35,269	19.0	31,553	18.5	5	31,919	18.9
	2	14,395	13.7	3	20,340	18.8	22,271	22.1	6	22,287	21.9
	3**	49,964	4.6	0	124,683	10.6	77,966	6.8	6	79,149	6.9
	4	22,039	2.6	0	47,706	5.3	38,779	4.4	0	39,385	4.4
KPOe	1	4,012	2.3	0	5,251	2.8	5,811	3.4	0	5,759	3.3
	2	2,516	2.3	0	3,172	2.9	2,432	2.4	0	2,435	2.4
	3	89,161	8.2	6	93,938	8.0	89,646	7.9	7	89,710	7.9
	4	49,641	5.8	3	56,303	6.2	48,217	5.5	3	48,459	5.5
FSOe	1	694	0.4	0	-	-	-	-	-	-	-
	2	-	-	-	-	-	-	-	-	-	-
	3**	13,408	1.2	0	-	-	-	-	-	-	-
	4	-	-	-	-	-	-	-	-	-	-

* *Die Wahlen in den Bundesländern.*
** *Die Presse*, October 19, 1954, p. 5. Official statistics were not used because they combine the FSOe vote with that of the VdU in Vienna.

zation. In the VdU however, the purgers became the purged in an endless, self-consuming cycle. This process seemed to end in the amity of the Bad Aussee convention, but the image was illusory. The VdU had found ideological purpose and increased enthusiasm among its nationalist membership, but the middle-class, moderate wing that had joined the movement out of a desire to exert a viable "third force" against the *Proporz* found no comfort in the new, homogeneous, ideological purity. These independents either refused to vote out of apathy for the VdU and enmity for the major parties, or joined the swelling ranks of the uncommitted center shifting with the times between the Socialists on the left and the OeVP on the right. They defected not out of sympathy for the *Proporz* but simply because the "third force" no longer offered any realistic promise of influence. They had expressed their discontent, but as prosperity and the easing of the de-Nazification robbed the "coalition of frustration" of the emotional cement of alienation, the bonds of the alliance dissolved, leaving only those whose principles precluded any other alternative. This was the process at work in the electoral defeats of 1953 and 1954.

The federal leadership understood the consequences of the *Landtag* elections and the Workers' Council elections which confirmed the defeat a week later. In a conference on October 25, the leadership correctly analyzed the reasons for the defeats and decided to reverse the recent trend in policy citing ". . . that a strong 'third force' is still a pressing demand for Austria and that the VdU as the central point for this 'third force' is questionable without a change in its goals."[36] It was decided that an extraordinary convention should be held in the near future to confirm the change in policy. In the meantime, a VdU propaganda campaign returned to the earlier emphasis on broadening the basis to include all elements not belonging to the major parties into one consolidated "third force" as the representative of the political center against the continuing dictatorship of the black-red *Proporz*.

But while the federal leadership was trying to shift the league away from the recent *völkisch* emphasis to recapture its moderate constituents who had defected to the major parties, a new threat to its right wing emerged in the consolidation of various nationalist organizations in Upper Austria. The leader of this movement was Anton Reinthaller, a former Nazi and the minister of agriculture in the *Anschluss* cabinet of Seyss-Inquart. For a time the VdU had wooed Reinthaller for his prestige value among nationalists and ex-Nazis. But Reinthaller rejected the gestures to remain free to create an entirely new agency of the "third force" for the Upper Austrian *Landtag* election scheduled for October of the next year.[37]

To counter this appeal from a purely nationalist party, the VdU again shifted its propaganda to integrate the nationalist and social-reformist appeals into an ideologically heterogeneous platform. In an attempt to reestablish the 1949 image of the VdU as the collecting point for all "neither black nor red" elements the VdU argued:

> It is clear and obvious that in a political community which emphasized the individual as does the VdU, that an intellectual uniformity and collectivism of ideas is undesirable. Therefore, every member and every functionary of this movement is free to give personal support to one or the other of the many ideas of the program without negating the other. . . .
> The program, if one will, the line of the VdU is firm. It can be outlined as follows: National and for this reason social, without being National Socialist in the sense of anachronistic tendencies. *Freiheitlich* in sharp contrast to collectivism and progressive in contrast to reactionary. Democratic in structure and in decision-making, without becoming formalistic and as a result irresponsible.[38]

Meanwhile, Reinthaller's efforts to consolidate a new party gained momentum with the incorporation of Action in January of 1955.[39] The Upper Austrian VdU itself threatened to split into two parties, one strongly nationalist and the other traditionally liberal. This threat evaporated at a provincial unity conference on January 23,[40] but another gesture was made towards Reinthaller suggesting the possibility of merging the various forces into a unified organization.[41] But Reinthaller, as the most charismatic leader on the scene at this time, remained cool to the VdU's overture and at a conference of the "Ring of National Associations" he openly declared that ". . . only in the founding of a new political community could the *freiheitlich* voters be assured of appropriate representation."[42] The *Salzburger Nachrichten,* reporting on the new activity towards broadening the third-party movement, speculated that the VdU, because of its continuing leadership and programmatic crises, was precluded as an agent for the revitalization of the "third force." Instead, the ". . . so-called Reinthaller work circles" appeared to be the most viable means ". . . for the reconstruction of the 'third force' and the reformation of the existing forces."[43] The so-called "Schwarzach decision" of elements from the Carinthian, Styrian, Tyrolean and Vorarlberg Leagues to join in support of Reinthaller provided further evidence of the threat to the VdU.

In order to block this erosion of its membership the VdU assembled an extraordinary convention on February 6, 1955 to discuss the new developments. There was a strong demand from the floor for the VdU to follow the example of Action and disband to facilitate the regrouping of all independent elements into a totally new political party. After a long and heated debate a majority of the delegates accepted a resolution rejecting dissolution and affirming the existing VdU as the logical point of origin for the new consolidation. In protest against this refusal to clear the way for a wholesale reorganization of the "third force," a substantial minority of the delegates left the assembly. Many of these were radical nationalists who strongly resented the federal leadership's retreat from the policies of the previous year. This group had no viable leadership or organization and if anything its departure was beneficial to the VdU. Much more important was the defection of the "Schwarzach Group" who formed a majority of the Tyrolean, Vorarlberg, Styrian and Carinthian delegations, on the grounds that the continued existence of the VdU could only serve to hinder the reorganization of the "third force." The assembly suspended the chairmen of these four provincial leagues, thereby barring any reconciliation and essentially converting their organizations into nuclei for the Reinthaller movement in their respective provinces.

With the dissidents gone, unity was quickly reached on the remaining issues. Stendebach was reelected chairman, confirming the policies of the past year. Recognizing the forces at work throughout the country to win the independent constituency away from the VdU, the assembly passed a resolution appealing for all available elements to join with the League of Independents in building "an effective 'third force in Austria.'" Because "the preconditions for this end will be different in the different provinces," the assembly decided to extend far-reaching autonomy to its regional organizations in order to facilitate the broadening of the basis ". . . from below, which would presumably prove itself healthier and more organic than a construction from above."[44] But what was intended as a revitalization of the organization from the foundation upwards, became in fact an invitation to collapse. In a gesture to the nationalists to compensate for the sharp tack back to the political center, Chairman Stendebach closed the convention with a moderate statement reaffirming the league's commitment to the German national ideal and expressing the hope that the assembly had established a set of principles upon which a regrouping of the "third force" could take place.

But even while the rump of the extraordinary assembly was optimistically declaring its reestablished unity, the cracks in the organization began to widen. In Carinthia, the provincial leadership disassociated itself from the federal organization and reaffirmed its support of the *Ausseer Programm* which it declared should be the basis for the broadening of the VdU, specifically in the direction of the Reinthaller group. In Vorarlberg, the provincial leaders were less hostile towards the federal leadership, but they nevertheless rejected the suspension of their chairman and urged that negotiations for strengthening the "third force" be carried out immediately.[45] In Styria, where Karl Hartleb had been sent as interim leader until a new provincial leadership could be elected, the suspended chairman called a meeting of his executive council to take a position on the actions of the general assembly. The council rejected the decisions of the convention as well as Hartleb's provisional leadership and issued an appeal for the expansion of the "third force," instructing its chairman to undertake negotiations with Reinthaller and other similar-minded groups to bring about such a consolidation in Styria.[46]

On February 15, these individual provincial movements were given additional impetus when representatives of the Vorarlberg, Tyrol, Carinthian and Salzburg provincial leagues met in Salzburg with former federal Deputy-Chairman Scheuch, FSOe Chairman Ursin, Dr. Gredler of the dissolved Action, Reinthaller and numerous other proponents of the "third force" from all provinces of Austria. As a consequence of this meeting a "third force" committee was created to "... harmoniously assemble all individuals, groups and associations of the 'third force.'" The four participating VdU provincial organizations joined by the Styrian League immediately welcomed the action and appointed liaison representatives to participate in further discussions.[47] Several days later four important leaders of the Tyrolean League joined with Dr. Canal, former leader of the BB committee and organizer of the "List of Those without a Party" for the 1953 *Landtag* election, and Drs. Ursin, Gredler and Anton Reinthaller to form the "Working Committee for the Creation of the 'Third Force' in Tyrol."[48]

In the meantime, while the disintegration of the VdU organization in the Alpine provinces was creating the building blocks for a new party, the various nationalist groups in Upper Austria finally constituted themselves as the "Provincial Committee of the 'Third Force' for Upper Austria" with the expressed purpose of creating a party organization for the *Landtag* election the coming October.[49]

Finally, Reinthaller drew all these groups together and on March 3 publicly announced that he had applied for permission from the Ministry of Interior to found the *Freiheitspartei* (FP).[50] In the next weeks organizers of the *Freiheitspartei* vigorously negotiated with other groups of the "third force" for a unification into one party. On March 24, these efforts bore their first significant fruit when Dr. Fritz Ursin resigned as chairman of the FSOe in order to "... devote his total strength to the construction of the *Freiheitspartei.*"[51] Although the FSOe was not formally dissolved, many of its supporters followed their chairman into the new party.[52] But discussions with the major agent of the "third force," the VdU, were not so successful. Contact with dissident provincial leagues continued, but although a general community of interest could be agreed upon, the leagues chose to await the results of discussions between the federal leadership and the *Freiheitspartei* before making any independent decisions.

In Salzburg, where sympathy was strong for a broadening of the independent party movement but had not led to the open defiance of the federal leadership, provincial Chairman and VdU *Nationalrat* Gustav Zeillinger met with Reinthaller to discuss the mechanics of a fusion. Although Zeillinger was unwilling to take any step that might contradict a subsequent decision by the federal leadership, he did work out an agreement with Reinthaller which ultimately transferred the Salzburg League *en bloc* into the new party.[53]

In Vienna, Lower Austria and Upper Austria where the federal leadership remained in control, the provincial organizations set up working and electoral committees "... to take the wind out of the sails of the *Freiheitspartei* ... [and create] a real and effective assembly of all Austrians who stand to the political center."[54]

At the federal level, Stendebach and Reinthaller struggled to negotiate a fusion of their two groups, but without success. Personality conflict and political ambition again blocked the broadening of the base. Fearful that Reinthaller's prominence as an *Anschluss* Nazi would seriously compromise the "third force," and convinced that he was motivated more by a desire to seize control of the movement than to broaden the base, VdU Chairman Stendebach placed such extensive conditions on a fusion of the two groups that *Freiheitspartei* declared that there was no common ground between the two and broke off the discussions.

Thus when a series of *Gemeinderat* elections in April in Styria, Vorarlberg and Lower Austria offered the voters a chance to express themselves on the recent political developments, the "third force" presented itself in a state of total disarray. The results were mixed. In Vorarlberg, although the VdU lost both seats and total votes from the *Gemeinderat* election of 1949, it nevertheless recovered somewhat from the *Landtag* election disaster of 1954.[55] In Styria the results were catastrophic. In the previous elections of 1950, the VdU had won over fifteen percent of the popular vote, carrying it to positions of responsibility in the local politics of many Styrian communities. In 1955 however, internal division had so debilitated the league that the VdU list won only 0.21 percent of the total vote.[56] In Lower Austria the VdU was able to achieve a modest increase in total votes, but due to a reapportionment of districts, received fewer seats in the local councils.[57]

Overall, the results illustrated not the recovery claimed by *Die Neue Front,* but simply a reaffirmation by a small segment of the population of the continued desire for an agency to exert a "third force" in Austrian politics. The only absolute progress was in Vorarlberg, where the VdU vote was strongly influenced by the movement of the provincial league in the direction of the Reinthaller consolidation. In Styria, where the VdU was in shambles due to the recent organizational split, it was almost totally rejected, but continued interest was expressed in the "third force" as evidenced in the ability of nonparty, independent and "homeland lists" to attract six percent of the vote. In Lower Austria, the VdU avoided risking an election defeat on a broad scale by campaigning in only five communities and, in the remaining communities, supported independent lists of candidates whose programs were amenable to the ideals of the VdU. As a result of this selective campaign, the VdU won seats in local assemblies where it had never before been represented and, claiming the independent lists, declared an electoral resurgence of the "third force" with 6,000 votes more than in the *Landtag* election of the previous year.[58] In general, the elections seemed to sustain the contention that some kind of political "third force" should exist; but that its sole agent should be the VdU no longer seemed clear.

While the movement for a regrouping of the "third force" remained in a high state of flux, another event captured the attention of all Austrians. On February 8, 1955, Soviet Foreign Minister Molotov surprised Austria and the world by agreeing that a state treaty with Austria could be concluded prior to a German peace treaty.[59] In April, a black-red negotiating team of Chancellor Raab, Vice-Chancellor Schärf, Foreign Minister Figil and State Secretary Kreisky traveled to Moscow where after three days of intensive negotiations the terms of the State Treaty were concluded.[60] On April 14, all of Austria was electrified by a terse, dramatic telegram from Raab via the OeVP Press Agency to the Austrian people: "Austria will be free; our native soil will be returned to us in its entirety; the prisoners of war will again see their homeland."[61]

The key to this generosity and sudden reversal of policy on the part of the Soviets was the condition that Austria declare absolute and perpetual neutrality along the Swiss pattern.[62] With the remilitarization of Germany a fact by the end of 1954, and the failure of the Soviet Union to ease Austria into its Eastern European orbit, the prospect of a neutral, demilitarized zone along the north-south military transportation routes of NATO in Central Europe was attractive. Nonalignment was of little concern to the Austrians and in any case was a small price to pay for freedom from the ten-year burden of occupation. The *Proporz* had achieved *the* political goal which stood above all others in the minds of virtually all Austrians. When the negotiators returned from Moscow on the afternoon of April 15, hundreds of thousands of Viennese flooded into the streets to celebrate the achievement, producing scenes of jubilation unknown in Austria since the days of the Third Reich.

The VdU was less enthusiastic. As an opposition party, it shared none of the responsibility for this magnificent success and indeed the neutrality clause violated some of the basic principles of the VdU program. In the parliamentary debate on ratification of the state treaty, VdU Chairman Stendebach stated the league's acceptance of the treaty subject to certain conditions on the neutrality clause:

> There are, however, deep fears in the people which have to be absolved, that Switzerland is to be used as a model for the kind of neutrality to which we are to dedicate ourselves.
> ... Switzerland, however, in the course of time has, ... out of self-interest, given up its freedom of negotiation on international law; that is, it has never made use of it and this always under the guise of neutrality. As a result, the opinion has been widely disseminated that surrender of freedom of negotiation on international law belongs to the concept of neutrality.
> If the model of Switzerland is set up for us, then the danger exists that also for us the surrender of freedom of negotiation on international law will be connected. That would mean, for example, we would lose the right to concern ourselves further with the fate of South Tyrol. ... We are not Switzerland. We have an entirely different historical development and we have a very different geopolitical situation.
> ....
> We have borne this Europe for a thousand years in our hearts and brains. We are a piece of it and Europe also bears Austrian characteristics. Just as Europe is inconceivable without Vienna, Paris and Rome, so is Vienna inconceivable without Europe. We could not shut ourselves out from Europe even if we wanted. But we do not want to.

> For to shut ourselves out from Europe would be to surrender a part of ourselves and our meaning for existence.
>
> ....
>
> The chancellor has again and again emphasized that Austria is viable. That is doubtlessly correct, but only under the precondition that we can dispose of a relatively large part of our social production ... outside our borders.... Our economic situation demands... participation in the emerging European Market Community.
>
> ... We want to live with our neighbors in peace.... But just by declaring that we do not want war, ... we do not assure peace. A neutral Austria on the dividing line of world political interest, on the old military road of the Danube valley, is still no guarantee for the security of peace. In contrast, a United Europe that declares itself neutral and whose territory is guaranteed by the power blocs in the East and West would be a real guarantee of peace. We want peace and we need peace.... The gate towards Europe must for these reasons remain open to us.[63]

In this manner, the VdU tried to reconcile its concept of *völkisch* unity and a united Europe with the conditions of a Russian dictated neutrality. Perhaps for the VdU, this statement rationalizing the compatibility of its united Europe goal with the requisite neutrality declaration was necessary to justify an affirmative vote on a question where opposition would have meant political suicide. For the average Austrian citizen, however, freedom was the only matter of importance and if it required a promise of perpetual neutrality with an implied exclusion from the developing Common Market with its political pretensions for a united Europe, it was worth the price. As a result the warnings of the VdU received no response from the public, and its grudging, unenthusiastic acceptance of the state treaty signed on May 15, 1955 amid general popular ecstasy only further emphasized the increasing estrangement of the VdU from political reality.

While the debate on the State Treaty occupied the attention of most Austrians, the disintegration of the VdU continued apace. At a provincial assembly in Vorarlberg, Chairman Seebacher, whose February expulsion by the extraordinary assembly had not been recognized, tried to gain approval for a secession from the federal VdU to lead the Vorarlberg League as a unit into the *Freiheitspartei*. When this motion failed to win the necessary two-thirds majority, Seebacher and his supporters split off from the VdU to form the Vorarlberg branch of the FP.[64] Although the majority of the Vorarlberg League remained intact, the relatively limited reservoir of the "third force" in this tiny province was hopelessly divided between two poles.

In other areas, the VdU organization simply ceased to function and new groups formed for the representation of the "third force." During May and June, *freiheitlich* clubs were founded in many communities throughout the country to provide all *freiheitlich*-oriented individuals a vehicle for cooperation. In some areas this involved VdU people who were seeking to find a means for coordinating all available elements either within the VdU or on a broadened base. In other areas it involved FP members trying to accomplish the same for their new party. But the effect of these discussions at the local level was to reverse the trend towards enmity between the two groups that had followed the breach of the Stendebach-Reinthaller negotiations in March.

The first positive result of this easing of tensions between the various elements of the "third force" came in September when the Upper Austrian VdU and FP announced that they would run a common list under the label *Freiheitlich Wahlgemeinschaft* (VdU-FP-*Parteilose*) in order to avoid the splintering of the national-*freiheitlich* vote bloc in the October *Landtag* election.[65] VdU Upper Austrian Chairman Grünbarth and FP Provincial Chairman Peter emphasized that this was a new political grouping involving non-partisan personalities who had joined together to form a "... strong, united collecting basin of the national-*freiheitlich* electorate so that the social ideal of a true *Volksgemeinschaft* will finally be established on the basis of the inalienable freedoms of the individual."[66]

Meanwhile, stimulated by the merger on the provincial levels and under heavy pressure from the nationalist wing of the VdU, Chairman Stendebach resumed negotiations with Reinthaller, but with sharply reduced demands.[67] On October 17, just six days before the Upper Austrian election, agreement was reached between leading personalities from the VdU, FP, Action and other independent *freiheitlich* clubs to fuse all the like-minded organizations into a single new party, the *Freiheitlich Partei Österreichs* (FPOe). A committee was established to serve as the interim party leadership and to work out a provisional program and statutes upon which a formal constitution could ultimately be based.[68]

But this consolidation of the "third force" came too late to bring any real upsurge of popular enthusiasm for the new party. The results of the Upper Austrian *Landtag* election showed a clear victory for the government parties and particularly for the OeVP whose campaign was based on federal politics and above all on the personality of Chancellor Raab, whose prestige had soared as a consequence of the State Treaty. (See Table IX.)

Despite the failure to achieve immediate success, the FPOe could

Table IX

Comparison of the 1949 and 1955 *Landtag* and the 1949 and 1953 *Nationalrat* Elections in Upper Austria*

Party	1955 *Landtag*			1949 *Landtag*			1953 *Nationalrat*		1949 *Nationalrat*	
	Votes	%	Mandates	Votes	%	Mandates	Votes	%	Votes	%
OeVP	295,292	49.1	25	268,578	45.0	23	285,308	46.2	268,578	45.0
SPOe	241,978	39.4	19	183,066	30.8	15	236,944	38.4	184,042	30.8
VdU-FP	58,936	9.6	4	124,520	20.8	10	75,065	12.2	124,520	20.8
KPOe	17,366	2.9	0	18,461	3.1	0	18,780	3.0	18,574	3.1

Die Wahlen in den Bundesländern, and "Die Nationalratswahlen vom 9. Oktober 1949," and "Die Nationalratswahlen vom 22. Februar 1953," *Wahlstatistik*, pp. C 127 and C 137.

find some cheer in the analysis of the independent press which found the results more favorable for the future of the *freiheitlich* movement than had been expected. As *Die Presse* pointed out, "... where zealous work and industrious speakers had been employed, something was still achieved. . . . The unification in the *freiheitlich* camp evidently came too late to be really effective."[69] Taking encouragement from its acceptable showing at the polls, the FPOe formally constituted itself as a political party on November 3, 1955. The membership of the provisional leadership reflected a true fusion of the hitherto existing agents of the "third force." The previously unaffiliated, but nationally oriented General-Major Franz Rainer was chosen as chairman with Stendebach of the VdU, Reinthaller of the FP and Gredler of Action as vice-chairmen.[70]

Noticeably absent from the leadership of the FPOe were the names of VdU founders Kraus and Reimann. Indeed both had been uncharacteristically quiet in recent months. The pages of *Die Neue Front* no longer carried the previously customary editorials of Dr. Kraus and even his name appeared in print only when coverage was given to his speeches in the *Nationalrat*. Likewise Dr. Reimann, although still chief editor of *Die Neue Front,* published few editorials and even these made no mention of the long-desired broadening of the base which was underway. In fact this silence was not so strange, for these two early proponents of the "third force" saw the new FPOe not as a consolidation of all independent elements, but rather as a regrouping of officials of the leading organizations, who were for the most part nationalists. After six years of struggle, the right wing took over complete control of the "third force."

In its goals (limitation of the two-party system and collectivism, the social *Volksgemeinschaft,* the social market economy and nonpartisan trade unions, Austria as an autonomous member of the German *Volks* and cultural community)[71] as well as in its program[72] the FPOe represented no real departure from the VdU. The change was in the leadership of the new party which was partially new and certainly more dominated by nationalist principles. As a result, the moderate, political and social reformist elements that had initially provided the leadership around which the VdU had originally formed, were either forced to adjust to the new conditions, or to retire.[73]

In order to consolidate the party and prepare for the *Nationalrat* elections the coming year, the FPOe began to draw its sympathizers in the various provinces into formal party organizations. In Salzburg, Carinthia and Vorarlberg the VdU organizations simply joined the

FPOe by carrying over their existing leadership into the new party. In other provinces the VdU refused to be subsumed into the FPOe and new splits occurred.[74] To formalize the new party structures assemblies were held at the local, regional and provincial levels to choose the new party leadership and to elect delegates to the forthcoming General Constituent Assembly. With the exception of Salzburg where the social-reformist faction carried over from the VdU was predominant, the new provincial leaderships that emerged from these elections were overwhelmingly nationalist in composition.[75] Drs. Kraus and Reimann, shut out of the leadership of the new party and tired of trying to hold together a party that was constantly on the edge of centrifugal disintegration, simply retired from the struggle.[76] As a result many of their supporters in the social-reformist wing of the VdU likewise declined involvement with the FPOe. Thus when the general assembly gathered on April 7, 8, 1956 to formally constitute the party, the "third force" represented by its new agent, the FPOe, was lacking its moderate wing. The dominant nationalist faction controlled the general assembly and elected as chairman Anton Reinthaller, the charismatic figure who had provided the attraction towards the nationalist pole. Former Action leader Dr. Wilfried Gredler, former VdU chairman Max Stendebach and the previously unaffiliated, former Nazi *Reichsbahn* director Heinrich Zechmann, who had led the consolidation of the FPOe in Carinthia, were elected as deputy-chairmen. In separate caucuses delegates from the VdU and the *Freiheitspartei* dissolved their respective organizations and announced their unification behind the FPOe.

But the congruence of the FPOe with the "third force" was not total. Shortly after the euphoric unanimity of the Constituent General Assembly, Dr. Kraus called a press conference in Vienna to declare that for himself and for Reimann "the results of the FPOe convention have occasioned me to reject the *[Nationalrat]* candidacy offered and to resign from the FPOe." He recounted their hopes in founding the movement and the bitter realization of the end to which it had come:

> This convention was the confirmation of the long prepared seizure of power by a small circle of right-extremists and former National Socialist leaders. Those moderate representatives who have remained in the FPOe have for all purposes been condemned to impotence.
>
> The responsibility which I feel to my former constituents demands that I not give my name and therewith my recommendation to a party that has struck out in a new direction. I never wanted to found a successor organization for the NSDAP, but rather a general, re-

spectable movement of social renewal with particular emphasis for those who after 1945 came under the wheel. Precisely these people, however, need a guarantee against suspicion and defamation and therefore within the larger framework of the one single party of renewal now being set aside.

Under the motto of an assembling on the broadest base, a party has now arisen on the narrowest base that is primarily directed at the past. The official declaration of the FPOe of a 'rejection of extremism' and a 'party of the center' come from the need for a masking that has become very necessary. Decisive is only the people who are in authority and the majority of those belong to the circle mentioned (former National Socialist Minister Reinthaller, van Tongel, Schweiger, etc.).

With the old spirit of impatience and the methods of total claim to power, they have misused the sincere efforts for a "third force" as well as the previous achievements of the VdU to create a new political platform for the once tumbled greats of the National Socialist regime. I will remain loyal to the convictions which I have previously represented and attach myself to no party.[77]

Dr. Reimann, whom Kraus committed to this statement without his prior consent, was less extreme in his condemnation of the new party, but no more willing to cooperate in its activities. Both men had seen their dreams of a "government of interests rather than a government of parties" crushed by the overwhelming power of the *Proporz*.[78] By 1956, the idealism that had motivated them to found the VdU had been killed by the realities of party politics and they no longer desired to fight against the darker forces of the movement which they had marshaled behind them.

The elements contained within the VdU had never really been united, and the League of Independents had at best been a movement, but never a real political party. After seven years of struggle, not only against the declared enemy of the black-red coalition, but also against constant attacks on their concept of the "third force" from within, Kraus and Reimann simply surrendered to the only unified element in the movement, the nationalists. FPOe *Nationalrat* Gustav Zeillinger, a VdU moderate who continued on with the movement to become a leader of the new party, feels that Kraus's bitter resignation stemmed more from personal reasons than from any significant deviation of the FPOe from the course set by the VdU. Zeillinger argues persuasively that although the leadership was partially new and much more dominantly nationalist than any VdU predecessor, it still represented an element that had been prominent in the League of Independents from its inception. Although the nationalist emphasis was distasteful to him, Dr. Kraus had been able to accept the increased appeal to *völkisch* nationalism in the *Ausseer Programm* of 1954, and had even cooperated in the negotiations in October, 1955 that set the terms for the founding of the FPOe. Rather, Zeillinger feels and on this Reimann agrees, Kraus was unable to continue in the movement out of a personal animosity and emotional inability to work in subordination to a former Nazi minister.[79] Regardless of their motivation, however, the abdication by Kraus and Reimann of any further responsibility for the political activity of the "third force" deprived the FPOe, as its new agent, of the most convincing proponents of a social-reformist interpretation of the third-party movement.

VIII

Conclusion and Epilogue

The essential difference between the VdU and its successor was one of emphasis rather than of substance; nevertheless, the 1956 *Nationalrat* election campaign was dominated by nationalist slogans to a degree unknown in the brief history of the league. The results proved that while stirring appeals to German nationalism could provide a satisfactory cohesive force for the relatively small organization of functionaries and registered members, as a broad electoral program it lacked any real appeal. (See Table X.)

Kraus's bitter repudiation of the FPOe as a successor to the VdU was paralleled by the Austrian electorate, but not because of its program or its leadership, both of which had been accommodated within the loose structure of the league. The reason lay primarily in a change in the mood of the Austrian electorate. The VdU's successes had been based, above all, on an appeal to a broad spectrum of dissatisfaction. To a large degree this dissatisfaction accrued from some aspect of the legacy of National Socialism and the Third Reich and provided a common denominator for the movement. But by 1956 the poverty of the early postwar years had given way to a "little economic wonder." The excessive severity of de-Nazification had eased to the point where it touched only a relative few, whom most Austrians regarded as deserving of their fate. After seventeen years of occupation (seven Nazi German and ten Allied) Austria was again an independent, but also prospering state. The question of whether Austria was a separate nation or a second German nation and the fine distinction between political and cultural unity of *Volk* concerned only a relative few. As a consequence, the dissatisfaction of 1949 evaporated. As the cohesion of mutual anger eroded away, the nationalists, as the only united element within this coalition of malcontents, increased their control. In 1956 the nationalist wing captured the political party representing the "third force." Thus when the Austrian people denied their continuing support to the FPOe, they rejected not the concept of a "third force" but rather the contemporary interpretation of it.

Table X

Comparison of the *Nationalrat* Election Results of 1956 with Those of 1949 and 1953*

Party	1956 Votes	1956 %	1956 Mandates	1953 Votes	1953 %	1953 Mandates	1949 Votes	1949 %	1949 Mandates
OeVP	1,999,986	46	82	1,781,777	41	74	1,846,581	44	77
SPOe	1,873,295	43	74	1,818,517	42	73	1,623,524	39	67
VdU-FP	283,749	7	6	472,866	11	14	489,273	12	16
KPOe	192,438	4	3	228,159	5	4	213,066	5	5

*"Die Nationalratswahlen vom 9. Oktober 1949," "Die Nationalratswahlen vom 22. Februar 1953," and "Die Nationalratswahlen vom 13. Mai 1956," reprinted in *Wahlstatistik* (Vol. III of *Wahlhandbuch*), pp. C 127, C 137 and C 147–166.

In the next few years, the nationalist emphasis was unable to provide any more cohesion to the FPOe than the moderates had for the VdU. In the wake of the election defeats of 1956 a new struggle for power occurred within the FPOe. This led to an exodus of the extreme rightists from the party, which intensified after the death of Chairman Reinthaller in 1959. Friedrich Peter, a traditional liberal, was elected chairman to succeed Reinthaller and led the FPOe back towards the political center in an effort to make the party into a viable representative of the "third force." In Parliament the FPOe pursued a policy of watchful opposition to the policies of the government parties with constant criticism of the *"Demokratur"* of the coalition. Ideologically the trend towards the political center definitively subordinated the German nationalist appeal to the European concept of the early years of the VdU.

The maturation of the Austrian Republic by the 1960's and the increasing discomfort of coalition politics led increasingly to a desire to abandon the cautious policy of *Proporz* designed for the precarious postwar years. The *Nationalrat* election of 1962 gave the OeVP an eighty-one to seventy-six seat advantage over the Socialists and could have led to a bourgeois coalition government with the eight man FPOe faction. But the OeVP chose not to deliver such political leverage into the hands of its rival for the middle-class vote and thereby risk the opposition of a seventy-six vote Socialist bloc in the *Nationalrat*. Instead, after four exhausting months of negotiation, a new cabinet was put together which differed little from its predecessors.

But the new coalition pact did not resolve the continuing dissatisfaction of each major party with having to constantly compromise with a partner of strikingly different ideological principles. In the OeVP this disenchantment led to dramatic internal reorganization in October of 1963 which brought Dr. Josef Klaus and Dr. Hermann Withalm into the leadership of the party on a program of bringing an early end to the practice of coalition government. With the days of the black-red coalition obviously numbered, elements within the SPOe began to look to the possibility of a small coalition with the newly respectable FPOe as a viable alternative. But when it was revealed that Minister of Interior Franz Olah, the principal proponent of the new alignment, had arranged, through his powerful position as president of the League of Trade Unions, for the financing of the 1962 FPOe *Nationalrat* campaign, a crisis ensued within the SPOe. The left wing of the party led the attack against the "practicalism" and the *"Führercult"* of Olah. Olah was ultimately driven out of the party and with him vanished the possibility for a small coalition. The FPOe for its part tried to compensate for its flirtation with the left by a renewed conservative emphasis.

In the *Nationalrat* election of 1966, the OeVP was the only party to derive any benefit from the intensive political maneuverings of the past few years. With exactly half of the seats in Parliament, OeVP Chairman Klaus translated his reform program of 1963 into reality by putting together a government composed exclusively of ministers from his party. Thus one of the demands that had served to crystallize the third-party movement twenty years before was finally realized: an end to the *Proporz*.

In the years since 1966 Austrian political parties have maneuvered vis-a-vis each other with a flexibility unknown in the days of the coalition pacts. As a consequence, the FPOe is finally in a position to potentially exert the balancing force that has long been the desire of the third-party movement. Furthermore, in the absence of the rigid government coalitions a new political dynamic seems to be operating which causes any public dissatisfaction to automatically devolve on the ruling governmental party. The result has been a trend away from the party in power in various off-year elections. While the obvious benefactor of this trend after 1966 was the SPOe, the FPOe registered significant successes as well. In March of 1969, the FPOe won a surprising eighteen percent of the total vote in the Salzburg *Landtag* election, and this "Salzburg trend" was confirmed the next month in Viennese municipal elections where inroads were made in traditional OeVP districts.

In the campaign propaganda for the 1970 elections each of the major parties exhorted the electorate to entrust it with the sole responsibility for government. But unofficially, functionaries of both parties let it be known they were leaving all options open regarding the potential shape of the new government.

The FPOe for its part attempted to make itself attractive as a future coalition partner by adopting a less contentious program at its October 1968 convention. A potential struggle between the liberal wing of the party led by Chairman Friedrich Peter and Gustav Zeillinger and the nationalists, Alexander Götz and Otto Scrinzi, did not materialize. Peter was overwhelmingly reelected as chairman with both Zeillinger and Scrinzi as deputy chairmen. In his speech to the convention Peter attempted to definitively end the continuing struggle between the liberal and national wings of the party. In response to a flier that had been circulated at the convention criticizing the FPOe for being insufficiently nationalist, Peter argued that German nationalism was a dead issue and in no way could be used as a basis for a meaningful political program. Instead of looking to the past, the FPOe must seek the support of the ideologically uncommitted youth of Austria and convince them that the party offers a real and viable alternative to the majority parties.[1] The convention closed with a press conference in which the newly elected officers declared their readiness to participate in a small coalition with either SPOe or the OeVP. Thus the FPOe approached the 1970 *Nationalrat* elections confident of a regeneration of the "third force" and optimistic about finally gaining a share in the governing of Austria. The expressed goal of the FPOe in the 1970 election campaign was to continue the apparent resurgence of the "third force" so as to increase its representation in the *Nationalrat* from six to at least eight or hopefully twelve mandates. In the anticipated fairly even balance between the OeVP and the SPOe this would finally make the FPOe a viable partner in either a large or small coalition or a powerful "weight on the political scale" should either major party try to rule alone. In order to woo the moderates and conservatives who were disillusioned by four years of OeVP government and rejected the Klaus campaign argument that Austria had never had it so good, the FPOe disassociated itself from its fellow opposition party for the last four years by declaring that it would be prepared only to enter into a coalition with the OeVP.[2]

The OeVP predictably posed the specter of a "red chancellor" if middle-class voters were to heed the FPOe's campaign for their support. Throughout the remainder of the campaign, the People's party repeatedly pointed to the 1963 SPOe-FPOe coalition negotiations and to the joint opposition of the two parties to Klaus government as proof of collusion. The offer of coalition to the OeVP could only be an "official" smokescreen for this conspiracy, since the FPOe knew full well that already in September of the previous year the OeVP Chairman Klaus had rejected a return to the politics of coalition.[3]

The SPOe reacted to the FPOe declaration and the OeVP charges with a bitter rejection of any idea of cooperation between the two parties. To undermine any appearance of similarity between such an arrangement and the Socialist-FDP coalition in the Federal Republic of Germany, the central organ of the SPOe denied that there was any left-liberalism in the Austrian third-party movement. Instead, as SPOe Chairman Bruno Kreisky argued: "The FPOe is not a liberal, but rather a conservative and in many aspects even a reactionary party."[4] The only unity between the two came from the fact that both were in opposition to the Klaus government. But this cooperation stemmed "... for the most part from different reasons. What in the government program was insufficiently progressive for the SPOe, was for the FPOe insufficiently conservative."[5] Despite the OeVP protestations to the contrary, the SPOe argued that the FPOe declaration was just what it appeared: an anti-progressive coalition that gave the voters only two choices on election day — conservative or socialist.[6]

The election results of March 1 revealed that the FPOe tactic of trying to take advantage of moderate and conservative dissatisfaction with the Klaus government of the past four years by offering the possibility of a conservative, yet redirected coalition clearly backfired. The anticlerical, liberal-national camp, when confronted with a choice between the conservative-Catholic and the socialist parties, followed its traditional preference: "red rather than black." Although the FPOe did slightly increase its vote count over the 1966 total, the gain was insignificant relative to representation in Parliament. To be sure, the FPOe probably did attract some opposition-minded OeVP voters as well as some of the independent youth, but the SPOe was the primary beneficiary of the increasingly large body of Austrians who are not firmly bound to either ideological camp.

Following his party's thin 81:79:6 victory, Socialist party Chairman Bruno Kreisky undertook lengthy negotiations for a renewal of coalition government in Austria. The FPOe, which might have been seriously considered as a partner had its representation in the *Nationalrat* been significantly increased, was again excluded from the coalition plans. But even the discussions with the OeVP were fruitless. The years of one-party rule have apparently reduced the ground for compromise between the two major parties and each ultimately decided to accept a minority Socialist government and point to a new election in the near future in hopes of strengthening its position. The FPOe seemingly held the balance of power, but with no popular mandate, and lacking even the representaiton in Parliament to have the right to initiate legislation, the Independents have had to maneuver cautiously. In this situation however, the FPOe, for the first time in the Second Republic, was able to play a significant role as the "balance on the scale." In return for the election law reform that guaranteed its continued survival, the FPOe lent the support to the minority Socialist government which permitted Chancellor Bruno Kreisky to declare after his first year in office that he had achieved one quarter of his party's program.[7] It was a measure of the cooperation by the FPOe and its acceptance by the SPOe that permitted Kreisky to suddenly dissolve his minority government in July of 1971 and reach for majority control in an October 10 election.

Kreisky's timing was excellent and the Socialists emerged from the election with the first absolute majority in the history of the Second Republic. The FPOe maintained the approximately 5.4 percent share of the vote it had won in 1966 and 1970, while the OeVP lost approximately 1.5 percent from its 1970 total.[8] The reelection of Socialist Franz Jonas to the largely ceremonial office of president in the spring of 1971 and following his death in the spring of 1974, the election of the non-party, but Socialist-aligned Rudolf Kirshschläger seems to confirm the Socialist dominance of the current Austrian political scene.[9] For the moment Chancellor Kreisky's brand of moderate socialism parallels the popular mood. But single-party rule carries with it sole responsibility for failures and discontent. In an era of economic uncertainty and severe shortages in food and raw materials, Austria is susceptible to future political uncertainty and the Socialist majority is slim. With the continuing example of a Social Democratic-liberal coalition in the Federal Republic of Germany and the possibility that either major Austrian party might need a few additional votes to control a majority in Parliament, the potential importance of a third party remains.

From an overview of Austrian political behavior since 1945 it can be posited that the "third force" has been a factor of continuing importance. It has, however, consistently defied attempts to be forced into the conventional constraints of a political party. During times of dissatisfaction, such as the VdU was able to exploit, it was possible to consolidate the independent vote into a political movement for the purpose of expressing opposition to the policies of the government coalition. But in the final analysis the League of Independents was a melting pot of heterogeneous and, to a degree, mutually opposed elements. The fires which in 1949 had promised to forge these elements into a unified political party were gradually extinguished by the reduction of the severity of the de-Nazification laws, by an end to the occupation and above all by the increasing prosperity of Austria. With access to neither the agencies of political responsibility nor with the opportunity to exert the hotly desired "weight on the political scale," the "third force" failed to develop into a meaningful political party capable of winning any support beyond that of the frustrated and dissatisfied. When the VdU, the only successful unifier of this movement, collapsed, however, the "third force" did not disappear; rather it dissolved into its component parts with only the nationalist wing and a few die-hard VdU liberals continuing the thread into the FPOe. The remainder of the VdU constituency became a floating body of between 200,000 and 300,000 independent voters, drifting between the OeVP and the SPOe, but remaining uncommitted to either and usually voting against the governing party. As succeeding generations of Austrian youth come of voting age both the appeal to German nationalism and the stigma of Nazism become increasingly meaningless. The steady decrease of strong, ideological, party alignment has indeed increased the strength of the "third force" in Austrian politics. The challenge of the FPOe is whether it can offer this fluctuating potential constituency of independent voters something more positive than the vocal opposition of the past and realize the quarter-century-old VdU dreams of becoming a party of the center and a meaningful "third force" to truly "balance the political scale."

Appendix A

The Program of the Verband der Unabhängigen, 1949*

I. General

1. We affirm true democracy and firmly reject every form of dictatorship.
2. Equality of all citizens must be restored by the abolition of all privilege and prejudices.
3. We avow existing republican forms of government and federal state organization, whose provincial rights must be preserved.
4. We avow the constitutional state. Therefore, the laws must be in accord with the people's convictions of justice and with the basic order of the state. All laws which contradict the basic principles of the legal Constitution of 1920/29, and all executive acts which are issued upon such a basis, are to be repealed as unconstitutional.
5. We strive for an active development of our Federal Constitution in the spirit of the direct influence of the people upon legislation and leadership of the state, especially through plebiscites and referenda. The right of accusation in matters of a breach of the constitution must be granted to the people themselves.
6. The basic rights are to be drafted anew and expanded. Especially, the following principles are to be set down: complete protection of the individual, no retroactive penal laws, no double jeopardy, no retroactive extraordinary judgments made after the fact, no extradition of a citizen to a foreign country.
7. The protection of law by the Constitution and administrative courts is to be expanded. Everyone who is directly affected by an unlawful administrative act must have the right to submit a grievance to one of the two judicial courts. Each court, each administrative

---

* *Die Neue Front,* July 30, 1949, pp. 1, 3.

authority and each directly concerned party must receive the right to propose the suspension of unconstitutional or unlawful acts at the constitutional court.

8. In criminal law, normal proceedings in all areas are to be restored. The so-called "People's Court" is to be eliminated. The maximum duration of imprisonment on remand is to be determined by law. Each unlawful limitation of personal freedom as well as the spiritual and corporal mistreatment of prisoners is to be severely punished.

9. We recognize the moral principles of true Christianity. We reject the misuse of religion for political purposes.

10. In full support of our state independence, we acknowledge ourselves as members of the German nationality.

II. Foreign Policy

11. In foreign policy, we strive for a good relationship with the other states and we reject reciprocal intervention in internal affairs.

12. As the best security for the preservation of peace and for a prosperous development of the economy, we aspire to the creation of the United States of Europe on the basis of equality.

III. Domestic Policy

13. We demand: the recognition of the principle of the common fate of the community of all creative professions and individuals in the state and in all individual business operations.

14. purity of character and professional skill as the sole criterion for the filling of all positions in all branches of public life. We reject party *Proporz* and protectionism.

15. the strong executive should be nonpolitical and should not act as a member of a political party during active service.

16. an honest, thrifty administration by the most energetic opposition of all corrupt phenomena.

17. a thorough administrative reform. For this purpose, the laws are to be simplified and newly drafted, superfluous administrative duties and positions are to be eliminated, the time limits for successive appeals and for the rendering of judgments are to be shortened.

18. the transference of superfluous civil employees to jobs within the productive economy and better salaries for the remaining officials.

Those trained and experienced officials who have been retired prematurely from active service are to assume posts appropriate to their abilities.

19. legal counsel independent from all political influences in justice and administration.

20. the use of the Incompatibility Law, so that the unauthorized occupation of the posts on the Administrative Board and other such posts by delegates of the people and elected representatives cease.

IV. Economic Policy

21. We see the best guarantee for the avoidance of economic and social crises in a planned direction for the entire economy including agriculture. We reject a bureaucratic control as well as an economy of unrestrained profit.

22. We see as the best prerequisite for a healthy economy, a currency with stable buying power and an absolutely balanced budget.

23. We are for the recognition of justly acquired private property and we reject open and hidden attacks upon the same.

24. We are fundamentally against the nationalization of businesses and institutions which can be led on the basis of private enterprise without endangering the general interests.

Insofar as businesses are already led by the state however, they must, of course, produce an appropriate profit by irreproachable and economically thrifty management — without special subsidies. The management of state enterprises must remain unconditionally free from all party political influences.

25. We reject exploitation by the misuse of cartels, monopolies and similar institutions.

26. We demand a reasonable price policy based on the principle of prices covering costs.

27. A credit policy which is just and uninfluenced by political parties should take into account all branches of the economy according to the same principles.

28. Tax policy must be socially just and may not be disturbing to the economy. It must therefore leave the individual businesses the means which are necessary for the continuance and improvement of their establishments. Above all, it must not thwart the joy of work, striving for increased efficiency and frugality. An equalization of the burden must be reached by raising the buying power of the masses. Tax legislation should be as simple as possible.

29. Lawful regulations concerning financial equalization must en-

sure the individual district corporations the income which is necessary for them to fulfill their legal tasks.

30. An agrarian policy sure of its goal, allowing for the Austrian economic situation, with appropriate protection for domestic production, is an absolute prerequisite for the development of the economy.

We regard it as a duty of the state to demand everything which can lead to an increase in agricultural production and reduction of the price of agricultural production.

The principle of prices covering costs must also be applied to agriculture.

31. Migration from the country to the towns can only be checked if agriculture has at its disposal the means which are necessary to improve the job training of people working in agriculture, and to create for them the conditions essential for life which in itself would put an end to the migration to the city.

32. The essential significance which our industry owes to business and trade for the provisioning of our country and for export, must be taken into account in our economic policy. We are therefore in favor of the extensive promotion of exports and the elimination of all provisions which retard exports as well as for an active trade policy. However, the adequate maintenance of the domestic market may not thereby be endangered.

33. As much as possible, an extensive modernization and improvement of industrial equipment and the best training of the professions in cooperation with the initiative of the entrepreneur must bring the increase in performance which would make Austrian products competitive at home and abroad.

34. We fully value the great significance of real trade, especially transit commerce. We reject unnecessary middlemen's business for the maintenance of the economy and for the sale of products, as well as the excessive tightening of trade, both of which produce an increase in prices.

35. The function of the economic associations are to be limited to the economically necessary proportions.

V. Social Policy

36. We assert the right of every person to work and we see one of the most important tasks in a general plan for the creation of work which continually guarantees full employment. Above all, this would serve

the creation of housing, the expansion of hydroelectric power plants, electrification as well as the creation of tourist facilities.

The moral duty of every healthy person capable of working must be to serve the general public by achievement of suitable work.

37. The health of the people is a special task of the welfare policy. Therefore, health education and guidance must be provided for the people.

38. Apartment houses and development projects are to be generously promoted. Middle and small apartment houses, small private homes and small development projects are to be favored.

39. We strive for fair rent and see an important prerequisite for a healthy development of the economy in a basic, just regulation of this question under the fair preservation of the protection of giving notice.

40. We see the means for advancement by ability and achievement in a thorough job training which ensures the possibility of advancement for every industrious person.

We direct our special attention to the youth who have left school.

41. As highest goal of our social policy, we see the attainment of a condition in which the just share of profit, and with that of the standard of living of the masses, is ensured, under which achievement is the valid criterion.

42. We strive for a progressive, social legislation, which, based on a healthy economic development, conforms to just social demands.

43. He who has honestly worked his life long, should enjoy a carefree old age.

Therefore, we strive for a generous old-age public assistance for all people who have been gainfully employed. In this program are especially to be included: the independently employed in small businesses and in free intellectual professions as well as mothers who have worked for their families.

44. In the case of disasters, the public welfare programs and public insurance must intervene quickly, helpfully and with understanding. We see a special responsibility in the war casualties and their dependents.

The management of social insurance demands strict supervision and must continually be subject to the Auditing Office. We demand a far-reaching debureaucratization of this service.

45. We are for the protection of the family and for the economic security of the family as the nucleus of the state, with regard to the number of children.

46. For reasons of justice, we are for the naturalization, the equal economic rights and the incorporation of the *Volksdeutschen*.

47. Internal peace, especially peace at work, is just as sacred to us as peace in foreign affairs. For this reason, we condemn incitement of people and class struggle.

VI. Cultural Policy

48. The task of our cultural policy must be to preserve and organically develop our inherited culture and to make our culture accessible to all the people.

49. We are proud of the creative powers of our peoples. The scientific and artistic rising generation and scientific research are to be promoted with all means.

50. In youth, which is healthy in body, intellectually open and spiritually pure, we see the citizens for a better future for our homeland.

51. The education of the young is the task of the parents as well as that of the school.

We are for the elimination of all harmful, one-sided party influences in the school.

Timely job guidance and selection of the talented should make possible the right choice of profession for the youth.

52. The freedom of voicing an opinion and especially freedom of scholarship as well as the freedom of the press is to be restored and ensured.

The preceding programmatic points originate from the three basic demands of the VdU:

        Justice, Purity, Achievement.

Appendix B

The *Ausseerer Programm*, 1954*

I

We demand the freedom for the development of the individual within the national community.

Active communities of free people and their intellectual and material further development must be the highest aim and ultimate goal of the policy. Only in the community is the existence of the individual person, his freedom and his opportunities for advancement ensured. However, just so the development and the strength of all true communities are dependent upon its own existence and the free development of the individual persons who form it. We see therefore, in the struggle for the freedom of the independent personage, one of the most critical tasks, especially at a time in which this freedom is threatened most severely by collectivism of all kinds with their spiritual leveling. The claim to freedom of each individual finds, however, its obvious limit in the likewise justified claim to freedom of every other person and in the exigencies of the community.

The basis of every policy must be the highest possible promotion of the organically developed communities of family, employment, home, state, nation and family of nations.

II

Austria is a German state. Its policy must serve the entire German *Volk* and may never be directed against another German state. We demand the unification of the European peoples on the basis of full equality.

---

* *Die Neue Front,* May 22, 1954, p. 1.

The year 1945 was not only a German, but also a European tragedy. As a result, the recognition that the fate of the European continent and that of the European nations can only be mastered in common was obscured. With anxiety we observe that this idea, born by the war generation of all peoples, is endangered by reactionaries and by politicians preoccupied with old concepts. Not only economic and national defense policies press towards the *Grossraum* [extraterritorial sphere of influence], also the preservation of the European way of life against every foreign influence requires the common effort of all European- and nationally-minded men. The freedom and existence of every European nation, in accordance with its particular racial character, are only ensured within the framework of a European community.

Therefore the VdU in this serious hour avows with particular emphasis the unification of Europe on the basis of the sovereign and equal rights of all *Völker*.

A common European cultural consciousness and a new spirit of mutual respect and understanding of peoples will only be actively experienced by him who is deeply pledged to his own nation. The European idea and the avowal of nation are not contradictions, but rather concepts of order which naturally complement each other. The true national ideal is a building block of the United Europe.

The VdU pursues a national policy, that is, it stands up for the preservation and strengthening of the German *Volk* in the Austrian area and with that, for its spiritual and material well-being. It sees therefore, the German task of Austria in the following:

1. in the encouragement of the consciousness of the solidarity of all Germans,

2. in the execution of a sincere, friendly cooperation with Germany,

3. in a generous family policy which promotes the formation of healthy, prolific families,

4. in the care for a bodily and spiritually healthy youth and its education to community spirit, self-discipline, sense of responsibility and unselfishness,

5. in the protection of the threatened boundaries of *Deutschtum* [organic German area],

6. in the just, occupational and economic incorporation and settling of the *Volksdeutschen* who were driven from their homes.

III

We demand freedom of the mind and tolerance in religious matters.

We fight with all force so that the creative cultural achievements of our peoples will again be valued as the highest national possession.

In the relationship of the people to religion, we demand the freedom of personal decision. The membership or nonmembership to particular religious communities may not become an advantage or disadvantage to anyone in our state community. We adhere to the Western Christian ethics; however we want to know that every confessional strife is banned from our people and want to allow the respect for each religion, regardless of its nature, to develop for the general good. Our traditional culture is to be cared for, further developed and made accessible to the entire people.

Only a just valuation of the intellectual achievement and a gradual increase in the lagging cultural budget can save Austria's cultural mission from decline. Art and scholarship as the creative forces, school and members of the teaching profession as the mediators of culture must again win back their central position in the life of the people.

IV

We fight for the equality of the citizen, for the true constitutional state, the independence of the courts and for the honesty of the administration.

We avow the republican form of government, democracy and the constitutional state. In a true democracy, all citizens must be able to take part equally, directly or indirectly, in the forming of the decisions of the state, so that nothing may happen against the will of the people. For this reason, direct democracy (plebiscite and referendum) is to be cultivated. Furthermore, we demand the increased responsibility of the leading persons in the state.

For the realization of the constitutional state, we demand the laws be in accord with the people's consciousness of law, the generally acknowledged legal maxims and human rights as well as with the Constitution. This constant harmony and the faithful observance of such laws must be tended to by truly independent courts. The right must be granted to the person directly concerned to propose the repeal of regulations which are contrary to the Constitution and to law at the Constitutional Court.

We have a special duty to restore the rights of those who because of their national views were persecuted and deprived of rights.

Purity of character and professional ability must be the only criteria in filling positions of public administration. We reject party *Proporz* and protection. The complete impartiality of the judge is to be ensured by the fact that the appointment and promotion may only result from binding suggestions from the body of judges.

The degraded dependence of the citizens upon the omnipotence of the state must be overcome. The VdU therefore considers it as an important task of its liberal and independent will to eliminate the intolerable condition that one is dependent upon the judgment of the authorities and even worse — upon the partiality of the political parties, in obtaining a position, a place to live, a permit to work and all kinds of other licenses. Its principle therefore reads: fewer regulations and in the necessary laws, fewer ambiguous regulations, but rather binding regulations.

V

We strive for a new, just social order, which guarantees to all workers without discrimination of class and according to achievement, a just share of the social product as well as the highest possible social security and possibility for advancement. Capital and the economy must serve the interests of all the people and its higher development. In a social market economy, planned economic policies of the state must work together with individual economic initiative for the good of the whole.

The VdU avows the economic order of the social market economy and the partnership of labor and capital.

Its principles are therefore: not class struggle and Marxist planned economy, not group egoism and denial of profession, but an economic order in which private property, unrestrained competition as well as freedom of work and trade are ensured.

Freedom is indivisible. Economic freedom is a prerequisite for political freedom.

The VdU therefore demands the elimination of monopolies and the opposition of cartels and unnecessary restrictions of freedom of industry. It demands — not for individual groups, but for the entire political economy — a planned effective economic policy which leads to the systematic enlargement and just distribution of the social product as well as to an effective provision of work for unemployed which offers the necessary motivation for higher achievement and overcomes the origins of class struggle by the creation of "property for all."

The VdU fights for the principle of social security which places the responsibility upon the state, for all people who through sickness, accident or other means through no fault of their own are in need, to guarantee the highest possible degree of social help and to ensure the workers in old age of all classes an adequate livelihood according to their earlier achievement. The VdU regards this economic and social task as a unity and differs basically in it from the other parties, which are only the merging of various interests on the basis of power political considerations. Whereas the others by splintering will make everyone poorer, we want to create prosperity and happiness for all by working together.

Appendix C

The Short Program of the Freiheitliche Partei Österreichs, 1955*

1.

We avow the principle of freedom and herewith the basic rights of men and peoples.

2.

We avow the social community of the *Volk* and oppose thinking and acting in class and group interests.

3.

We avow the unrestricted state independence of Austria.

4.

We oppose the omnipotence of the state and the power apparatus connected with it which threatens all freedoms of men.

We avow the democratic constitutional state of free men and women standing before the law and demand therefore the elimination of the demoralizing party *Proporz*.

5.

We demand simple and understandable laws, an honest and frugal administration and a social tax system.

We want a responsibility-conscious officialdom as counsel for the people and not the parties.

---

* *Die Neue Front,* November 12, 1955, p. 1.

6.

We demand the promotion of early marriages and families with many children as the foundation of our people by adequate aid and improved tax incentives.

7.

We want an education conscious of the *Volk* for our youth to a moral behavior and conscious of its obligation to the community.

8.

We demand the promotion of all the creative powers of our *Volk*.

9.

We avow a social market economy, which serves the community in true competitive achievement without restraint from cartels, unjust monopolies and the dictatorship of the Chambers.

We demand the safety of the constancy of the value of money as a necessary prerequisite for social and economic safety.

10.

We struggle against the party-political misuse of the chambers and organs of professional representation. Trade unions and the local workers' representatives must be independent of party policy and belong in an apolitical area.

11.

We want the just wage based on achievement and the true industrial community for blue- and white-collar workers.

12.

We want a free, economically independent and stable class of peasants and an economically healthy industrial and commercial class.

13.

We demand the just evaluation and promotion of intellectual work and the complete protection of the independence of the free professions.

14.

We avow our membership in the German *Volks* and cultural community.

15.

We reject war as a tool of policy. In the spirit of freedom, we avow ourselves to be part of the West and desire therefore the European Confederation of free and equal nations and states.

Notes

Preface

1. League of Independents.

Chapter 1

1. Klaus Berchtold, ed., "Schönerers 'Mein Programm,' 1879," *Österreichische Parteiprogramme 1868-1966* (Vienna: Verlag für Geschichte und Politik, 1967), pp. 183-185.
2. *Ibid.*, "Kundgebung des 'Deutschnationalen Vereins', 1882," pp. 195-197.
3. *Ibid.*, "Das Linzer Programm der Deutschnationalen, 1882," pp. 198-203.
4. *Ibid.*, "Schönerers Wahlaufruf, 1885," p. 204. This and all subsequent translations from the original German were made by the author unless otherwise noted.
5. Peter G. J. Pulzer, *The Rise of Political Anti-Semitism in Germany and Austria* (New York: John Wiley & Sons, 1964), p. 156.
6. Berchtold, "Das Salzburg Programm der Grossdeutschen Volkspartei, 1920," pp. 439-482.
7. After World War I, a number of German-nationally oriented peasant organizations were able to organize a German Peasants' party for the parliamentary elections of 1920. In the next two years, it strove to create a general peasants' party, but succeeded only in unifying the nationalist and anticlerical groups into the *Landbund für Österreich* in 1923.

Chapter 2

1. United States Department of State, "The Moscow Conference, October 19-30, 1943, Declaration on Austria, November 1, 1943," *Department of State Bulletin*, Vol. IX, No. 228, Publication 2021 (Washington: United States Government Printing Office, 1943), p. 310.
2. Oskar Helmer, *Fünfzig Jahre erlebte Geschichte* (Vienna: Verlag der Wiener Buchhandlung, 1957), p. 191. Wine and *Schnapps* which had been hoarded in the wine cellars in and around Vienna throughout the war were given to anyone who came with a bucket to carry the liquid away during the period after the German withdrawal and before the occupation by the Red Army. Despite a monumental "binge" by the Viennese during the siege of the city, the supply had not been exhausted by the time the Russians arrived, a factor which served to complicate an already difficult discipline problem.

3. *Ibid.*, p. 197.
4. Adolf Schärf, *April 1945 in Wien* (Vienna: Verlag der Wiener Volksbuchhandlung, 1948), p. 54. The zero represented the letter O and the 5 the fifth letter of the alphabet e, that is: Oe for *Österreich*.
5. *Ibid.*, p. 53.
6. *Ibid.*, p. 56.
7. *Ibid.*, pp. 60-61.
8. *Ibid.*, p. 66.
9. Lois Weinberger, *Tatsachen, Begegnungen und Gespräche: Ein Buch um Österreich* (Vienna: Österreichische Verlag, 1948), pp. 245-246.
10. *Ibid.*, p. 247.
11. *Ibid.*
12. Ernst Fischer, *Das Jahr der Befreiung aus Reden und Aufsätzen* (Vienna: Stern Verlag, 1946), pp. 13-14 citing a lead article from *Neues Österreich*, April 23, 1945.
13. Weinberger, p. 250.
14. Karl Renner, *Denkschrift über die Geschichte der Unabhänigkeitserklärung Österreichs* (Zurich: Europa Verlag, 1946), p. 14.
15. Jacques Hannak, *Karl Renner und seine Zeit: Versuch einer Biographie* (Vienna: Europa Verlag, 1965), p. 670.
16. *Ibid.*, p. 671, citing an unidentified article in the *London Observer*.
17. Adolf Schärf, *Österreichs Erneuerung 1945-1955: Das Erste Jahrzehnte der Zweiten Republik* (Vienna: Verlag der Wiener Volksbuchhandlung, 1955), pp. 35-36.
18. Renner, *Denkschrift*, p. 31.
19. Schärf, *April*, p. 98.
20. *Ibid.*, 99, 101.
21. Renner, *Denkschrift*, pp. 71-74.
22. Such a fortress of natural mountain barriers and the most fanatical divisions of the German army had been planned, but the necessary funds and supplies were never delivered. About the only result this "fortress" had was to cause the Western Allies to overestimate the German resistance to their advance, a factor which must certainly have influenced the military plans decided upon at Yalta, which left the entire liberation of Eastern Europe to the Soviets.
23. Karl Renner, *Österreich von der Ersten zur Zweiten Republik* (Vienna: Verlag der Wiener Volksbuchhandlung, 1960), p. 235.
24. Karl Gruber, *Zwischen Befreiung und Freiheit: Der Sonderfall Österreichs* (Vienna: Ulstein, 1953), p. 28 and Adolf Schärf, *Zwischen Demokratie und Volksdemokratie: Österreichs Wiederaufrichtung im Jahre 1945* (Vienna: Verlag der Wienervolksbuchhandlung, 1960), p. 25.
25. Renner, *Österreich*, p. 235. One courier whom Dr. Renner dispatched in May to go to the Tyrol required seventeen days for the journey and even had to swim the Danube at Emms to get past the Russian boundary sentries, reported by Richard Hiscocks, *Österreichs Wiedergeburt*, trans. by Dr. Inge Lehne (Vienna: Hermes-Verlag, 1954), p. 55.
26. Allied Commission for Austria, Minutes of the Meetings of the Allied Council, ALCO/M(45)1, Annex 1, "The Commencement and Method of Operation of the Allied Commission," *Eight Reels of Allied Council (ALCO)*

and Fifteen Reels of Executive Committee (EXCO) Minutes (M) and U.S. Unofficial Minutes (UM), (Washington, and Vienna, Austria: Microfilmed with the Cooperation of the United States Department of State and the Austrian State Archives, 1958-1960), Vienna, 11 September, 1945.
27. ALCO/M(45)1, Vienna, 11 September, 1945, pp. 4-7.
28. ALCO/M(45)1, Annex 5, "Allied Council Proclamation to the Austrian People," Vienna, 11 September, 1945.
29. ALCO/M(45)1, Annex 3, "Decision of the Allied Council Concerning Political Activity of the Democratic Parties in Austria," Vienna, 11 September, 1945.
30. Schärf, *Zwischen Demokratie,* p. 22.
31. Gruber, p. 30.
32. *Ibid.*
33. Weinberger, p. 268.
34. ALCO/UM(45)3, pp. 5010, "Detail of the Meeting of the Allied Council," Vienna, 20 September, 1945.
35. Weinberger, 268-269.
36. Gruber, p. 36; and *Wiener Zeitung,* September 27, 1945, p. 8. *Wiener Zeitung* is the official organ of the Austrian Government.
37. Schärf, *Österreichs Erneuerung,* p. 25.
38. ALCO/M(45)6, Annex 1, "Memorandum by the Allied Council to Dr. Renner," Vienna, 20 October, 1945.
39. *Wiener Zeitung,* October 28, 1945, p. 1.
40. "Verfassungsgesetz vom 19. Oktober 1945 über die erste Wahl des Nationalrates, der Landtage, und des Gemeinderates der Stadt Wien in der befreiten Republik Österreich (Wahlgesetz)," *Staatsgesetzblatt und Bundesgesetzblatt für die Republik Österreich,* 51. Stück, 198. Gesetz, October 21, 1945 (Vienna: Österreichische Staatsdruckerei, 1945), pp. 317-324, hereafter referred to as *Stgbl.* and *Bgbl.*
41. *Kleines Volksblatt* (Vienna), October 11, 1945, p. 1. This is the Vienna organ of the OeVP.
42. Fischer, pp. 139-141, reprint of an article published in *Neues Österreich,* October 3, 1945.
43. Schärf, *Österreichs Erneuerung,* pp. 80-81.
44. Weinberger, p. 276, reports that the Communists figured on at least twenty and some as many as thirty seats in the *Nationalrat.*
45. *Die Nationalratswahlen vom 25. November 1945* (Vol. II of *Beiträge zur Österreichischen Statistik,* ed. by the Österreichischen Statistischen Zentralamt. vols. ff., Vienna: Carl Überreuter Verlag, 1946), pp. 9-16.
46. Schärf, *Österreichs Erneuerung,* p. 85.
47. *Ibid.*
48. The existence of these pacts was common knowledge, but the exact text was never revealed until the periodical *Aktion,* in a journalistic coup, published the 1953 Raab-Schärf agreement on January 9, 1954. Vice-Chancellor Schärf subsequently corroborated this exposé by publishing the substance of the 1949 agreement and the text of the 1953 agreement. Schärf, *Österreichs Erneuerung,* pp. 336-338.
49. *Wiener Zeitung,* November 29, 1945, p. 1.
50. ALCO/M(45)12, Vienna, 18 December, 1945, p. 1.

51. *Salzburger Nachrichten,* December 20, 1945, p. 1.

52. *Nationalrat* of the Republic of Austria, *Stenographisches Protokoll,* 64. Sitzung des Nationalrates der Republik Österreich, V. Gesetzgebungsperiode, Mitwoch den 19. November 1947 (Vienna Staatsdruckerei, 1945ff.), pp. 1702–1728.

53. The term "third force" which was commonly applied to this movement and which I have adopted throughout this study is actually a misnomer. In Austria in 1945, the Allied decision to accept only three parties calcified the political structure into a two-party system based on the traditional major parties, with a built-in opposition from the KPOe. The Communists did and still do speak of their party as an opposition "third force." As a consequence, when the opposition movement with which this study is concerned developed, it was originally called the "fourth party." Only after its success at the polls and the Communist electoral catastrophe in 1949 did it become common to the right, or as they preferred, the center party opposition as the "third force."

Chapter 3

1. A combination of the word *Demokratie* (democracy) with *Diktatur* (dictatorship).

2. A generic term used by the Austrians to half-laughingly and half-derisively refer to anyone from north of the Salzach river which forms the border between Bavaria and Austria.

3. "Verfassungsgesetz vom 9. Mai 1945 über das Verbot der NSDAP," *Stgbl. und Bgbl.,* 4. Stück, Nr. 13, June 6, 1945, pp. 19–22.

4. Report of Chancellor Figil to the Council of Ministers on the results of de-Nazification, *Wiener Zeitung,* June 13, 1946, p. 1.

5. Helmut Andics, *50 Jahre Unseres Lebens: Österreichs Schicksal seit 1918* (Vienna: Fritz Molden Verlag, 1968), p. 533.

6. ALCO/M(46)26, pp. 2–3, Vienna, 12 July, 1946. During this meeting a discussion took place regarding Austrian de-Nazification methods and concluded with a draft of a letter to the Austrian government expressing dissatisfaction with the progress made to date.

7. *Wiener Zeitung,* July 25, 1946, p. 1.

8. ALCO/M(46)38, Annex B, "Resolution on De-Nazification Law," Vienna, 11 December, 1946.

9. "Bundesverfassungsgesetz vom 6. Februar 1947, über die Behandlung der National Sozialisten," *Bgbl. und Stgbl.,* 8 Stück, Nr. 25, February 17, 1947, pp. 277–303.

10. ALCO/M(48)69, Annex B, "Amnesty for Less Implicated Nazis — Statement by the Soviet Member," Vienna, 4 March, 1948.

11. "Bundesverfassungsgesetz vom 22. April 1948 über die vorzeitige Beendigung der im Nationalsozialistengesetz vorgesehenen Sühnefolge für jugendliche Personen," *Bgbl.,* 16 Stück, Nr. 70, April 28, 1948, p. 331.

12. "Bundesverfassungsgesetz vom 21. April 1948 über die vorzeitige Beendigung der im NS Gesetz vorgesehene Sühnefolgen für minderbelastete Personen," *Bgbl.,* 22. Stück, Nr. 88, June 5, 1948, p. 449.

13. *Wiener Zeitung,* June 25, 1948, p. 1.

14. Viktor Reimann, "Die Demokratische Presse," *Salzburger Nachrichten*, October 23, 1945, p. 1. This was the lead article in the first issue of the newspaper after it was relinquished by the American occupation authorities.

15. Alexander Vodopivec, *Wer regiert in Österreich?* (Vienna: Verlag für Geschichte und Politik, 1962), I, 100.

16. Berchtold, "Die Programmatischen Leitsätze der Österreichischen Volkspartei, 1945," p. 378.

17. Wolfgang Drexler, "Die Partei der Parteilosen," *Salzburger Nachrichten*, November 12, 1945, p. 1.

18. In personal discussions with former Nazis who were interned as political prisoners at the American concentration camp at Glasenbach south of Salzburg, I have been told that both Reimann and Canaval were thoroughly hated by a large segment of the prisoners for their uncompromising condemnation of the National Socialist ideologies in which they had been so deeply indoctrinated.

19. Herbert A. Kraus, "Die Ziele unseres Institutes," *Berichte und Informationen des Österreichischen Forschungsinstitutes für Wirtschaft und Politik*, I (May 3, 1946), 1. Hereafter referred to as *Berichte und Informationen*.

20. H. A. Kraus, "Das fluktuierende und das bleibende Stimmkapital der drei Parteien," *Berichte und Informationen*, I, II (May 3, 10, 1946).

21. H. A. Kraus, "Das National Sozialistengesetz," *Berichte und Informationen*, XLIII (February 21, 1947), pp. 1–4.

22. Statement by Dr. Herbert A. Kraus, personal interview.

23. H. A. Kraus, "Die Forumrede im Sender Rot-Weiss-Rot: Die Bürukratizierung Österreichs," *Berichte und Informationen*, XLI (February 7, 1947). An exact reprint of the Forum debate.

24. *Salzburger Nachrichten*, April 5, 1946, p. 1.

25. Statement by Dr. Viktor Reimann, personal interview.

26. Dr. A., "Erste Ergebnisse der Volksbefragung: Wie eine Neuwahl ausgehen würde," *Berichte und Informationen*, LXXI (September 5, 1947), 1–2.

27. Dr. A., "Die Ergebnisse unserer Volksbefragung (2): Rund die Hälfte der Befragten für eine 4. Partei," *Berichte und Informationen*, LXXII (September 12, 1947), 5–6.

28. Dr. A., "Wie sich die einzelnen eine vierte Partei vorstellen: Nicht die 'Neuwähler,' — die Heimkehrer werden das politische Bild prägen," *Berichte und Informationen*, LXII (September 19, 1947), 3–4.

29. Statement by Dr. Kraus, personal interview.

30. H. A. Kraus, "Zwei Jahre Forschungsinstitut: Idee, Arbeitsprogramm und Aufbau unseres Institutes," *Berichte und Informationen*, LXXXVIII (January 2, 1948), 1–4.

31. *Ibid.*

32. H. T. Porta, "Parteien im Schatten," *Salzburger Nachrichten*, September 30, 1948, p. 1.

33. Report of Minister Helmer of September 22, 1948 in *Wiener Zeitung*, September 23, 1948, p. 1. This action was later ruled unconstitutional as reported in *Salzburger Nachrichten*, March 30, 1949, p. 3.

34. EXCO/M(48)122, "Soviet Proposal for the Suppression of the Newspaper *Alpenländischer Heimatsruf*," Vienna, 8 October, 1945, p. 5.

35. H. T. Porta, "Parteien im Schaten," and Viktor Reimann, "Gefährdete Demokratie," *Salzburger Nachrichten,* October 4, 1948, pp. 1–2.
36. H. A. Kraus, "Die Aussichten für die kommende Wahl (II): Die möglichen Wege der vierten Partei," *Berichte und Informationen,* CXXXV (November 26, 1948), 30.
37. *Ibid.*
38. *Ibid.*

Chapter 4

1. *Salzburger Nachrichten,* December 1, 1948, p. 2.
2. Statement by Dr. Kraus, personal interview.
3. *Salzburger Nachrichten,* February 5, 1949, p. 4.
4. *Demokratisches Volksblatt,* February 5, 1949, p. 2. This newspaper is the Salzburg organ of the SPOe.
5. *Salzburger Nachrichten,* February 5, 1949, p. 4.
6. H. A. Kraus, "Vorhut einer neuen Ordnung," *Die Neue Front,* August 2, 1952, the official organ of the VdU published weekly in Salzburg.
7. Statement by Dr. Viktor Reimann, personal interview.
8. Speech of Minister Helmer to Socialist city and town representatives on February 7, 1949, quoted in the *Demokratisches Volksblatt,* February 7, 1949, p. 1.
9. *Wiener Illustrierte,* March 12, 1949, p. 2.
10. Statement by Dr. Kraus, personal interview.
11. ALCO/UM(49)113, Annex B, "Statement by the US Member" in response to "The Danger of a Nazi Revival in Austria — Statement by the Soviet Member," Vienna, 22 December, 1949.
15. EXCO/M(49)135, "Violations of the Allied Council Decision on 'The Press in Austria' by the periodical *Berichte und Informationen,*" Vienna, April 22, 1949, p. 18.
13. EXCO/M(49)144, "Nazi and Military Propaganda in the Periodical '*Berichte und Informationen,*'" Vienna, August 19, 1949, pp. 20–21.
14. ALCO/M(45)1, "Decision of the Allied Council Concerning the Democratic Press in Austria," Annex 1, Vienna, September 11, 1945.
15. Viktor Reimann, "Offener Brief an den Wiener Kurier," *Die Neue Front,* May 13, 1949, p. 1. This newspaper was the weekly organ of the VdU.
16. Quoted from a letter by Mr. D. C. Watt, formerly of the British Intelligence Corps in Styria, relating his personal reminiscences regarding the VdU, communicated to me by A. Taylor Milne, Secretary and Librarian for the Institute of Historical Research, University of London.
17. Statement by *Nationalrat* Gustav Zeillinger, personal interview.
18. Statement by Dr. Kraus, personal interview.
19. Paragraph #2 of the *Verband* statutes, *Die Neue Front,* April 1, 1949, p. 3.
20. Helfried Pfeifer, "Österreichs Parteien und Parlament," pp. 417–475 in *Jahrbuch des öffentlichen Rechtes der Gegenwart,* ed. Gerhard Leibholz (Tübingen, J.C.B. Mohr, 1962), p. 445.
21. "Wovon die 'Unabhängige' Presse abhängig ist," *Die Neue Front,* April 1, 1949, p. 2.

22. *Salzburger Nachrichten,* April 1, 1949, p. 2.
23. Maintained by Drs. Kraus and Reimann, and corroborated by *Nationalrat* Zeillinger in separate interviews without the knowledge of the testimony of the others.
24. *Ibid.*
25. Statement by Dr. Reimann, personal interview.
26. The program was published in full in *Die Neue Front,* July 30, 1949, p. 2; see Appendix A for the complete, translated text.
27. Decision of the constituent assembly of March 26, 1949, *Die Neue Front,* April 1, 1949, p. 3. At the 1949 rate of exchange this amounted to approximately eight cents.
28. Statement by Dr. Reimann, personal interview.
29. Statement by Dr. Kraus, personal interview.
30. *Ibid.*
31. William Lloyd Stearman, *Die Sowjetunion und Österreich 1945–1955: Ein Beispiel für die Sowjetpolitik gegenüber dem Westen,* trans. Hanswilhelm Häfs (Vienna: Verlag für Zeitarchiv, 1962), p. 105.
32. See above, p. 36.
33. Alfred Missong, "Die vierte Partei," *Österreichische Monatshefte,* II (November, 1948), p. 55. This is the monthly ideological journal of the OeVP.
34. *Demokratisches Volksblatt,* May 2, 1949, p. 2.
35. ALCO/M(49)99, "Memorandum to the Federal Chancellor of the Austrian Republic, Ing. L. Figil," Vienna, May 27, 1949.
36. Pfeifer, *Österreichs Parteien,* pp. 445–446.
37. Helmer, *50 Jahre,* p. 332.
38. Interview with Minister Helmer in *Die Neue Front,* July 23, 1949, p. 1.
39. Statement by Dr. Reimann, personal interview.
40. Elenore Gläser, "Die Propaganda für die österreichischen Wahlen 1949, Parteien, Propaganda, Verlauf," unpublished Ph.D. dissertation, the University of Vienna, 1951, reprinted in part pp. 466–479 of Waine Marvich, et al., *Wahlwerber* (Vol. II of *Wahlen und Parteien in Österreich: Österreichisches Wahlhandbuch,* 3 vols., Vienna: Österreichischer Bundesverlag: Verlag für Jugend und Volk, 1966), p. B472. Hereafter the collective work will be cited as *Wahlhandbuch.*
41. There is considerable disagreement regarding the extent of circulation. In an interview twenty years later when Dr. Kraus could be expected to be objective but perhaps forgetful on this matter, he placed circulation at a high of 70,000 issues. In April of 1949 when the VdU was trying to tout itself as a truly new front for political renewal, the party organ boasted a circulation of 243,000 and claimed to reach a million people because of wide readership in restaurants, *Gasthäuser* and other watering holes and because of the tendency of subscribers to pass their copies along to friends unable to afford to subscribe, *Die Neue Front,* April 29, 1949, p. 1. In any case all independent interviews confirm that the party organ was financially self-sufficient and was able to contribute earnings to the league treasury in 1949.
42. Statement by Dr. Reimann, personal interview.
43. *Ibid.*
44. Gläser, *Wahlhandbuch,* II, B478. See below, n. 47.
45. *Ibid.*

46. Statement by Dr. Kraus, personal interview.
47. Gläser, *Wahlhandbuch,* II, 478. Although Dr. Gläser emphasized the significance of OeVP attendance at mass meetings, it can be seen by averaging her own figures that proportionally, VdU attendance was by far the highest among all the parties, further seeming to confirm Kraus's and Reimann's claims that they were the greatest single means of publicity for the league.

Party	Number of Meetings Sept. 1–Oct. 1, 1949	Attendance	Average (not supplied by Gläser)
SPOe	1,056	291,889	276
KPOe	551	79,600	144
OeVP	371	116,698	314
VdU	85	47,511	588

48. H. A. Kraus, "Die Grundsätze unserer Arbeiterpolitik," *Die Neue Front,* March 25, 1949, p. 3.
49. For the best statement of the VdU policy on European integration see, Speech of Ernst Roden, "Um ein geeintes Europa," *Die Neue Front,* April 22, 1949, p. 3, and the text of a speech delivered by Viktor Reimann in Innsbruck, "Staatspolitik staat Parteipolitik," *Die Neue Front,* June 24, 1949, p. 1.
50. ALCO/M(45)1, Annex 5, "Allied Council Proclamation to the Austrian People," Vienna, 11 September, 1945.
51. Simply translated as the language of instruction.
52. Dr. Walter Fessel, "Querschnitte der öffentlichen Meinung," in *Wahlwerber* (Vol. II of *Wahlhandbuch*), pp. B 584–585.
53. Point 9 of the VdU program. See Appendix A.
54. Walter B. Simon, "Politische Ethik und Politische Struktur," *Kölner Zeitschrift für Soziologie und Sozialpsychologie,* XI (1959), pp. 450–454.
55. Speech of Dr. Reimann, "Staatspolitik statt Parteipolitik," *Die Neue Front,* June 24, 1949, p. 1.
56. Statement by Dr. Reimann, personal interview.
57. *Ibid.*
58. Dr. A., "Wie sich die einzelnen eine vierte Partei vorstellen: Nicht die 'Neuwähler,' — die Heimkehrer werden das politische Bild prägen," *Berichte und Informationen,* LXIII (September 19, 1947), 3.
59. Ernst Roden, "Weder Proletar noch Bürger," *Die Neue Front,* February 25, 1949, p. 1.
60. Statement by Dr. Reimann, personal interview.
61. Ernst Roden, "Um ein geeinigtes Europa," *Die Neue Front,* April 1, 1949, p. 1.
62. "Hoffnung der 80,000 Rückwanderer," *Die Neue Front,* September 24, 1949, p. 5.
63. Helmer, pp. 279–286. By the end of 1954 Helmer puts the total *Volksdeutsch* immigration at 159,576 and the *Reichsdeutsch* immigration at 264,155.
64. Statement by Dr. Reimann, personal interview.
65. Councils elected in business, industry as well as in government enterprises for local representation of workers and employees.

66. "Wahlflugblatt unserer Parteiorganization in Steyr," *Welt der Arbeit: Sozialistische Betriebszeitung* (Vienna), LIV (October 28, 1949), 16. Monthly ideological publication of the Socialist trade unions.
67. Statement by Dr. Reimann, personal interview.
68. Speech of Minister Helmer, "Der Wahlkampf," delivered to functionaries of the Lower Austrian Socialist party, *Arbeiter Zeitung: Zentral Organ der Sozialistischen Partei Österreichs* (Vienna), October 4, 1949, p. 2.
69. ALCO/M(45)1, Annex 5, "Allied Council Proclamation to the Austrian People," Vienna, 11 September, 1945.
70. Leader of the provincial government, selected by the majority party in the *Landtag*.
71. *New York Times*, June 10, 1949, p. 5.
72. *Arbeiter Zeitung*, August 23, 1949, p. 1.
73. Interview with the OeVP leadership, *Salzburger Nachrichten*, August 24, 1949, p. 2.
74. "Das Wort der OeVP an die Wähler," *Österreichische Monatshefte*, XII (September, 1949), 498. Monthly ideological organ of the OeVP.
75. "VdU Skandal auf dem Höhepunkt," *Wiener Tageszeitung*, August 27, 1949, p. 1. Central organ of the OeVP.
76. *Wiener Tageszeitung*, October 1, 1949, p. 1.
77. "VdU Skandal auf dem Höhepunkt," *Wiener Tageszeitung*, August 27, 1949, p. 1.
78. *Ibid.*
79. "Dr. Kraus, Feingold & Co.," *Wiener Tageszeitung*, October 5, 1949, p. 1.
80. "Spinne und VdU," *Wiener Tageszeitung*, October 8, 1949, p. 1.
81. After the election nothing more was heard of the "Spider" affair.
82. *Die Neue Front*, October 8, 1949, Extra Edition, p. 1; corroborated twenty years later in a personal interview with Dr. Kraus.
83. *Wiener Tageszeitung*, October 9, 1949, p. 2.
84. "Beiträge zur Österreichischen Statistik, 4. Heft: Der Nationalratswahlen vom 9. Oktober," ed. Österreichische Statistisches Zentralamt (Vienna: Österreichische Staatsdruckerei, 1949), reprinted in *Wahlstatistik* (Vol. II of *Wahlhandbuch*), p. C125.
85. "Fruchtbare Enttäuschung am Tage nach der Wahl," *Arbeiter Zeitung*, October 11, 1949, p. 1.
86. *Ibid.*
87. Viktor Reimann, "Waren es frei Wahlen?," *Die Neue Front*, October 15, 1949, p. 1.
88. Statement by Dr. Kraus, personal interview.
89. See above, p. 67.
90. Statements by Drs. Kraus and Reimann, personal interviews.
91. *Die Neue Front*, October 15, 1949, p. 1.
92. Dr. H. A. Kraus, "Appel an die staatspolitische Vernunft," *Die Neue Front*, October 21, 1949, p. 1.
93. Schärf, *Österreichs Erneuerung*, p. 254.
94. *Wiener Zeitung*, November 8, 1949, p. 1.

Chapter 5

1. The *Nationalrat* of the Republic of Austria, *Stenographisches Protokoll*, 2. Sitzung des Nationalrates der Republik Österreich, VI Gesetzgebungsperiode. Mitwoch 9, November, 1949, p. 24.
2. *Ibid.* Summary of the KdU parliamentary program.
3. *Salzburger Nachrichten,* November 9, 1949, p. 1.
4. *Stenographisches Protokoll,* p. 24.
5. *Ibid.,* p. 38. Speech of Hartleb in response to Figil's "Declaration of Government."
6. *Wiener Zeitung,* May 29, 1953, pp. 2–3.
7. Karl Blecha, "Wähler und Parteien," in *Wahlwerber* (Vol. II of *Wahlhandbuch*), p. B 596. The conclusion of a poll conducted on the public images of the various parties.
8. The exact terms of this pact are not known. The assumptions here are made on the basis of the terms of the 1953 pact, first published by the VdU as the result of a journalistic coup and later by SPOe Chairman Dr. Schärf in *Österreichs Erneuerung,* pp. 336–338. Judging from the operation of the two pacts, the 1953 agreement seems even somewhat more elastic than that of 1949.
9. Statement by Dr. Kraus, personal interview. This was one of the goals expressed by Dr. Kraus in his initial parliamentary speech of November 9, 1949, see point four of the speech summary above, p. 75.
10. See above, p. 74.
11. *Welt der Arbeit,* XIV (October 28, 1949), p. 16.
12. *Ibid.*
13. *Österreichische Allgemeine Zeitung,* December 9, 1949.
14. *Welt der Arbeit,* XV (November 11, 1949), 2.
15. *Ibid.,* XIV (October 28, 1949), 16.
16. Karl Czernetz, "Die Welt — Die Wahl — Die Zukunft," *Die Zukunft: Sozialistische Monatsschrift für Politik und Kultur,* X/XI (November, 1949), 293.
17. Vodopevic, I, 100.
18. See above, pp. 50–51.
19. Statement by Dr. Kraus, personal interview.
20. *Salzburger Nachrichten,* February 25/26, 1950, p. 4.
21. *Ibid.*
22. *Salzburger Nachrichten,* February 28, 1950, p. 2.
23. *Die Neue Front,* March 23, 1950, p. 2.
24. *Ibid.*
25. *Salzburger Volkszeitung,* February 22, 1950, p. 2.
26. *Ibid.*
27. *Die Neue Front,* April 6, 1950, p. 1.
28. *Demokratisches Volksblatt,* May 12, 1950, p. 2.
29. "Götterdämerung im VdU," *Österreichische Monatshefte,* IV (April, 1950), 261.
30. *Salzburger Volkszeitung,* March 9, 1950, p. 2.
31. *Wiener Zeitung,* July 2, 1950, p. 1. In response to this incident and previous accusations by the Soviet element in the Allied Council that the VdU

represented a revival of Nazi activity, the three western Occupying Powers conducted investigations of the VdU and other allegedly neo-Nazi groups. When on July 13, 1950 the Soviet representative to the Allied Council, Maslov, charged that the incident in Graz "... left no doubt that its [the VdU] aim was to revive the National Socialist party, to make propaganda for Nazi ideology and to restore a Fascist regime in Austria," the three western representatives absolutely rejected the accusation. The statement by the French element, Bouthouart, recorded in the unofficial minutes, best summarizes the posture of the three: "We all know the VdU is a league composed of various elements, that certain parts of it are Nazi, but other members are not Nazi. Three of the elements consider that the measure taken by the Austrian Government was sufficient and that it will not be necessary or justified to request further information from the Austrian government." ALCO/UM(50)126, p. 4. The official minutes of the discussion are contained within ALCO/M(50) 126, pp. 1–5, "Nazi Provocation in the British Zone of Occupation in Austria," Vienna, 13 July, 1950.

32. *Die Neue Front,* July 13, 1950, p. 1.
33. *Salzburger Nachrichten,* July 22/23, 1950, p. 4.
34. Statement by *Nationalrat* Zeillinger, personal interview.
35. *Salzburger Nachrichten,* July 22/23, 1950, p. 4.
36. *Salzburger Nachrichten,* July 24, 1950, p. 2.
37. *Ibid.*
38. *Die Neue Front,* August 25, 1950, p. 2.
39. *Salzburger Nachrichten,* September 6, 1950, p. 2.
40. Statement by Dr. Reimann, personal interview.
41. *Die Neue Front,* October 7, 1950, p. 1.
42. *Salzburger Nachrichten,* October 3, 1950, p. 2.
43. Statement by Dr. Reimann, personal interview.
44. Statement by *Nationalrat* Zeillinger, personal interview.
45. Statement by Dr. Reimann, personal interview.
46. *Ibid.*
47. Schärf, *Österreichs Erneuerung,* p. 259.
48. *Demokratisches Volksblatt,* September 27, 1950, p. 1. According to investigations conducted by the three western Occupying Powers, the Red Army encouraged subversive elements in demonstrations and acts of violence, transported rioters around the city in army trucks and thwarted the movement of Austrian police units in the Soviet zone of the city to the sites of the disturbances. These charges were made by U.S. representative Lt. General Geoffrey Keyes, then serving as Chairman of the Allied Council, and corroborated by the British and French delegates. ALCO/M(50)131, "Soviet Interference in Austrian Law Enforcement Agencies," Vienna, 29 September, 1950, pp. 15–19.
49. Gruber, p. 231.
50. Press release of September 26, 1950 by the "Independent Representatives of the Industrial Council of VOeST," *Die Neue Front,* September 30, 1950, p. 1.
51. Report of the VOeST strike committee of September 28, 1950, *Die Neue Front,* October 7, 1950, p. 3.
52. Schärf, *Österreichs Erneuerung,* p. 261.

53. *Salzburger Neue Zeit und Tagblatt,* October 2, 1950. Official organ of the Austrian Communist Party in Salzburg.
54. Charge made by Federal Chancellor Figl in a letter of October 5 to N.J.A. Cheetham, representative of the United Kingdom serving as chairman of the Allied Council for the October 6, 1950 meeting. Chairman Cheetham accepted these charges as well substantiated. EXCOM(50)172, "Protest by the Federal Chancellor Alleging Breach of the Control Agreement by the Soviet Element. Statement by the Chairman," Vienna, 6 October, 1950, pp. 9–13.
55. *Ibid.,* pp. 12–13.
56. Gruber, pp. 234–235.
57. *Ibid.*
58. Ludwig Adamovic (ed.), *Die Bundesverfassungsgesetze samt Ausführungs- und Nebengesetze,* 5th ed. (Vienna: Verlag der Österreichischen Staatsdruckerei, 1947), p. 83.
59. "Verfassungsgesetz vom 13. Dezember 1945 womit verfassungsrechtliche anordnungen aus Anlass des Zusammentrittes des Nationalrates und der Landtage getroffen werden: Verfassungs-Überleitungsgesetz 1945," *Staatsgesetzblatt für die Republik Österreich,* 60. Stück, Nr. 232, December 18, 1945 (Vienna: Österreichische Staatsdruckerei, 1945), p. 423.
60. Bundesgesetz vom 22. April 1948 womit die Vertretung des Bundespräsidenten in Ausführung des Artikels geregelt wird," *Bundesgesetzblatt für die Republik Österreich,* Nr. 84, April 27, 1948 (Vienna: Österreichische Staatsdruckerei, 1948), p. 435.
61. Schärf, *Österreichs Erneuerung,* p. 270.
62. Gruber, p. 250.
63. *Wiener Zeitung,* January 3, 1950, p. 2.
64. Schärf, *Österreichs Erneuerung,* p. 271, see also Gruber, p. 250.
65. The Nationalrat of the Republic of Austria, *Stenographisches Protokoll,* 44. Sitzung des Nationalrates der Republik Österreich, Montag 12. January 1951, pp. 1791–1794. Speech of SPOe delegate Pittermann stating the Socialist demand for a popular election.
66. *Die Neue Front,* January 6, 1951.
67. "Bundesgesetz: Wahl des Bundespräsidenten," *Bundesgesetzblatt für die Republik Österreich,* 8 Stück, Nr. 42, February 19, 1951 (Vienna: Österreichische Staatsdruckerei, 1951), pp. 215–219.
68. Gruber, p. 250.
69. *Die Neue Front,* January 20, 1951, p. 1.
70. Gruber, p. 250.
71. Interview with an anonymous OeVP functionary, *Salzburger Nachrichten,* February 21, 1950, p. 2.
72. Walter Jambor, "Junge Generation im Aufbruch," *Österreichische Monatshefte,* VI (June, 1950), 373–374.
73. *Salzburger Nachrichten,* March 3/4, 1951, p. 4.
74. *Salzburger Nachrichten,* March 3/4, 1951, p. 2.
75. *Salzburger Nachrichten,* March 3/4, 1951, p. 4.
76. Statement by *Nationalrat* Zeillinger, personal interview. Zeillinger was a member of the "Committee" and present at the meeting.
77. G. A. Canaval, "Die einigende Idee," *Salzburger Nachrichten,* January 7/8, 1951, p. 1.

78. Statement by *Nationalrat* Zeillinger, personal interview.
79. *Wiener Zeitung,* March 23, 1951, p. 3.
80. *Salzburger Nachrichten,* April 25, 1951, p. 2.
81. From a Breitner radio speech on station *Rot-Weiss-Rot,* the text of which was published in the *Salzburger Nachrichten,* April 28/29, 1951, p. 4.
82. Interview with Dr. Breitner by Ludwig Canal, Chairman of the Breitner Committee, *Die Neue Front,* March 31, 1951, p. 1.
83. Breitner interview with Ludwig Canal, *Die Neue Front,* April 14, 1951, p. 3.
84. G. A. Canaval, "Dieses BB," *Salzburger Nachrichten,* April 14/15, 1951, p. 4.
85. From a Breitner radio speech on station *Rot-Weiss-Rot,* the text of which was published in the *Salzburger Nachrichten,* April 28/29, 1951, p. 4.
86. Schärf, *Österreichs Erneuerung,* p. 272.
87. *Salzburger Volkszeitung,* April 27, 1951, p. 1.
88. H. T. Porta, "Varianten einer Wahl," *Salzburger Nachrichten,* April 28/29, 1951, p. 1.
89. *Salzburger Volkszeitung,* April 27, 1951, p. 1.
90. *Salzburger Nachrichten,* March 31/April 1, 1951, p. 1.
91. H. T. Porta, "Varianten einer Wahl," *Salzburger Nachrichten,* April 28/29, 1951, p. 1.
92. "Die Wahl des Bundespräsidenten am 6. und 27. Mai 1951," ed. Bundesministerium für Inneres: Österreichischen Statistischen Zentralamt (Vienna, 1959), pp. VII–XII reprinted in *Wahlstatistik* (Vol. III of *Wahlhandbuch*), pp. 207–208.
93. *Die Neue Front,* May 12, 1951, p. 1.
94. See above, p. 100.
95. Gruber, p. 251.
96. Report of the May 18 meeting of the VdU federal leadership and the KdU in Vienna, *Salzburger Nachrichten,* May 19/20, 1951, p. 4.
97. *Die Neue Front,* May 26, 1951, p. 1.
98. *Salzburger Nachrichten,* May 22, 1951, p. 1.
99. *Ibid.*
100. *Demokratisches Volksblatt,* May 12, 1951, p. 1.
101. Anonymous article, "Mein Tagebuch," by "an ex-Nazi," *Demokratisches Volksblatt,* May 22, 1951, p. 1.
102. *Demokratisches Volksblatt,* May 18, 1951, p. 1.
103. "Die Angekündigte Empfehlung," *Die Neue Front,* May 19, 1951, p. 1.
104. *Ibid.*
105. *Demokratisches Volksblatt,* May 26, 1951; and Schärf, *Österreichs Erneuerung,* p. 275.
106. Statement by Dr. Reimann, personal interview.
107. Statement by Dr. Kraus, personal interview.
108. Herbert Kraus, "Ich Wähle Gleissner," *Die Presse,* May 24, 1951, p. 3.
109. *Ibid.*
110. "Die Wahl des Bundespräsidenten am 6. und 27. Mai 1951," *Wahlstatistik,* pp. C 207–208.
111. G. A. Canaval, "Die Wahlbedeutung," *Salzburger Nachrichten,* May 30, 1951, pp. 1–2. The percentages were calculated from raw figures provided

in the article. The totals estimated by Canaval were Gleissner: 281,900, Körner: 289,000, invalid: 92,000.

112. V. Reimann, "Die fünf Erkenntnisse aus der Wahl," *Die Neue Front,* June 2, 1951, p. 1.

Chapter 6

1. V. Reimann, "Die fünf Erkenntnisse aus der Wahl," *Die Neue Front,* June 2, 1951, p. 1. In this reference to Salzburg, Dr. Reimann was pointing to the fact that despite the support of the *Salzburger Nachrichten* for Gleissner in the runoff election, the OeVP candidate polled only 91,848 votes for 48.16 percent of the vote. Körner received 79,045 votes for 41.66 percent while a decisive 19,310 ballots, 19.18 percent, were left blank. In the first election, with the support of the *Salzburger Nachrichten* and the VdU, Breitner won 67,037 votes for 35.33 percent, against Gleissner with 64,849 votes for 34.38 percent and Körner with 48,424 votes for 25.68 percent. These statistics were taken from "Die Wahl des Bundespräsidenten am 6. und 27. Mai 1951," *Wahlstatistik,* pp. 207-208.

2. See above, p. 159.

3. V. Reimann, "Die fünf Erkenntnisse aus der Wahl," *Die Neue Front,* June 2, 1951, p. 1.

4. "Der Weg des VdU als Partei der Mitte," *Die Neue Front,* July 7, 1951, p. 1.

5. V. Reimann, "Das neue Antlitz," *Die Neue Front,* June 16, 1951, p. 1.

6. V. Reimann, "Probleme der erweiterten Basis," *Die Neue Front,* June 23, 1951, p. 1.

7. *Die Neue Front,* July 14, 1951, p. 1.

8. Statement by Dr. Reimann, personal interview.

9. Fritz Stüber, "Unser Bekenntniss zur deutschen Nation," *Die Neue Front,* September 8, 1951, p. 5.

10. *Ibid.*

11. See above, p. 55.

12. Fritz Stüber, "Universal Menschheit der Gemeinschaft der Nationen," *Die Neue Front,* September 15, 1951, p. 5.

13. V. Reimann, "Sozialisten in der Defensive," *Die Neue Front,* October 6, 1951, p. 1.

14. V. Reimann, "Vor dem Bundesverbandstag," *Die Neue Front,* December 1, 1951, p. 1.

15. Schärf, *Österreichs Erneuerung,* p. 276; and from the text of a speech by Schärf at a SPOe convention in which he raised the rumor of inclusion of the VdU in the coalition and rejected the possibility, *Demokratisches Volksblatt,* November 13, 1951, p. 1.

16. *Die Presse: Morgenblatt* (Vienna), December 2, 1951, p. 2.

17. *Salzburger Nachrichten,* December 3, 1951, p. 2.

18. *Ibid.*

19. Speech of FDP *Bundestag* faction chairman Dr. Euler, *Die Neue Front,* December 3, 1951, p. 2.

20. *Die Presse: Morgenblatt,* December 4, 1951, p. 2.

21. *Die Neue Front,* December 8, 1951, p. 2.

22. H. A. Kraus, "Unsere Aufgaben für 1952," *Die Neue Front*, December 29, 1951, p. 1.
23. *Ibid.*
24. See above, pp. 95-96.
25. *Salzburger Nachrichten*, May 18, 1951, p. 2.
26. *Salzburger Nachrichten*, October 22, 1951, p. 1.
27. *Salzburger Nachrichten*, January 16, 1952, p. 2.
28. *Die Presse: Morgenblatt*, June 14, 1952, p. 1.
29. *Salzburger Nachrichten*, July 23, 1952, p. 2.
30. *Demokratisches Volksblatt*, July 23, 1952, p. 2.
31. *Salzburger Volkszeitung*, July 23, 1952, p. 2.
32. *Salzburger Nachrichten*, October 13, 1952, p. 2.
33. *Wiener Zeitung*, October 24, 1952, p. 1.
34. *Wiener Zeitung*, October 29, 1952, p. 1.
35. *Die Neue Front*, October 31, 1952, p. 1.
36. *Salzburger Nachrichten*, November 10, 1952, p. 2.
37. *Die Presse: Morgenblatt*, December 17, 1952, p. 2.
38. *Die Neue Front*, December 20, 1952, p. 2.
39. *Ibid.*
40. *Die Presse: Morgenblatt*, December 17, 1952.
41. *Ibid.*
42. Gruber, p. 297.
43. *Salzburger Volkszeitung*, January 10, 1953, p. 1.
44. Schärf, *Österreichs Erneuerung*, pp. 328-329.
45. V. Reimann, "Versprechungen der Regierungsparteien: Sieben Jahre hätten sie Zeit gehabt!," *Die Neue Front*, January 17, 1953, p. 1.
46. *Die Neue Front*, January 24, 1953, p. 1.
47. "Wahlt Wahlpartei der Unabhängigen," *Die Neue Front*, February 7, 1953, p. 1.
48. *Ibid.*
49. *Ibid.*
50. Speech of Foreign Minister Gruber in Salzburg, *Salzburger Volkszeitung*, January 26, 1953, p. 2.
51. V. Reimann, "Unsere Stellung zu Deutschland," *Die Neue Front*, February 7, 1953, p. 2.
52. *Ibid.*
53. *Ibid.*
54. This charge was initially published in the Socialist press, *Demokratisches Volksblatt*, January 31, 1953, p. 1, and was later picked up by the OeVP *Salzburger Volkszeitung*, February 3, 1953, p. 2. The charge was later disproved in a libel proceeding in the Mittersill District Court, April 2, 1953.
55. *Salzburger Volkszeitung*, January 12, 1953, p. 2.
56. *Salzburger Volkszeitung*, February 23, 1953, p. 1.
57. *Demokratisches Volksblatt*, February 23, 1953, p. 1.
58. V. Reimann, "Und erst Recht," *Die Neue Front*, February 28, 1953, p. 1. "Ruah" is the word *Ruhe*, peace and/or quiet, rendered in Austrian dialect.
59. Gruber, p. 298.
60. *Die Presse, Morgenblatt*, March 3, 1953.
61. *Salzburger Volkszeitung*, March 2, 1953, p. 1.

62. *Die Presse, Morgenblatt,* March 4, 1953, p. 1.
63. Schärf, *Österreichs Erneuerung,* p. 333.
64. *Die Presse, Morgenblatt,* March 10, 1953, p. 1.
65. The Nationalrat of the Republic of Austria, *Stenographisches Protokoll,* I. Sitzung des Nationalrates der Republik Österreich, VII Gesetzgebungsperiode, March 18, 1953, p. 8.
66. Schärf, *Österreichs Erneuerung,* pp. 333-334.
67. *Salzburger Volkszeitung,* March 23, 1953, p. 1.
68. Schärf, *Österreichs Erneuerung,* p. 334.
69. Gruber, p. 299.
70. Text of the Körner speech in *Wiener Zeitung,* March 28, 1953, p. 1.
71. Schärf, *Österreichs Erneuerung,* p. 337.
72. "Das Vetorecht ist gefallen," *Die Neue Front,* April 11, 1953, p. 1.
73. Schärf, *Österreichs Erneuerung,* p. 337.
74. *Ibid.* Both Drs. Kraus and Reimann feel that Raab was initially sincere in his efforts to include the VdU in the coalition, but was willing to renege on his promises when a solution emerged that was acceptable to his party and the SPOe. Statements by Drs. Kraus and Reimann, personal interviews.

Chapter 7

1. Statement by Dr. Reimann, personal interview.
2. Statement by Thomas Neuwirth upon reentering the VdU in 1953, *Die Neue Front,* February 5, 1953, p. 3.
3. *Salzburger Nachrichten,* April 21, 1953, p. 2.
4. *Salzburger Nachrichten,* May 8, 1953, p. 4.
5. *Salzburger Nachrichten,* May 18, 1953, p. 2.
6. *Die Presse,* July 14, 1953, p. 2.
7. *Salzburger Nachrichten,* July 13, 1953, p. 2.
8. Speech by Dr. Rudolf Lodgemann in Salzburg, May 16, 1953, *Die Neue Front,* May 23, 1953, p. 3.
9. *Die Neue Front,* July 11, 1953, p. 1.
10. *Die Neue Front,* October 24, 1953, p. 2.
11. *Die Neue Front,* November 28, 1953, p. 1.
12. *Die Presse,* November 26, 1953, p. 2.
13. *Salzburger Nachrichten,* December 15, 1953, p. 1.
14. *Salzburger Nachrichten,* December 15, 1953, p. 1.
15. Text of a speech delivered by Kraus to a mass meeting on January 22, 1954, *Die Neue Front,* January 23, 1954, p. 2.
16. V. Reimann, "Neues Verhältnis zu Deutschland," *Die Neue Front,* January 16, 1954, p. 1.
17. Text of a speech delivered by Kandutsch to a mass meeting on January 12, 1954, *Die Neue Front,* January 23, 1954, p. 2. The emphasis is Kandutsch's.
18. Evaluation by Dr. Kraus, personal interview.
19. H. A. Kraus, "Das Aktive Programm des VdU für 1954," *Die Neue Front,* January 1, 1954, p. 1.
20. *Die Neue Front,* May 22, 1954, p. 1.
21. *Ibid.* For the complete text of the *Ausseer Programm* see Appendix B.
22. See Paragraphs I and V, Appendix B.

23. See Paragraph IV, Appendix B.
24. Point 10 of the 1949 Program, See Appendix A.
25. See Paragraph II, Appendix B for the complete statement.
26. Point 12 of the 1949 Program, See Appendix A.
27. See Paragraph II, Appendix B.
28. See Paragraph III, Appendix B.
29. *Die Neue Front,* May 15, 1954, p. 1.
30. Pfeifer, p. 447.
31. *Die Neue Front,* September 4, 1954, p. 10.
32. *Die Neue Front,* October 16, 1954, p. 1.
33. *Die Neue Front,* October 13, 1954, Special Election Edition.
34. *Die Presse,* October 19, 1954, p. 1.
35. V. Reimann, "Mutlosigkeit der Entrechten," *Die Neue Front,* October 23, 1954, p. 1.
36. *Die Neue Front,* October 30, 1954, p. 1.
37. *Salzburger Nachrichten,* January 7, 1955, p. 2.
38. "National oder Sozial?," *Die Neue Front,* January 22, 1955, p. 1.
39. *Salzburger Nachrichten,* January 17, 1955, p. 2.
40. *Salzburger Nachrichten,* January 22/23, 1955, p. 2.
41. *Die Neue Front,* January 29, 1955, p. 1.
42. "Nationale drängen auf Auflösung des VdU," *Salzburger Nachrichten,* January 28, 1955, p. 2.
43. Eberhard Zwink, "Reinthallers Kraft," *Salzburger Nachrichten,* January 28, 1955, p. 1.
44. Text of a resolution passed by the general assembly, *Die Neue Front,* February 12, 1955, p. 2.
45. *Salzburger Nachrichten,* February 14, 1955, p. 2.
46. *Salzburger Nachrichten,* February 15, 1955, p. 2.
47. *Salzburger Nachrichten,* February 19/20, 1955, p. 4.
48. *Salzburger Nachrichten,* March 1, 1955, p. 2.
49. *Die Presse,* February 25, 1955, p. 1.
50. *Salzburger Nachrichten,* March 4, 1955, p. 2.
51. *Salzburger Nachrichten,* March 25, 1955, p. 2.
52. Stüber, co-founder with Ursin of the FSOe, although expressing sympathy for the new movement, made no recommendations and personally remained aloof from the FP. After failing to gain a leading position in the expanded "third force" he founded a new party with the dubious name DNAP (Demokratische Nationale Arbeiter Partei) which, after its total defeat in the *Nationalrat* election in 1956, disappeared without a trace. See *Salzburger Nachrichten,* January 9, 1956, p. 6.
53. *Salzburger Nachrichten,* March 10, 1955, p. 2 and statement by *Nationalrat* Zeillinger, personal interview.
54. *Salzburger Nachrichten,* March 14, 1955, p. 2.
55. *Die Presse,* April 5, 1955, p. 2.
56. *Ibid.*
57. *Die Presse,* April 26, 1955.
58. The Styrian and Vorarlberg elections are analyzed in *Die Neue Front,* April 9, 1955, p. 2; the Lower Austrian election in *Die Neue Front,* April 30, 1955, p. 1.

59. *Die Presse,* February 10, 1955, p. 1.
60. Actually most of the terms of the state treaty had been hammered out in arduous negotiations in the climate of Cold War beginning in 1947. An excellent book on these negotiations which appeared too late for serious consideration in this study is Gerald Stourzh, *Kleine Geschichte des Österreichischen Staatsvertrages, Mit Dokumententeil* (Graz: Styria Verlag, 1975).
61. *Salzburger Volkszeitung,* April 15, 1955, p. 1.
62. Schärf, *Österreichs Erneuerung,* p. 440.
63. The Nationalrat of the Republic of Austria, *Stenographisches Protokoll,* 66. Sitzung des Nationalrates der Republik Österreich, VII Gesetzgebungsperiode, April 28, 1955, pp. 1062–1063.
64. *Salzburger Nachrichten,* May 10, 1955, p. 2.
65. *Die Neue Front,* September 10, 1955, p. 2.
66. *Ibid.*
67. Pfeifer, p. 447.
68. *Salzburger Nachrichten,* October 19, 1955, p. 2.
69. *Die Presse,* October 25, 1955, p. 1.
70. *Salzburger Nachrichten,* October 19, 1955, p. 2.
71. *Die Neue Front,* October 22, 1955, p. 1.
72. "Kurzprogramm der Freiheitlichen Partei Österreichs," *Die Neue Front,* November 12, 1955, p. 1. See Appendix C.
73. Statement by *Nationalrat* Zeillinger, personal interview.
74. Pfeifer, p. 447.
75. Statement by *Nationalrat* Zeillinger, personal interview.
76. Statement by Dr. Reimann, personal interview.
77. Press Conference by Dr. Kraus, *Wiener Zeitung,* April 13, 1956, p. 2.
78. Statement by Dr. Reimann, personal interview.
79. Statements by Dr. Reimann and *Nationalrat* Zeillinger, personal interviews.

Chapter 8

1. *Salzburger Nachrichten,* October 14, 1968, p. 2.
2. *Volksblatt,* January 17, 1970, p. 1.
3. *Ibid.*
4. *Arbeiter Zeitung,* February 2, 1970, p. 3.
5. *Ibid.,* January 20, 1970, p. 2.
6. *Ibid.,* February 1, 1970, p. 1.
7. *Die Zeit* (Hamburg), July 16, 1971.
8. Election statistics derived from coverage by *Volksblatt* and *Arbeiter Zeitung* for both elections.
9. *Die Zeit,* July 9, 1974, p. 2.

Selected Bibliography

Primary Sources

1. Official Publications, Documentary Collections, Handbooks, and Unpublished Statistics

Adamovic, Ludwig (ed.). *Grundriss des Österreichischen Staatsrechtes: Verfassung und Verwaltungsrechte nach dem Stande der Gesetzgebung vom 1. August 1935*. Vienna: Druck und Verlag der Österreichischen Staatsdruckerei, 1935.

The Allied Commission for Austria. *Gazette of the Allied Commission for Austria*. Vienna: 1945–1955.

The Allied Commission for Austria. Minutes of the Meetings of the Allied Council. *Eight Reels of Allied Council (ALCO) and Fifteen Reels of Executive Committee (EXCO) Minutes (M) and U.S. Unofficial Minutes (UM)*. Washington and Vienna, Austria: Microfilmed with the cooperation of the United States Department of State and the Austrian State Archives, 1958–1960.

Keesings Archiv der Gegenwart. Vienna: Siegler Verlag, 1946ff.

Marvich, Waine, et al. *Wahlrecht*, Vol. I, *Wahlwerber*, Vol. II, and *Wahlstatistik*, Vol. III of *Wahlen und Parteien in Österreich: Österreichisches Wahlhandbuch*. Vienna: Österreichischer Bundesverlag, Verlag für Jugend und Volk, 1966.

The Nationalrat of the Republic of Austria. *Beilagen zu den Stenographischen Protokollen des Nationalrates der Republik Österreich*. Vienna: Österreichisches Staatsdruckerei, 1946ff.

The Nationalrat of the Republic of Austria. *Nationalrat und Bundesrat: Büro, Mitglieder, Ausschüsse, Klubs*. Vienna: Österreichische Staatsdruckerei, 1947ff.

The Nationalrat of the Republic of Austria. *Stenographisches Protokoll... Sitzung des Nationalrates der Republik Österreich*. Vienna: Österreichische Staatsdruckerei, 1945ff.

Oberleitner, Wolfgang (ed.). *Politisches Handbuch der Republik Österreich 1945–1960*. Vienna: Guardaval; Vereinigung zur Herausgabe von Zeitungen und Zeitschriften Gesellschaft M.B.H., 1960.

The Press Service of the Republic of Austria. *Österreichisches Jahrbuch 1949 nach ämtlichen Quellen*. ed. Bundespressedienst. Vienna: Druck und Verlag der Österreichischen Staatsdruckerei, 1950.

The Provincial Government of Lower Austria. *Die Wahlen in den Bundesländern seit 1945: Nationalrat und Landtage*. Vienna: Selbstverlag, 1962.

The Provincial Government of Salzburg. *Die Landtagswahlen im Bundesland Salzburg 1945–1959.* Vol. III of *Salzburger Landesstatistik.* ed. Amt der Salzburger Landesregierung, Abteilung X, vols. ff. Salzburg: Salzburger Landesstatistik, 1962. (Unpublished, mimeographed.)

The Provincial Government of Salzburg. *Die Gemeinderatswahlen im Bundesland Salzburg 1949–1962.* Vol. IV of *Salzburger Landesstatistik.* ed. Amt der Salzburger Landesregierung, Abteilung X, vols. ff. Salzburg: Salz: burger Landesstatistik, 1962. (Unpublished, mimeographed.)

The Provincial Government of Salzburg. *Die Nationalratswahlen in Salzburg 1945–1962.* Vol. V of *Salzburger Landesstatistik.* ed. Amt der Salzburger Landesregierung, Abteilung X, vols. ff. Salzburg: Salzburger Landesstatistik, 1962. (Unpublished, mimeographed.)

The Provincial Government of Salzburg. *Die Nationalratswahl am 22. Februar 1953: Wahlergebnisse von Stadt und Land Salzburg. Gesamt ergebnis von Österreich.* Amtsblatt der Landeshauptstadt, 4. Jahrgang, Nr. 9. Salzburg: 1953.

2. *Memoirs, Speeches and Collected Writings*

Fischer, Ernst. *Das Jahr der Befreiung: Aus Reden und Aufsätzen.* Vienna: Stern Verlag, 1946.

Gruber, Karl. *Zwischen Befreiung und Freiheit: Der Sonderfall Österreichs.* Vienna: Ullstein Verlag, 1953.

Hannak, Jacques (ed.). *Leopold Figl: Reden für Österreich.* Vienna: Europa Verlag, 1965.

Hannak, Jacques (ed.). *Oskar Helmer: Ausgewählte Reden und Schriften.* Vienna: Europa Verlag, 1965.

Helmer, Oskar. *Fünfzig Jahre Erlebte Geschichte.* Vienna: Verlag der Wiener Buchhandlung, 1957.

Malata, Alfred. *Entscheidung für Morgen: Christliche Demokratie im Herzen Europas.* Vienna: Fritz Molden Verlag, 1968.

Pfeifer, Helfried. "Österreichs Parteien und Parlament," *Jahrbuch des öffentlichen Rechtes der Gegenwart,* XI, vols. ff. Tübingen: J.C.B. Mohr (P. Siebeck), 1962, pp. 417–475.

Pittermann, Bruno (ed.). *Mensch und Staat: Handbuch der österreichischen Politik.* 2 vols. Vienna: Danubia Verlag, 1962.

Raab, Julius. *Selbstportrait einer Politiker.* Vienna: Europa Verlag, 1965.

Raab, Julius. *Verantwortung für Österreich.* Vienna: Österreichischer Wirtschaftsverlag, 1961.

Renner, Karl. *Denkschrift über die Geschichte der Unabhängigkeitserklärung Österreichs.* Zurich: Europa Verlag, 1946.

Renner, Karl. *Österreich von der Ersten zur Zweiten Republik.* Vienna: Verlag der Wiener Volksbuchhandlung, 1960.

Schärf, Adolf. *April 1945 in Wien.* Vienna: Verlag der Wiener Volksbuchhandlung, 1948.

Schärf, Adolf. *Österreichs Erneuerung 1945–1955: Das erste Jahrzehnte der Zweiten Republik.* 7th ed. Vienna: Verlag der Wiener Volksbuchhandlung, 1955.

Schärf, Adolf. *Zwischen Demokratie und Volksdemokratie: Österreichs Wiederaufrichtung im Jahre 1945.* Vienna: Verlag der Wiener Volksbuchhandlung, 1960.

Weinberger, Lois. *Tatsachen, Begegnungen und Gespräche: Ein Buch um Österreich.* Vienna: Österreichischer Verlag, 1948.

3. Newspapers

AKTION für soziale Erneuerung, Vienna. Weekly organ of Aktion zur politischen Erneuerung.

Alpenruf: Unabhängiges Wochenblatt für Heimatpolitik, Graz. After 1949 affiliated with, but never an official organ of the Verband der Unabhängigen.

Arbeiter Zeitung: Zentralorgan der Sozialistischen Partei Österreichs, Vienna.

Demokratisches Volksblatt: Organ der Sozialistischen Partei Salzburgs.

Freie Stimmen Österreichs: Kampfblatt für nationale Politik, Vienna. Weekly organ of the Freiheitliche Sammlung Österreichs (FSOe).

Kleines Volksblatt, Vienna. Daily Viennese organ of the Österreichisches Volkspartei.

Österreichische Allgemeine Zeitung, Salzburg. Daily organ affiliated with the Verband der Unabhängigen.

Österreichischer Beobachter: Kampfblatt der Nationalen Liga, Vienna. Weekly organ of the Nationale Liga.

Österreichische Volksstimme: Zentralorgan der Kommunistischenpartei Österreichs, Vienna.

Die Presse: Morgenblatt, Vienna.

Die Neue Front: Zeitung der Unabhänigen, Salzburg. Central weekly organ of the Verband der Unabhängigen.

The New York Times.

Salzburger Volkszeitung. Affiliated with the Österreichische Volkspartei.

Salzburger VdU-Nachrichten: Kampfblatt der national-freiheitlichen Bevölkerung Salzburgs. After 1956 known as the *Salzburger FPOe-Nachrichten.*

Salzburger Volksblatt.

Salzburger Nachrichten: Unabhängige Demokratische Zeitung.

Stimme Salzburg: Berichte und Kommentare aus Politik, Wirtschaft und Kultur.

Salzburger Neue Zeit und Tagblatt. Daily Salzburg organ of the Kommunistischenpartei Österreichs.

Die Union: Wochenblatt der Demokratischen Union, Vienna.

Unser Weg, Salzburg. Quarterly organ of the Verband der Unabhängigen Jugend.

Wiener Illustrierte.

Wiener Kurier. Organ of the American Occupation Authorities.

Wiener Tageszeitung: Zentralorgan der Österreichischen Volkspartei.

Wiener Zeitung. Official newspaper of the Austrian Government.

4. Political Periodicals

Berichte und Informationen des Österreichischen Forschungsinstituts für Wirtschaft und Politik, Salzburg.
Österreichische Monatshefte: Blätter für Politik, Vienna. Monthly ideological organ of the OeVP.
Welt der Arbeit: Sozialistische Betriebszeitung, Vienna. Bimonthly Socialist industrial periodical.
Die Zukunft: Sozialistische Monatsschrift für Politik und Kultur. Monthly ideological organ of the SPOe.

5. Other Primary Sources: Unpublished

Personal letter from A. Taylor Milne, Secretary and Librarian of the Institute of Historical Research, University of London, of December 23, 1968, quoting the reminiscences of Mr. D. C. Watt, a member of the British Intelligence Corps in Austria during the time of occupation.
Personal interview with Dr. Herbert Kraus, April 4, 1969, in the offices of Donau Finanz, Vienna.
Personal interview with Dr. Viktor Reimann, December 11, 1968, Cafe Mozart, Vienna.
Personal interview with *Nationalrat* Gustav Zeillinger, January 19, 1969, Cafe Bazar, Salzburg.

Secondary Sources

1. Books and Monographs

Ableitinger, Alfred. *Liberalismus-Nationalismus-nationale Strömungen.* Vol. IV of the Retzhofschriften. vols. ff. Graz: Selbstverlag, 1968.
Andics, Helmut. *50 Jahre Unseres Lebens: Österreichs Schicksal seit 1918.* Vienna: Verlag Fritz Molden, 1962.
Andics, Helmut. *Staat, den keiner wollte.* Vienna: Verlag Fritz Molden, 1962.
Ausch, Karl. *Österreichs Wirtschaft seit 1945.* Vienna: Europa Verlag, 1963.
Bader, William B. *Austria between East and West 1945-1955.* Stanford: Stanford University Press, 1966.
Benedikt, Heinrich (ed.). *Geschichte der Republik Österreich.* Vienna: Verlag für Geschichte und Politik, 1954.
Braunthal, Julius. *The Tragedy of Austria.* London: V. Gollancz, 1948.
Ciller, Alois. *Die Vorläufer des Nationalsozialismus: Geschichte und Entwicklung der nationalen Arbeiterbewegung im deutschen Grenzland.* Vienna: Ertl Verlag, 1932.

Diamant, Alfred. *Austrian Catholics and the First Republic.* Princeton, N.J.: Princeton University Press, 1960.
Eichstädt, Ulrich. *Von Dolfuss zu Hitler: Geschichte des Anschlusses Österreichs 1933-1938.* Wiesbaden: F. Steiner, 1955.
Eisenberg, Dennis. *The Reemergence of Fascism.* New York: A. S. Barnes and Co., 1968.
Funder, Friedrich. *Als Österreich den Sturm Bestand: Aus der Ersten in die Zweite Republik.* Vienna: Herold Verlag, 1957.
Goldinger, Walter. *Geschichte der Republik Österreich.* Vienna: Verlag für Geschichte und Politik, 1962.
Gulick, Charles A. *Austria from Habsburg to Hitler.* 2 vols. Berkeley: University of California Press, 1948.
Hammerschmidt, Helmut, and Michael Mansfield. *Der Kurs ist Falsch.* Heft XI of Europaische Dokumente: Kulturschriftenreihe des Verlages Kurt Desch. vols. ff. Munich: Verlag Kurt Desch, 1956.
Hannak, Jacques. *Karl Renner und seine Zeit: Versuch einer Biographie.* Vienna: Europa Verlag, 1965.
Hannak, Jacques. *Vier Jahre Zweite Republik: Ein Rechenschaftsbericht der Sozialistischen Partei.* Vienna: Verlag der Wiener Volksbuchhandlung, 1949.
Hantsch, Hugo. *Die Geschichte Österreichs.* 2 vols. Graz: Steirische Verlagsanstalt, 1947.
Hantsch, Hugo. *Die Nationalitätenfrage im Alten Österreich: Das Problem der konstruktiven Reichsstaltung.* Vienna: Verlag Herold, 1953.
Hindels, Josef, "Nationale Strömungen," in *Bestandaufnahme Österreich 1945-1963.* ed. Jacques Hannak. Vienna: Forum Verlag, 1963. Pp. 83-111.
Hiscocks, Richard. *Österreichs Wiedergeburt.* trans. from the English by Inge Lehne. Vienna: Hermes Verlag, 1954.
Jaszi, Oscar. *The Dissolution of the Habsburg Monarchy.* Chicago: The University of Chicago Press, 1929.
Jedlicka, Ludwig. *Ein Heer im Schatten der Parteien: die militärpolitische Lage Österreich 1918-1938.* Graz: H. Böhlaus, 1955.
Kann, Robert A. *The Habsburg Monarchy: A Study in Integration and Disintegration.* New York: Praeger, 1957.
Kann, Robert A. *The Multinational Empire: Nationalism and National Reform in the Habsburg Monarchy 1848-1919.* New York: Octagon Press, 1964.
Klenner, Fritz. *Die Österreichischen Gewerkschaften.* 2 vols. Vienna: Verlag des Österreichischen Gewerkschaftsbundes, 1951, 1953.
Klenner, Fritz. *Putsch Versuch — Oder Nicht?* Vienna: Pressreferat des Österreichischen Gewerkschaftsbundes, 1950.
Kohn, Hans. *The Idea of Nationalism: A Study in its Origins and its Background.* New York: Macmillan & Co., 1961.
Mikoletzky, Hans Leo. *Österreichische Zeitgeschichte: Vom Ende der Monarchie bis zum Abschluss des Staatsvertrages 1955.* Vienna: Österreichischer Bundesverlag, 1962.
Nolte, Ernst. *Three Faces of Fascism: Action Francaise: Italian Fascism: National Socialism.* trans. from the German by Leila Lennewitz. New York: Holt, Rinehart and Winston, 1966.

Pulzer, P. G. *The Rise of Political Anti-Semitism in Germany and Austria.* New York: John Wiley & Sons, 1964.
Reichhold, Ludwig. *Zwanzig Jahre Zweite Republik: Österreich findet zu sich selbst.* Vienna: Herder Verlag, 1965.
Schroth, Alois. *Das Nationalsozialistengesetz.* 7. Vortrag erster Gewerkschaftlicherkurs. Vienna: Selbstverlag der Gewerkschaft der öffentlichen Angestellten, 1947.
Schorske, Carl E. "Politics in a New Key: Schönerer," in *The Responsibility of Power.* ed. Leonard Krieger and Fritz Stern. New York: Doubleday & Co., 1969.
Schuschnigg, Kurt. *My Austria.* trans. from the German by John Segrue. New York: A. A. Knopf, 1938.
Schuschnigg, Kurt. *Austrian Requiem.* trans. from the German by Franz von Hildebrand. New York: G. P. Putnam's Sons, 1946.
Seltenreich, Susan. *Leopold Figil: Austrian Patriot and Statesman.* Vienna: Erwin Mitlen Verlag, 1966.
Shell, Kurt L. *The Transformation of Austrian Socialism.* New York: State University of New York, 1962.
Shepherd, Gordon Brook. *Der Anschluss.* trans. from the English by Gerolf Coudenhove. Graz: Verlag Styria, 1963.
Shepherd, Gordon Brook. *Die Österreichische Odyssee.* trans. from the English by Johann Heinrich Blumenthal. Vienna: Quintus Verlag, 1958.
Siegler, Heinrich. *Österreichs Weg zur Souveränität, Neutralität und Prosperität 1945-1959.* Vienna: Verlag für Zeitarchiv, 1959.
Stearman, William Lloyd. *Die Sowjetunion und Österreich 1945-1955: Ein Beispiel für die Sowjetpolitik gegenüber dem Westen.* trans. from the English by Hanswilhelm Häfs. Vienna: Verlag für Zeitarchiv, 1962.
Veiter, Theodor. *Gesetz als Unrecht: Die Österreichische Nationalsozialistengesetzgebung.* Vienna: Verlag Wilhelm Braumüller, 1949.
Vodopivec, Alexander. *Wer Regiert in Österreich?* 2 vols. Vienna: Verlag für Geschichte und Politik, 1960, 1962.
Vodopivec, Alexander. *Die Balkanisierung Österreichs: Folgen einer grossen Koalition.* Vienna: Verlag Fritz Molden, 1966.
Wandruska, Adam. "Österreichs politische Struktur: Die Entwicklung der Parteien und politischen Bewegungen," *Geschichte der Republik Österreich.* ed. Heinrich Benedikt. Vienna: Verlag für Geschichte und Politik, 1954. Pp. 291-485.
Whiteside, Andrew. "Austria," *The European Right: A Historical Profile.* eds. Hans Rogger and Eugene Weber. Berkeley and Los Angeles: University of California Press, 1966.
Whiteside, Andrew. *Austrian National Socialism before 1918.* The Hague: Martinus Nijhoff, 1962.
Zöllner, Erich. *Geschichte Österreichs von den Anfängen bis zur Gegenwart.* 3d ed. Vienna: Verlag für Geschichte und Politik, 1966.

2. Periodical Literature

Karbach, Oscar. "The Founder of Political Anti-Semitism: Georg von Schönerer," *Jewish Social Studies,* VII (January, 1945), pp. 3–30.

Kuhnelt-Leddihn, Erik. "The Bohemian Background of National Socialism," *Journal of the History of Ideas,* IX (June, 1948), pp. 339–371.

MacCormac, John. "The Improbable Coalition that rules Austria," *The Reporter,* XVIII (January 23, 1958), pp. 33–36.

Secher, Herbert P. "Representative Democracy or 'Chamber State.' The Ambiguous Role of Interest Groups in Austrian Politics," *The Western Political Quarterly,* XIII, No. 4 (December, 1960), pp. 890–909.

Simon, Walter B. "Politische Ethik und Politische Struktur," *Kölner Zeitschrift füt Soziologie und Sozialpsychologie,* XI (1959), pp. 450–454.

Sugar, Peter F. "The Rise of Nationalism in the Habsburg Empire," *Austrian History Yearbook,* III (1967), pp. 91–120.

Whiteside, Andrew G. "The Deutsche Arbeiterpartei 1904–1918: A Contribution to the Origins of Fascism," *Austrian History Newsletter,* IV (1963), pp. 3–14.

Zöllner, Erich. "The Germans as an Integrating and Disintegrating Force," *Austrian History Yearbook,* III (1967), pp. 201–233.

Index

Action for Political Renewal: emerges out of the OeVP Youth Front, 113; negotiations for fusion with the VdU, 113-116, 132-133; election of 1953, 116, 118-119; supports Reinthaller, 148; mentioned, 118-119, 124, 129-131, 150. See also Youth Front.

Anschluss: nullified by Moscow Declaration of the Allied Powers, 12; mentioned, 2, 3, 6-8, 11, 19, 28, 54, 58, 60, 120, 147, 151.

Allied Council: first meeting of, 20; Proclamation to the Austrian people, 20-21, 63; acceptance of first Austrian government, 25; protest about de-Nazification, 30; approval of 1947 de-Nazification Law, 30; control over party political activity, ix, 21, 30, 36, 41-42, 44, 47-49, 68; reaction to the founding of the VdU, 42-44; reaction to Soviet charge that the VdU was guilty of Nazi activity, 192n-193n; Chancellor Figil protests Soviet aid to the Communist putsch attempt of 1950 to, 90, 194n; mentioned, 22-23, 36, 41-42, 56.

Alpenruf, Der (independent but pro-VdU newspaper in Graz), 50

Anticlericalism, 3, 6, 8, 16, 24, 30, 46, 52, 57, 131, 135, 143, 166. See also *Freiheitlich.*

Association of German Nationalists, 5.

Association of those loyal to the Constitution, 36, 37.

Austrian Resistance Movement, 12, 40, 42.

Balance on the political scale, 7, 26, 68, 77, 121, 127, 130, 164-168.

Belastete (incriminated) National Socialists: as specified by the Law about the treatment of Nationalists, 30; mentioned, 112.

Breitner, Dr. Burghard (presidential candidate of the VdU and other independent groups in 1951), 97-107, 111-114.

Canal, Dr. Ludwig (Chairman of the Burghard Breitner for President Committee): as organizer of the presidential campaign of 1951, 195n; in *Landtag* election in Tyrol in 1953, 135; joins with Reinthaller in forming the *Freiheitspartei* in 1956, 150.

Canaval, Gustav (editor of the *Salzburger Nachrichten*): opposes de-Nazification laws, 33, 187n; defects from the VdU, 45; leads campaign for the election of Burghard Breitner to president, 100; analyzes the presidential run-off election of 1951, 106; mentioned, 31.

Christian Socialist Party (forerunner of the Austrian Peoples Party during the First Republic): resistance movement, 15; reorganized as the Austrian Peoples Party, 15; mentioned, 6-9, 11-12.

Clark, General Mark (U.S. High Commissioner in the Allied Council), 50.

Coalition Pacts: of 1945, 16, 24-25, 52; of 1949, 74, 76-77, 192n; dissolution of, 115, 117; of 1953, 124-127, 185n; of 1962, 163; an end to, 164.

Committee of above party Unity (Burghard Breitner, or BB Committee), 97-99, 101-104, 107-108, 135, 150.

Communist putsch of 1950: VdU action in, 89; mentioned, 87-91.

Conference of the Provinces, 21, 22.

Demokratur, 27, 186n, 33, 76, 127, 129, 163.

De-Nazification: required by the Allied Council, 21; review of by Allied Council, 30, 186n; Verbot Law of 1945, 29–30, 32–33; results of, 29–30, 63; 1947 Law about the treatment of National Socialists, 30, 34, 125, 160; modification of, 77–78; opposition to, 32–33, 38, 41, 57–60, 113; easing of, 147, 161; mentioned, ix–x, 21, 23, 28, 38, 41, 43, 51, 53, 56–61, 74.

Elections: parliamentary of 1945, 23, 24; campaign of 1949, 39, 49–74; results of 1949, 66, 69, 70–73, 107; industrial council of 1949, 78–79, 104; presidential campaign of 1951, 95–101; presidential results, 101, 105, 107, 196n, 111; VdU calls for new parliamentary, 111, 113, 115, 118; campaign of 1953, 116–121; 1953 results, 121–123; Salzburg *Gemeinderat* of 1953, 135; Tyrolean *Landtag* of 1953, 135; *Landtag* and *Gemeinderat* of 1954, 143–146, 154; *Gemeinderat* in Lower Austria, Styria in 1955, 151–152; *Landtag* in Upper Austria in 1955, 155–156; Parliament, 1956, 161–162; Parliament, 1962, 163; Parliament, 1966, 164; Parliament, 1970, 165–166; Parliament, 1971, 167.

Election Law: franchise, ix, 23, 26, 30, 34, 41; presidential of 1929, 92; of 1920, 92–93; of 1951, 94.

Europeanism: expressed as international *Volkstum,* 55, 109, 130; and the State Treaty, 153–154; mentioned, 26, 56, 60–61, 111–113, 119–120, 128, 133–134, 139, 142–143.

Figl, Leopold (OeVP Chairman and Austrian Chancellor): meeting with Helmer to reestablish government for Lower Austria in April 1945, 13; negotiations for fusion of the OeVP with the Tyrolean Party, 22; forms a government, 1945, 24–25; 1949, 74; declaration of government, 1949, 75; resigns as chancellor, 115; attempts to form a government, 1953, 124; loses party support, 126; mentioned, 21, 186n, 40, 125, 152.

Fischer, Ernst (Prominent Austrian Communist), 16.

FPOe *(Freiheitliche Partei Oesterreichs):* preliminary organization of, 148–150, 154; initial organization as *Freiheitspartei,* 150–151; negotiations with the VdU, 151, 154–155; consolidation with the VdU, 155; constitution as a political party, 157; General Constituent Assembly of, 158; Program of, 157, 180–182; in elections, 1955, 155–157; 1962, 163; 1969, 164; 1970, 166; denounced by Kraus, 158–159; negotiations with the SPOe for a small coalition, 163–164; support of SPOe, 166–167; 1968 convention, 164–165.

Freiheitlich (free thinking), 111, 134, 139, 142–145, 148, 155, 157. See also anti-clericalism and national-liberal principles.

FSOe *(Freiheitliche Sammlung Oesterreichs):* founded by Stüber and Ursin in 1953, 139–140; negotiations with the VdU for cooperation in 1954 elections, 144; absorbed by the *Freiheitspartei,* 151; mentioned, 143–144.

FDP (Free Democratic Party), 111.

Gleissner, Dr. Heinrich (OeVP candidate for the presidency in 1951), 94, 96, 100–108, 110, 196n.

Gollob, Col. Gordon (VdU General Secretary): as nationalist orator, 63; challenges moderate leadership, 81, 83, 84–85, 110; expelled, 84; elected deputy chairman, 86–87; bolts 1951 general assembly, 110; mentioned, 51, 140.

Graf, Ferdinand (OeVP leader and Austrian State Secretary), 40, 45.

Gredler, Wilfred (leader of Action), 113, 124, 132, 150, 157–158.

Grossdeutsch sentiment, 2, 3, 28, 37, 53–58, 78, 83–84, 109, 114, 143.

Grossdeutsche Volkspartei (precursor of the VdU during the First Republic): absorbed by the NSDAP, 9; mentioned, 7–8, 183n, 27.

Gruber, Dr. Karl (OeVP leader and Austrian Foreign Minister): negotiations with Renner about the inclusion of western representatives in the provisional government, 21; negotiations with the OeVP for the inclusion of the Tyrolean Party, 22; appeal to western Allies for aid in the Communist putsch of 1950, 89, 91; protests to Soviet occupation authorities about the obstructionism of the Red Army, 91; mentioned, 94, 95.

Hartleb, Karl (VdU leader): elected deputy chairman of the VdU, 44; coauthor of the 1949 VdU program, 46; reelected deputy chairman 1950, 86; as the balancing force in the VdU executive committee, 87; critical of Kraus, 110, 115; elected Third President of the Nationalrat, 1953, 125; negotiations with Reinthaller, 151; mentioned, 76, 150.

Heger, Josef (VdU leader): resigns to form the *Nationaldemokratischer Verband,* 82.

Helmer, Oskar (SPOe leader and Austrian Minister of Interior): meeting with Figil to restore government for Lower Austria in April, 1945, 13; encourages a new, middle-class party, 36, 42; as protector of the VdU, 48–49, 62–63, 65; challenges the right of the Allied Council to forbid new political parties, 48, 62; dissolves the Styrian VdU for neo-Nazi activity, 84.

Hümer, Oskar (VdU leader in Upper Austria), 80–83.

Hurdes, Felix (OeVP leader and Austrian Minister of Education), 56, 124.

Kandutsch, Jörg (VdU leader): elected as deputy chairman, 1951, 110; 1952, 116; 1953, 132; mentioned, 140–141.

KdU: *Klub der Unabhängigen* (VdU parliamentary faction), 75–77, 117, 130, 132.

Konev, Marshal Ivan (Soviet High Commissioner in the Allied Council), 20, 22.

Koplenig, Johann (Austrian Communist), 16.

Körner, Theodor (SPOe leader and Austrian President): becomes mayor of Vienna, 1945, in presidential election of 1951, 94, 100–106, 196n, 115, 124, 126.

KPOe (Communist Party of Austria): and the formation of the provisional government, 14, 16, 18–19; sanctioned by the Allied Council, 21; demands disenfranchisement of former Nazis, 23; in first Austrian government, 25; opposition to VdU, 43–44; in 1949 election, 66; attempted putsch of 1950, 87–92; endorsement of SPOe candidate Körner for the presidency in 1951, 103; mentioned, 22, 34.

Kraus, Dr. Herbert (co-founder of the VdU): founds Austrian Research Institute for Economics and Politics, 33; opposes de-Nazification laws, 34; public opinion polls on political climate, 34–35, 37, 59; criticizes the *Proporz,* 34; posits a program for a new, fourth party, 35–37; supports the creation of a new party, 37; at the Congress of those without a Party, 39–40; founds the VdU, 44; accused of violating the de-Nazification laws, 42–43, 63; elected chairman of VdU, 44; negotiates with the SPOe for participation in government, 49; forbids negotiations for the ex-Nazi vote, 58, 84; contacted by OeVP for inclusion in the government, 65; statement of parliamentary policy, 75; leadership challenged, 83–96, 108–111; reelected chairman, 1950, 86, 1951, 110; opposes government's 1950 wage-price agreement, 88; endorses Burghard Breitner for president, 97; *Presse* article endorsing Gleissner in the 1951 presidential run-off election, 105, 110; enunciates VdU goals for 1952, 111–112; negotiates with Action for fusion with VdU, 114–116, 131–133; withdraws as chairman of VdU in 1952, 116; elected deputy chairman, 116; reelected deputy chairman, 1953, 132; on inclusion of the VdU in the government coalition, 1953, 124-125, 129; reelected chairman of KdU, 1953, 130; declines reelection as deputy chairman, 1954, 141; resigns from FPOe, 158; denounces FPOe, 158-159; mentioned, 45, 50, 189n, 51, 190n, 64, 67, 76, 80-82, 117, 140, 157, 160.

Kreisky, Dr. Bruno (SPOe leader and Austrian State Secretary, later Chancellor), 152, 165-167.

Landbund (Agrarian League during the First Republic): decision not to reactivate in 1945, 16; mentioned, 8, 183n, 30, 37, 40, 44, 54, 58.

League of Independents (VdU: Verband der Unabhängigen): founding of, 40; American, British, French and Soviet policies on, 42-43; Allied Council reaction to the founding of, 44; Statutes of, 44; registers with the Allied Council, 45; 1949 "Action Program" of, 46, 169-174; financial support of, 44, 46-47, 189n, 65; opposition to de-Nazification laws, 41-42, 51, 57-59; as an electoral party *(Wahlpartei),* 48-49; defections from, 45, 80-84, 139-141, 148-151, 154-155; negotiations with the SPOe, 49; election campaign of 1949, 49-66; issue of inclusion in government, 49, 74, 115, 124, 130; denied entrance into government, 74, 127; election campaign of 1949, 49 66, constituency in the 1949 election, 52-62; accused of neo-Nazism, 46, 51, 62-68, 76, 84, 111; mass meeting as a campaign weapon, 50-51, 190n, 140; appeal to *Grossdeutschen,* 53, 78; peasants, 54; German nationalists, 54-57, 119-120, 128, 134-135, 140-142; anti-clericals, 57; ex-Nazis, 57-60, 140, 144-145, 147-148; veterans, 59; youth, 59-60; *Volksdeutschen,* 53, 60-61, 78, 118; 1949 election results, 69-73; loss of worker support in 1950, 79-81; organizational crises, 80-87, 108-111, 115, 131, 139-140, 145, 147-151, 154-155, 157-160; in the presidential campaign of 1951, 94-106; negotiations with the OeVP in the presidential campaign of 1951, 95; endorses Burghard Breitner for president, 97; stance in presidential run-off election of 1951, 101-105; discussions with OeVP for supporting Gleissner, 102; negotiations for fusion with Action, 113-116, 132-133; in elections of 1953, 116, 118-121, 128, 135-139; Ausseer Program of 1954, 142-144, 150, 175-179; 1954 *Landtag* elections, 144-146; negotiations with Anton Reinthaller, 148, 151, 155; dilemma on State Treaty, 153-154; absorption into the FPOe, 157-158; General Assemblies of, 1949, 44; 1950, 85-87; 1951, 109-111; 1952, 115-116; 1953, 131-132; Bad Aussee Convention, 1954, 141-144; Extraordinary Convention of 1955, 147-149; mentioned, x, 183n, 43, 76, 80, 107, 159-160, 163, 167-168.

Minderbelastete (less incriminated) National Socialists: as amnestied by the Law about the treatment of National Socialists, 30; VdU appeal to, 57-60; influence on election of 1949, 67, 69-73; mentioned, 34. See also de-Nazification.

Mitteleuropa, 2-3, 28, 134.

Moscow Declaration of 1943, 12, 19-20, 183n.

McCreery (British High Commissioner in the Allied Council), 20.

National-liberal principles: 1949 VdU program statement of, 46, 52, 54-57, 170; 1954 Ausseer Program statement of, 142-143, 174-176; role of in 1949 election, 67-68; role of in 1951 presidential election, 104, 106; role of in 1953 election, 119-121; role of in 1954 *Landtag* elections, 144-145; an end to as a political issue, 165; mentioned, x, 3, 5, 7, 9-10, 16, 24, 27, 30-31, 43, 52, 54-55, 57-58, 61, 104, 106, 130, 142-143, 147-150, 154-157, 159, 163. See also *freiheitlich.*

Nationale Liga, 82, 135–136.

Neue Front, Die (Party Organ of VdU): founded, 44, 189n; confiscation of, 62–63; moratorium on in presidential election of 1951, 94–95; analysis of 1951 presidential election run-off, 106; *völkisch* articles in, 108–109, 133; redefinition of VdU ideology, 140; mentioned, 64, 68, 80, 118, 120, 152, 157.

Neo-Nazism: as a campaign issue, 23, 62–66; significance in 1949 election, 67; Styrian VdU dissolved for, 84; Allied Council position on charge against VdU, 192–193n; as an issue in the 1951 presidential campaign, 99–100, 121; mentioned, 33, 36–37, 41–49, 51, 58, 61, 68, 76, 78, 84, 111, 159.

Neuwirth, Thomas (VdU leader): elected deputy chairman, 86; mentioned, 130.

O 5 (Austrian resistance group), 14, 184n, 15, 21, 28.

Österreichische Allgemeine Zeitung: founded, 50.

OeVP (Austrian Peoples Party): founded, 15, 16; negotiations on a new provisional government, 18; sanctioned by the Allied Council, 21; opposition to disenfranchisement of former Nazis, 23; campaign of 1945, 24; in first Austrian government, 24; cooperation with the SPOe in socialization programs, 31–32; supported by *Minderbelasteten,* 34; on accommodating the "third force" within the party, 40, 133; opposition to the formation of a new, fourth party, 36, 44; attitude toward the VdU, 41–42, 45, 47–48, 114–115; appeal to ex-Nazis, 42, 63, 121; accuses VdU of neo-Nazism, 46–49, 51, 58, 62–65, 99; attitude towards inclusion of the VdU in the government, 65, 74, 115, 120–121, 124, 125; in 1949 election results, 66, 68; position on the manner of selecting a president, 93–94; seeks VdU support in presidential election of 1951, 95, 102–104, 108, 110; presidential campaign of 1951, 99–100, 102–105; in elections of 1953, 117–121, 135–138; negotiations on a new coalition in 1953, 124–127, 130; coalition of 1962, 163; majority government 1966–1970, 164; mentioned, 33, 36, 40, 46–47, 49, 54, 57, 112–113, 145, 147, 165–168.

Pan-German, 4, 5, 6, 37, 43, 76.

Party of those without a Party: congress of the, 39–40; mentioned, 32, 33.

Peter, Friedrich (FPOe Chairman), 155, 163–164.

Pfeifer, Dr. Helfried (VdU leader): suggests the VdU run as a *Wahlpartei,* 48–49; mentioned, 51, 63, 76, 144.

Proclamation to the Austrian People, 20, 21.

Proporz: the beginning of, 19, 24–25; opposition to, 31, 41; VdU interest in joining, 117; an end to, 163–164; mentioned, 27, 32, 34, 41, 74, 118, 127, 143, 147, 153, 159.

Provisional government: maneuvers for representation in, 14; declaration of, 19; relations with provisional provincial governments, 21; inclusion of "westerners" in, 22–23; calls for elections, 23; mentioned, 18, 20–21, 25, 29.

Raab, Julius (OeVP leader and Austrian Chancellor): negotiates the 1953 coalition, 125; made chancellor-designate by OeVP, 126; negotiates the Austrian State Treaty, 152; mentioned, 64, 126–127, 152, 155.

Red Army: liberation of Vienna, 13; harassment of VdU, 43–44; aid to Communist putsch attempt of 1950, 89–91, 193n; mentioned, 14, 16–17, 19, 44.

Reinthaller, Anton (FPOe founder), 147–150, 155, 157–158, 163.

Reimann, Dr. Viktor (co-founder of VdU): assistant editor of the *Salzburger Nachrichten,* opposes de-Nazification laws, 33, 187n, 42, 57–58, 60, 63; accused of Nazi sympathies, 63; begins publication of the VdU organ, *Die Neue Front*, 44; elected deputy chairman of VdU, 44; co-author of 1949 "Action Program of the VdU," 46; attempts to resolve organizational crisis in Upper Austria, 81; leadership challenged, 83–86; declines to continue as deputy chairman, 86–87; endorses Körner for president, 105; analyzes the 1951 presidential run-off election results, 106–107, 196n; on German nationalism, 109, 120, 140; retires from political activity, 158–159; mentioned, 45, 49–51, 190n, 66–67, 76, 80, 82, 110, 121, 141, 145, 157, 160.

Renner, Dr. Karl (SPOe leader, Austrian State Chancellor, and later President): as state chancellor of the provisional government, 17–18; declaration of the independence of the Second Austrian Republic, 19; dissolves the provisional government, 25; dies, 92; mentioned, 20, 184n, 23, 92, 94.

Salzburg Circle, 35, 40.

Salzburger Nachrichten (independent Salzburg daily): as impetus for the independent party movement, 31–32, 34, 36; supports the election of an above-party president, 94, 97, 100–101, 107; analysis of the presidential run-off election of 1951, 106–107, 196n; mentioned, 110, 148.

Schönerer, see von Schönerer, Georg.

Schärf, Dr. Adolf (SPOe Chairman and Austrian Vice-Chancellor): becomes chairman of SPOe in 1945, 15; negotiates with the VdU for inclusion in a coalition, 49; rejects VdU participation in a coalition government, 74; negotiates a coalition pact with the OeVP, 74; becomes vice-chancellor, 1949, 74; proposes a means of selecting the president in joint session of the parliament, 93; resigns as vice-chancellor in 1953, 115; mentioned, 14–15, 18, 49, 66, 92–93, 126, 152.

Scheuch, Dr. (VdU leader): elected deputy chairman, 86–87; boycotts the 1951 general assembly, 110; re-elected deputy chairman, 1954, 141; mentioned, 150.

Slavik, Dr. Felix (Leader of the *Nationale Liga*), 82.

Social Democratic Party (forerunner of the SPOe): resistance movement, 12; participates in the founding of a provisional government, 14; mentioned, 6–7, 11, 17–18.

SPOe (Socialist Party of Austria): founding of, 15; negotiations on the formation of a new provisional government, 18; sanctioned by the Allied Council, 21; supports the disenfranchisement of former Nazis, 23; in the first Austrian government, 25; cooperation with the OeVP on socialization programs, 32; degree of support from the *Minderbelasteten*, 34; policy on admission of a new, fourth party, 42, 48, 62; encouragement for a new, fourth party, 36, 42, 44; attitude towards the VdU, 62, 114; accuses the VdU of neo-Nazism, 62, 66–67, 121, 197n; election results of 1949, 66, 68; rejection of VdU participation in government, 74; competition with the VdU in industrial council elections, 78; woos back worker support from VdU, 82; challenged by KPOe for worker support on the issue of the 1950 wage-price agreement, 88; resistance to the Communist putsch of 1950, 90–91; position on the manner in which a president should be selected, 92–94; protests against OeVP discussions with VdU, 95, 110, 196n; presidential campaign of 1951, 99–100, 102–105; appeal for ex-Nazi vote, 104; elections of 1953, 117–118, 121, 135–138; 1953 negotiations on a new coalition, 124–127, 130; support of the FPOe, 163; minority government, 166; majority government, 167; mentioned, 113, 145, 147, 165–168.

State Treaty: VdU dilemma on, 153–

154; mentioned, 56, 87, 152, 200n, 155.
Stendebach, Max (VdU Chairman): election as deputy chairman in 1951, 110; elected chairman in 1952, 116; reelected chairman in 1953, 132; reelected chairman in 1954, 141; reelected chairman in 1955, 149; position on the State Treaty, 153–154; negotiations with Reinthaller for fusion with the *Freiheitspartei,* 151, 155; chosen vice-chairman of FPOe, 157; elected deputy chairman of FPOe, 158; mentioned, 112, 116–117, 121, 131–132, 134, 141, 149, 151, 153, 155, 157–158.
Strachwitz, Dr. Ernst (leader of the Youth Front and Action): leads the Youth Front out of the OeVP, 96, 113; founds Action, 113; negotiations with Kraus for fusion with the VdU, 114, 116; mentioned, 96, 124.
Stüber, Dr. Fritz (VdU leader and founder of the FSOe): leads a nationalist challenge to the moderate VdU leadership, 108–110, 115, 131, 139; elected deputy chairman of VdU, 1952, 116; elected deputy chairman of VdU in 1953, 132; opposes joining a government coalition, 124, 129; expelled from the VdU, 139–140; founds the FSOe, 140–141; mentioned, 51, 63–64, 76, 108, 110, 115–, 116, 120, 124, 129, 131, 144.
Third Force: becomes a political reality, Ch. 4; fragmentation of, 128, Ch. 7; reconsolidation under Reinthaller and the FPOe, 148–149, 161–168; mentioned, x, 26–27, 30, 33–35, 106–107, 114–115, 119, 124, 128, 130, 133–135, 139, 144, 161, 167.
Tyrolean Party: founded, 21; mentioned, 22.
Ursin, Dr. Fritz (VdU leader): resigns from VdU, 139; resigns from FSOe to join *Freiheitspartei,* 151; mentioned, 129, 132, 150.
VdU *(Verband der Unabhängigen).* See League of Independents.

Volksdeutschen: VdU appeal to, 53, 60, 61, 190n, 78; role of in 1949 election, 67; mentioned, 31, 38–39, 79, 118, 133.
von Schönerer, Georg, 4–6, 183n.
WdU *(Wahlpartei der Unabhängigen),* 48–49, 116.
Weber, Anton (Social Democratic Councilman of Vienna), 14.
Weinberger, Lois (OeVP leader), 15–16, 22, 185n.
Youth Front (OeVP youth organization): founded in 1949, 95; principles, 96; defects from the OeVP, 96–97; supports the VdU candidate for president in 1951, 97; reorganized as Action for Political Renewal, 113; mentioned, 118, 133. See Action for Political Renewal.
Zeillinger, Gustav (VdU and later FPOe parliamentary representative from Salzburg): expelled from VdU, 85; reinstated, 85; negotiations with the *Freiheitspartei,* 151; mentioned, 159, 164.